CHRIST-CENTERED HEALING OF TRAUMA

HEALING A BROKEN HEART

NORM WIELSCH

ENDORSEMENTS

"Throughout biblical history, many great men of God were broken down by divine or consequential circumstances. One was taken from his land and sent to prison, while another was knocked off a horse and blinded by a divine light.

Norm Wielsch, a well-respected law enforcement veteran, received many awards and accolades from local, state, and federal agencies during his twenty-six-year law enforcement career. He has experienced a wide range of life traumas, everything from being the commander of a multi-agency narcotics task force, being shot at, to walking out of his home in handcuffs.

After receiving a fourteen-year prison sentence, he was committed to the Federal Bureau of Prisons. It was in a federal prison cell, by divine intervention, God used inmate and former Los Angeles PD Officer Ruben Palomares to enlighten and heal the heart and soul of Norm Wielsch.

Christ-Centered Healing of Trauma: Healing a Broken Heart, is a book written by a man who experienced traumas and their after-effects first-hand. He experienced both the challenges and the tools used in his healing process.

I am a retired San Diego Police Department Detective Sergeant with over thirty-two years of law enforcement experience. Today, I am the CEO of Sheepdog Active Critical Incident Trauma. I offer counseling and services to active and Christ-Centered Healing of Trauma retired first responders, military, clergy, medical staff, and victims of traumatic incidents. I also provide PTSD training and seminars on prevention, detection, and intervention. During my training and counseling sessions, I quote and highly recommend this book *Christ-Centered Healing of Trauma: Healing a Broken Heart.*

This is a book every Pastor, Christian Counselor, and anyone that is in pain from PTSD should read and have. This book is for the person suffering from PTSD and for their family and loved ones. It describes the healing process and the pain, sorrow, and destruction associated with PTSD.
This book has been instrumental in my own personal healing. I highly recommend this book and commend Norm Wielsch for his passion, dedication, and perseverance."

Retired Sergeant David Contreras
San Diego Police Department

"Norm does a great job detailing and getting deep to the root of one's healing. A must-read and apply for one's journey into wholeness. Awesome work, Norm!"

Former Los Angeles Police Department
Ruben Palomares
Christian Counselor

DEDICATION

I dedicate this book to my Lord and Savior, Jesus Christ.

And,

To the brave men and women who protect and serve our communities, who risk their lives daily, who place the welfare of others before their own without the thought of the physical and emotional damage they may suffer.

And,

To my family who stood by me when no one else did. They endured more pain than I did during those long years I was in prison. Thank you for your unconditional love.

 For Worldwide Distribution through Ingram

978-1-951648-06-0 (hardcover)
978-1-951648-25-1 (paperback)
978-1-951648-26-8 (ebook)

FOREWORD

I met Norm Wielsch at perhaps the lowest point in his life. His name and face were on every Bay Area news station for weeks on end. His story would be shared nationally as well, on Dr. Phil, Dateline, and more. I didn't know the elite police officer and "top cop" who was the head of the drug task force: the man who made all who knew him proud to be his friend or family member. No, I was introduced to the broken man, one battling suicidal thoughts, shame, guilt, loneliness, and, if the news reports were accurate, even worse. But, on that Monday night, when we first talked on the phone, I sensed a man on the other end of the line who was filled with sorrow. He talked more about his family and their pain than the painful case that enveloped him. He was more concerned about all of them than his own judicial fate. He was out on bail while awaiting his trial and eventual sentencing. And he wanted restoration and healing for his family more than his own. He did the crime and was willing to do the time. That Monday night, as the opportunity presented itself, I had the amazing privilege of introducing him to someone he had never known personally. This man would be willing to do the time, even though Norm had done the crime. That introduction to Jesus would be the beginning of a healing and rebuilding process that would take years to accomplish. You hold in your hands a resource and tool that could become a lifesaver for you or someone you deeply care about.

The steps and invaluable resources in Norm's incredible guide to restoring mental health are a must-read for anyone who has found themselves at a low point in life. So, read it, and by all means, share it with others. Lean into the painstaking information found in every chapter. The healing may come quicker than it did for Norm, or it may take even longer, but if you read with diligence, the good news is that the healing will come. And, when it does, can I be bold enough to ask you to do exactly what my good friend has done. Would you share this with someone whom you know will benefit from it? You see, Norm was never content to just find healing for himself. He desired healing for others as well. He wanted healing for first responders, leaders, politicians, counselors, pastors, family, and friends. And perhaps Norm was one of the millions of people in history whom God had in mind when he inspired the Apostle Paul to write the words found in 2 Corinthians 1:4, " . . . He comforts us in all our troubles so that we can comfort others. When they are troubled, we will be able to give them the same comfort God has given us . . . " (NLT).

Retired Pastor Jeff Kenney

In police academy 1985

Patrol 1989

Undercover 1994

Task Force Commander

Seizure 2009

Team Photo 2010

Norm and Ruben 2014

Racing at Sonoma Raceway 2006

TABLE OF CONTENTS

INTRODUCTION

> *"I have said these things to you, that in Me you may have peace. In the world you will have tribulations [troubles]. But take heart; I have overcome the world."*
>
> *John 16:33*

Jesus tells us that we will experience tough times in life. There will be traumatic events and overwhelming circumstances that will come into our lives. No one will go unscathed. Life is a journey that will take us through a series of disappointments, loses, traumas, and crises. Some are predictable and expected, but most are total surprises.

During life we must always resolve issues that have the potential to wound us. Every potential crisis provides an opportunity to learn new ways of using resources that God provided for us to succeed and overcome. Many times, this requires several tries to get it right. But through Jesus Christ we will overcome. As we overcome our trials, we learn and grow to resolve future crises much easier.

> *"Between stimulus and response there is a space. In that space is our power to choose our response. In our response lies our growth and freedom."—Victor Frankl*

We all have experienced trauma, some more than others. If you have not yet experienced an overwhelming life event, don't worry, you will! So why do some of us live defeated lives after going through a traumatic event? Why can't some people shake it off and move forward after trauma? Why are we often held captive by the memories of our past and fear of the future?

Experiencing a traumatic event, causes a wounding of the heart. The initial wound is like a seed planted in the heart. A seed grows when it's fed. It is how we feed the seed that determines how it grows. It is not the traumatic incident that leaves us in pain, anger, and bitterness. No, it is our sinful response.

Our sinful response opens the door to Satan and allows him to begin his oppression. Merriam Webster defines oppression as a spiritual burden, or a sense of being weighted down in body or mind. Once wounded, if we feed that seed with anger, judgment, and unforgiveness, the seed will grow into what the Bible refers to as a "Bitter Root." Left unchecked, that root will continue to grow taking over our heart and eventually all aspects of our lives. But if we feed that seed with forgiveness, understanding, and love, the seed will grow into a beautiful tree producing good fruit.

In the Bible, good and bad fruit is an analogy for good and bad character traits or structures. For example, bad fruit is likened to a person who exhibits anger, hate, resentment, bitterness, and is unforgiving. Good fruit is likened to a character that exhibits peace, joy, forgiveness, and love. Sin is the culprit that leads us into oppression. So, when we are in unrepented sin, we have given Satan the authority to oppress us.

Before we became Christians, we were slaves to sin. But then, because of Christ's work on the cross, sin no longer has the power to control us. Christ defeated sin and its pusher—Satan. However, Satan's goal is to prevent us from understanding and accepting who we are "in Christ." He wants to deceive us into believing that we are a product of our past, and that all our disappointments and wounds should be carried as a weight on our shoulders, pressing us down—defeating us.

But as a Christian, you are in Christ, and He is in you. You are the victor. Nothing can defeat you!

As Christians, we are all children of God. We have been forgiven of our sins: past, present, and future. Once we learn the essential spiritual laws and principles, as well as the power of forgiveness, confession, and repentance—we will be free of the sin that weighs us down and blocks our healing. We also become free from our anger and bitterness that negatively affects our lives.

Some people are perfectly comfortable living their lives oppressed by their sins. They have endured the pain for years, if not decades, of being oppressed by their guilt, shame, doubt, fear, and unforgiveness. In fact, they've done it for so long that it has become second nature to them to live with the pain daily. They do not know what it feels like to be free. They may not even know that it's possible.

But the truth is that Jesus has set us free from the emotional baggage we carry. He has broken the bars of the prison of anger and bitterness that binds us, so we can live the abundant life that is only in Christ. Our position is free! And to experience this freedom, we must remove the obstacle that blocks our liberation, release, and restoration. This obstacle is the sin that separates us from God and blocks our healing.

This book is intended for those who suffer from past trauma or overwhelming life events that are preventing you from moving forward and enjoying life again. I call these the woundings of the heart, or a broken heart. We will look at how we are wounded and how we respond to those situations that break our heart.

We will learn about strongholds and why they keep us under the thumb of Satan's oppression and how the biblical laws and principles help us overcome these strongholds and promote healing. This is not a self-help book. There is no magic pill that will fix our emotional and spiritual problems. It is only God that can heal a broken heart.

It is not by accident you are reading this book; God has placed it in your hands to begin the healing process. The Christ-Centered Healing method was originally designed to minister to first responders and combat veterans. As I ministered to traumatized inmates, I realized that trauma was widespread among the inmate population. As I learned more, I saw that every person has had an overwhelming life event or a traumatic circumstance. I thought it was just me.

In ancient times, God ordered that any member of Israelite army who killed another or touched a dead body was to purify themselves. These people would camp outside of the city to purify and cleanse themselves through prayer and fellowship for seven days. This same treatment that was given back then, applies for us today too. It was simply spending time fellowshipping with others, God, and prayer that heals. [See Numbers 31:19-20]

This book is not only for the victims of trauma, but for their husbands, wives, daughters, sons, and parents who suffer right along with them. They are all wounded people. Because hurt people hurt people. Since our families are the closest to us, we tend to hurt them more than we know or intend.

Christ-Centered Healing is a discipline of self-examination, repentance, prayer, and sanctification that forces us to look at our character structures to discover strongholds and obstacles to healing never brought to the cross since we received Jesus Christ as our Lord and Savior. Strongholds keep us in pain. As we destroy the strongholds, we are transformed in our inner man/woman.

Broken hearts and the emotional pain they bring, when left unchecked keep us in a defeated state. The pain and suffering in our lives can either paralyze us or be a catalyst for growth. Pain drives us to God and His healing comfort. We learn to see our pain from a different perspective, God's perspective. God often uses pain and sorrow to achieve His will. God is sovereign and in control. When we understand and accept this truth, our anxiety and fear are removed.

When we respond to our pain in a sinful manner, it festers and develops a stronghold in our lives (more on strongholds later). We often deny the pain because it is too difficult to deal with. It is easier to drink your pain away than to do the work to heal it. It is important that we face the pain to determine the initial wounding and then evaluate our response to the wound.
It is essential that we are honest with ourselves during this process. If we are honest, we will see the sinful response and its affect in our lives. It is our sin that separates us from God. It is our sin that takes us out of His will and limits our blessing and healing.

In order to heal spiritually, emotionally, and physically, we must return to doing God's will for our lives. We must realign ourselves with His will and restore our relationship with Him. The greatest obstacle to our spiritual and emotional health is the sin we harbor in our hearts. The bitterness and anger towards the person who hurt us will take over our lives and negatively impact every one of our relationships. To restore our relationship with God, we renounce our sinful responses, forgive when required, confess, and repent our sin.

The Bible teaches that when we are obedient to God with no unrepented sin, we are considered "in fellowship" with Him. Healing occurs when we are in fellowship with God. We will learn that Jesus healed people after their sins were forgiven.

Mark chapter two tells us that one day Jesus was teaching in a house. The house was full of people—standing room only. Four men wanted Jesus to heal their paralyzed friend but could not get close to Him. So, they carried the paralytic man onto the roof of the house. They broke open the roof and lowered the man down to where Jesus was teaching.

When Jesus saw what they were doing, He said, "Son, your sins are forgiven." The man was then healed. And in John chapter five we see the story of Jesus healing an invalid. After Jesus healed the man, He said, "See, you are well! Sin no more, that nothing worse will happen to you." We see the correlation between the forgiveness of sins and our healing. Healing begins when our relationship with God is restored.

Christ-Centered Healing incorporates the mind and spirit. The mind and spirit working in concert strengthens the spirit, body, and soul. Our minds are very powerful; we possess the mind of Christ (1 Corinthians 2:16). Living life stuck in habitual sin causes stress, depression, anger, and bitterness that can affect our physical health and can cause diseases like heart disease, cancer, or diabetes.[1] We have all been wounded in some form or fashion.

This book is meant to provide you with hope. Jeremiah 29:11 says, "For I know the plans I have for you, declares the LORD, plans for welfare, not for evil, to give you a future and a hope." Jesus Christ is that hope.

---

[1] "Happiness is a State of Mind," Psychology Today, accessed July 7, 2023, https://www.psychologytoday.com/us/blog/happiness-is-state-mind/202010/breast-cancer-and-mental-health

Study after study shows us that long-term negative thoughts and emotions such as worry, stress, anger, depression, and bitterness can kill us. How we emotionally respond to the storms in our lives affects our healing. Emotions are good. God designed us with emotions for a reason. As a physical injury to the body signals pain in an area indicating that something is wrong, so, our emotions signal that something is wrong in our heart and spirit.

Emotions are normal, they should never be suppressed or denied. When we try to escape the negative emotions, we are in sin. The sin often results in poor coping mechanisms like self-destructive behavior or substance use/abuse. It is not our emotions that cause us to be oppressed, it is our response to our emotions that keep us in pain.

I hope to show you that trauma, emotional pain, grief, and our failures can be key factors to our spiritual growth and maturity. God created mankind with the freedom of choice to respond in a way that benefits us or causes us to suffer pain. Our normal, even automatic response is based on many things. Some include events in our childhood, education, spirituality, previous events in trauma, age, gender, and our worldview, among other things.

Our prior wounds normally dictate a response to a new wound. Since the fall of man, we tend to respond sinfully to almost all situations. Sinful responses include: unforgiveness, forming of inner vows, bitter root judgments, and unrealistic expectancies.

The author of Hebrews tells us to set aside our emotional baggage that festers within us and to stay focused on Jesus to bring the peace and joy we crave. Since the fall of man, we are all born in sin, spiritually dead, separated from our creator. Because of this imputed sin, a piece of our heart is missing, so we are born with this void in our heart. We know something is missing from our lives, but don't know what. We search our entire life for something to fill that hole to make us feel better.

We often try to fill it with money, possessions, social status, sex, drugs, alcohol, and gambling, just to name a few. But as we go along in life, we find that these things cannot make us feel better. We feel no better than before. Nothing except a relationship with God will fill this void because the piece that is missing is God shaped! Once we humble ourselves before God, our heart will be made whole.

There is no psychologist, psychiatrist, doctor, or self-help book can heal your heart. Secular methods can provide a temporary distraction from the pain, but it's not lasting. It is only God that can heal. Remember, your trauma does not define you. You are not your trauma, what defines you is who you are, a child of God.

CHAPTER 1

A NARCOTICS OFFICER

In the fall of 2010, I was parked on the side of a dark frontage road off a highway in the San Francisco Bay Area. It was about 9:00 p.m. I had just finished helping another narcotic team serving narcotic search warrants in the West County area. I was writing a letter to my wife and family on my note pad—a suicide letter. I placed the notepad on the passenger side seat and clipped my badge onto the notepad. I cleaned up my department issued under-cover police car. I cleaned up all the empty bags of fast food—the cop's food of choice. I didn't want the cops that responded to my suicide to think I was a pig—no pun intended.

I pulled out my duty weapon, a Glock .40 caliber handgun. I was contemplating the most effective way to shoot myself to ensure a quick and painless death. I wiped the tears from my face on my sleeve.

I had been a police officer for about twenty-six years. I responded and investigated dozens of suicides; some successful, some not. Most were horrific scenes, some appeared tranquil.

How was I going to do it? How did I get to this point? How did my life spiral down to contemplate suicide?

PART 1: HOW I ARRIVED AT MY DARKEST HOUR

I was an only child who grew up in a middle-class family. My father was an ex-military disciplinarian and my mother a stay-at-home mom. My father owned an auto repair shop, where I got my love of cars, especially classic and racing cars. My parents identified themselves as Christians, but like most only went to church on Easter and Christmas.

I remember going to a church service only about two times because most of the time I stayed home. I still remember to this day a bedtime prayer my mom taught me in German. It's funny what we remember.

I learned how to be a mechanic from my father. I worked with him after school and on Saturdays. After I graduated high school, I worked for him full-time.

I built and raced cars at nineteen years old. I began road racing on tracks like Sonoma Raceway and Laguna Seca Raceway. After a few years, I moved to NASCAR oval track racing. I raced all over Northern California.

When I was twenty-one years old my father retired, so I took over the business. My father was so proud of me following in his footsteps. I loved working on cars, but I knew this was not what I was meant to do for a living.

At twenty-one, I married my high school sweetheart. A few years later, we had our first daughter. One night, I went on a police ride-a-long. I loved it! The excitement was great.

I knew I had found my calling. I did not want to disappoint my father, so I decided to become a police reserve first. A reserve officer is a volunteer who wears a police uniform and has full police powers while being supervised by a full-time paid police officer. I went to an evening police academy. After graduation, I worked in the city in which I lived.

I excelled at police work and eventually became a Level I Reserve. This meant that I was approved to work unsupervised. I volunteered many hours on evenings and weekends.

Police officers protect the thin line between good and evil. They witness the worst that Satan can give. It is a difficult job requiring the patience of a pastor, the wisdom of a judge, and the strength and stamina of a professional athlete. One minute you are driving a patrol car eating fast food or donuts, the next you're chasing a burglar over fences. Very few people are able to endure the emotional stress and physical wear and tear on the body.

Many recruits are let go after a few months. Very few officers retire from a twenty or thirty plus year career without many scars: internal and external. There is a very high rate of suicide for law enforcement officers—even higher for retired officers. The job announcements for police recruits do not mention the likelihood of PTSD.

After volunteering for a few months, I was dispatched to the scene of a small plane crash. It was December 23, 1985 in the late afternoon. The city next to us had a municipal airport next to a busy freeway. On the other side of the freeway was a huge two-story shopping mall. This was the day before Christmas Eve, and the shopping center was full of last-minute shoppers.

A small plane intended to land at the airport, but it appeared that the pilot had some sort of medical issue. The plane crashed into the roof of the shopping center. It went through the ceiling about twenty-five yards from where Santa was meeting with kids listening to their gift requests. Fourteen people died and over eighty-eight more suffered injuries.

When I arrived, it looked like a war zone. It's been over thirty years and those images are still burned in my memory.

I was taught at an early age from my father (a veteran of WWII), and then later in the police academy to suppress my emotions—never show them to anyone. We were taught to "Just put it out of your mind," and go to the next call. Looking back, I don't know how I did it, but I did. I was good at it. Never in a million years did I think that those emotions would surface at some point.

Death was common, some natural and some violent. I handled the calls well with what I thought had no negative effects. I loved the job and decided to change careers and become a full-time officer.

I was hired by a different city than I volunteered at. They sent me to the police academy again. My father was really disappointed, because he had built his business to hand over to me to follow in his footsteps.

I began to work as a full-time paid officer in 1985. I had no idea what I was getting myself into. One of my first calls was a suicide by shotgun. At that time, it was the worst crime scene that I had ever seen, worse than the plane crash. I could barely hold down my lunch.

After about a year on the job, I was assigned to the Traffic Division. The mission of a traffic officer is to respond to and investigate traffic collisions. We do not call them traffic "accidents" because they are never accidents, there is always one driver who is at fault. I was sent to special schools and became an expert in collision investigation.

Our secondary mission is to determine where collisions occur most, then ascertain and conclude the reason for the collisions. This is done primarily through issuing traffic citations. Yes, that makes me one of the evil cops who write traffic tickets! Sorry!

During my five years assigned to the Traffic Division, I investigated dozens of fatal collisions. I won't go into detail here, but the body goes through extreme forces during a collision causing severe injuries or death. Some of these fatal collisions included child victims; these are the worst for officers to respond to because most cops have children.

I also investigated several train versus pedestrian collisions. Again, I will not go into detail, but you can imagine what a train traveling sixty mph can do to a human body. It is a horrific sight.

One of the collisions I responded to was on the freeway at about 4:00 a.m. while a reserve officer was riding with me. A semitruck was carrying a load of square tubing on a flatbed trailer. The truck had mechanical issues and broke down in the fast lane but the driver could not get the trailer all the way out of the fast lane.

A young man driving at freeway speeds in the fast lane did not see the trailer for whatever reason. His car crashed into the rear of the trailer. The square tubing that was hanging off the back of the trailer pierced the windshield right where the driver was sitting. Upon our arrival, we saw that the driver had been decapitated.

Needless to say, the reserve officer never rode with me again. These calls are common for all police officers. They witness tragic deaths on a daily basis.

I can still see every fatal collision and its victim in my mind. These images will never leave me. After five years I wanted out of this position, so I returned to the Patrol Division.

In the Patrol Division, officers respond to citizen's calls for service. The best part was there was something different every day. During this time, I was assigned secondary duty as a Special Weapons and Tactics (SWAT) officer. I was on SWAT for eight years. Some of the traumatic incidents included:

1. A male who took his two toddler sons hostage in retaliation for his estranged wife filing for divorce. He locked himself into the master bedroom of their residence upstairs. He was threatening to kill the kids and himself. Negotiators were trying to get the man to surrender. After a few hours, the man shot and killed both boys and himself. Our SWAT team was not able to get into the room in time to save anyone. All officers on the team had children, and were devastated.

2. Another time, a woman who held her two children hostage in their downstairs apartment. She was suffering from mental illness. She locked herself and the kids in the bedroom with a rifle. The SWAT team was in the apartment just outside her room waiting for hostage negotiators. I was close enough to hear the kids crying, saying, "Mommy, please don't kill me." She replied. "The police will kill you, not me." Other SWAT officers were positioning themselves outside her bedroom window trying to get a vantage point in the apartment. The woman either saw them or heard them and began shooting through the wall. One bullet went through the wall striking an officer just under his helmet in his forehead. Thank God the officer survived. When we heard the shot, we forced entry into the bedroom. She then began shooting at us. However, we were able to subdue her without injuring her or the children.

3. In another incident, late one night, I responded to a report of domestic abuse a man beating his wife. When I was about one block away from

the house, I saw the taillights of a car driving away. As I arrived, a small crowd pointed to the car and said, "The guy is getting away." I tried to catch up with the car. I saw the taillights turn onto the main road. I followed. There was a slight grade, and as I crested this grade, I saw headlights coming at my direction. I had my emergency lights and siren on. At the last minute, I saw the car veer towards me, and it rammed me in my driver's door. There was no place for me to go. I was traveling about forty mph and it was later determined that he was going over sixty mph. He intentionally rammed my car. Both cars were destroyed. I was dazed and had to climb out the passenger side window. For a few seconds I did not know where I was. People began to come out of their homes. The driver of the other car ran at me and attacked me. As we fought, he tried to take my gun away. The fight now turned deadly. Finally, some bystanders helped me and pulled him me. The guy tried to run away, but the bystanders ran after him and detained him for other responding officers. I passed out and woke up in the hospital. The collision crushed two discs in my spine and still causes me problems today.

4. Finally, I was dispatched to a call of a bank robbery in progress only a block away. The bank was located at a large four-way intersection. On one corner was the bank, on the others were a fast-food restaurant, a gas station, and a small strip mall. This call drew a response from all officers in the area as well as neighboring cities. As I approached the intersection, I saw a box truck parked in the lot of the strip mall. I decided to pull into the lot and conceal myself behind the truck so I could watch the bank across the street. As I entered this parking lot. I looked ahead to make sure I was not going to run over anyone. As I looked straight ahead, I saw two males running out of a storefront in this mall. I forgot that there was a small credit union in this mall! I was dispatched to the wrong bank. The men ran right at my marked patrol car. When they were less than ten feet away, they pointed guns at me. The barrels looked like huge pipes! I ducked under the dashboard, trying to pull out my gun. I thought they were going to kill me and I would never see my family again. As I looked up to shoot, I saw them running away and jumping a fence into a residential area. I drove around the corner and chased them on foot through backyards and over fences. I was much younger back then. I was able to catch one of them in a backyard. He still had the gun in his waistband. Other responding officers caught the other bank robber hiding in another

> backyard. Two handguns and the stolen money from the bank were recovered. No one was injured. I had nightmares over this incident until Jesus healed me. The dispatcher made a mistake and sent me to the bank that saw the masked armed robbers and called the police, instead of the bank that was being robbed. This mistake could have cost me my life.

All these incidents are considered traumatic. There are other calls that police respond to every day that may not be as exciting but still can overwhelm their emotions. I remember calls that affected me included child abuse, and physical and sexual abuse. It is very difficult to listen to a five-year-old girl tell you about how her uncle sexually abused her, then going and talking to the uncle who you know did horrible things and not show emotion.

Any death involving a child, especially Sudden Infant Death Syndrome (SIDS), and child drownings are extremely difficult to handle emotionally. We must always remember that this world is currently being ruled by Satan. He causes death and havoc daily. Every broken heart and traumatic incident are from Satan.

The birth of my second daughter turned out to be an overwhelming life event. When she was born, the doctors immediately saw something concerning and took her away. They later diagnosed her with aplastic anemia. Her body was not producing white blood cells. Without white cells, the immune system cannot fight off illness.

They transferred her to three different hospitals finally arriving at the University of San Francisco Medical Center (UCSF). She required a bone marrow transplant in order to survive. Fortunately, I was a direct DNA match with my daughter and was able to donate bone marrow to her. Before the surgery, she was in isolation for three months. When we visited, we were required to wear personal protective paper clothing, so no germs entered her room. This period caused a lot of stress for my wife and I that negatively affected our marriage. While she showed her emotions, I did not. I appeared callus, but inside I was a mess.

UCSF was wonderful and provided the best care. My daughter's picture is still up in the transplant wing. She recovered and is healthy today. I did not realize it then, but God was with her back then and even today.

Once that event was behind me, I felt I needed a change. I believed in my heart that drugs were society's number one problem. I made a lot of narcotic arrests and became an expert in almost all areas of narcotic enforcement. I requested to be reassigned to the Narcotic Division. It was a three-year assignment, and I got it. I was excited because I thought the calls to unattended deaths were over. Although I did not know it at the time, PTSD had already taken its toll on my heart. From the outside, I appeared to have it all, two beautiful daughters, married to my high school sweetheart, had a great job, and a nice house. But inside I was a mess, I suffered from depression and lashed out in anger at minute things but did not know why. My wife could only take so much. We divorced. We shared custody of the girls 50/50.

I excelled in narcotics. It seemed a good fit for me and my personality. The narcotic team had four detectives and a supervisor. We had a good team; everyone pulled their weight, and more.

Each year, one of us would be assigned to work undercover for six to nine months purchasing drugs all over the city. In 1994, it was my turn. I spent nine months undercover. I was given an undercover car and was followed by a small team of officers in case something went wrong. I purchased almost every illicit drug except for PCP and LSD.

I no longer had to respond to calls of death, but now was on the front lines of child neglect and abuse. I learned that people addicted to drugs will do almost anything necessary to obtain their next high. Any amount of cash they earned or stole went to purchasing drugs. Parents who were addicts would buy drugs instead of diapers, milk, or food for their children.

During my time in narcotics, I ordered the removal of dozens of children from their parents for their own safety and wellbeing. It was a difficult experience because the child does not understand the situation. They love their parents unconditionally.

When there was no food, utilities, or responsible parent or family member available, we were forced to have child protective services remove the child and place them in temporary foster care until the parents could properly care for them. I saw the darker side of the drug world where children were physically, emotionally, and sexually abused by their caregivers and those whom they associate. There are incidents that I will never forget.

Narcotics was a very busy assignment that required lots of overtime. For three years straight, we averaged over 100 search warrants per year between four detectives. We also responded to more than fifty methamphetamine laboratories per year. Clandestine meth labs were discovered every week. Search warrants and meth labs were very dangerous operations.

We were all trained SWAT personnel. A judge would authorize the forceable entry into a residence suspected of selling or manufacturing drugs. Our team of officers would surround the house and another team would be assigned to enter by force if necessary. The entry team would approach the front door not knowing if the occupants inside had seen our approach.

We would knock on the door, announce that we are the police and advise them of the search warrant. This was the most dangerous time of the operation because most drug dealers have a weapon to protect their drugs and/or profits from would-be robbers. Many officers have been shot and killed by suspects shooting through the closed door. This is common because targets either do not want to go out without a fight, or did not believe the police were really the police, but instead robbers acting like police.

After the knock and notice is given, our entry team waited a brief time for the suspects to open the door voluntarily. Timing is crucial here. The suspects may be asleep, not at home, destroying evidence, or arming themselves preparing for a confrontation we could not know.

When there is no answer at the door after a reasonable time, we forced the door open and made entry into the residence. The entry team must then search each room for suspects who may be hiding or lying in wait to harm an officer. This is a very dangerous time, but also a very exciting one. The adrenaline rush is indescribable and very addicting. There is nothing like it in this world. You do not know if this will be your last day on this earth or not.

In 2008, my team was serving a search warrant at an apartment. The man inside opened the door for the agents. For an unknown reason, the resident grabbed the handgun of the first officer in the residence. A fight for the weapon ensued. The agent ordered him to let go, but the resident did not.

The agent feared that the gun may be taken was forced to shoot. The resident did not survive. This was a very stressful incident. We do not know why this young man tried to take the officer's weapon.

Search warrant services are very dangerous and stressful generally. As I said, the adrenaline puts you in a hypervigilant state. Many officers suffer from depression after being taken out of the narcotic unit due to the loss of this excitement and rush.

Combat veterans tell me they feel the same way while in combat. It is so dangerous, but the adrenaline is addicting. So much that they often sign up for more deployments.

I became a recognized expert in both state and federal courts on the subject of narcotic enforcement. I testified regarding surveillance techniques, search warrant service, under-cover drug purchases, possession for sales, and drug influence. I wrote a book that was published by LawTech Publishing called, *The Patrol Officer's Guide to Narcotic Enforcement.* Many police departments purchased that book for their patrol officers.

I was due to rotate back to patrol in 1997. I did not want to return to uniformed patrol. So, I applied to be a full-time narcotic officer with the California Department of Justice, Bureau of Narcotic Enforcement.

I met my current wife during this time. She had three children and was recently divorced. We combined our families. In 1998, I was hired by the state and went to work as a full-time undercover narcotic agent.

It was in 1998 when I was diagnosed with a neuro-muscular disease. I was losing all feeling in my feet and began to develop blisters on the bottom of my feet. The blisters were so deep that you could see the tissue of the foot. The blisters would not heal without the pressure being taken off the surrounding skin. This disease is called Peripheral Neuropathy.

The neuropathy was complicated by a degenerative muscular disease called Charcot-Marie-Tooth disease. This disease caused atrophy of the muscles in the extremities. The diagnosis caused a large amount of distress. I would go to work with these quarter-sized blisters on the bottom of my feet; the blood would soak through my socks and would get bone infections in the foot due to the open wounds.

Surgery was required to remove pieces of bone that were infected. Doctors would cast up one foot or sometimes both on a Friday afternoon to relieve the pressure off the wound. On the way to work on Monday morning, the doctors would remove the casts so I could go to work. My wife had to sew Velcro into my shirts and pants because I could no longer button buttons with my fingers. I was required to undergo over twenty-five-foot surgeries in a ten-year period.

These surgeries caused me to fall into a deep depression. I began to experience anxiety and panic attacks. I did not know it at the time, but this was PTSD rearing its ugly head. I later found out that PTSD can lay dormant until another traumatic incident triggers it.

Every time a surgery would fix whatever the problem was at that time, it took five to six weeks to heal. I used up all my sick leave and vacation time. Since I was well-liked and respected, my supervisors always let me work light duty so as not to use more sick time. Light duty is where you are allowed to work administrative duty only.

As I look back, I am concerned that my supervisors never investigated if I was fit for duty. I think they failed me and the agency. However, I do know that officers do not want to know about another officer's illnesses. I believe it is because it will make them come to grips with their own mortality. Soon after I healed and went back to full duty, another medical issue or infection would come up requiring yet another surgery. All these incidents brought me to a very dark place. I was plagued with horrific nightmares about work-related incidents.

One of my dreams is where I was working in uniform. I conducted a traffic stop on a car and I saw a male get out of the car. He pointed a gun at me and began shooting. The bullets first bounced off the windshield of my patrol car, then they began to come through the windshield. I opened my door, drew my handgun, and began to shoot at him. I saw the bullets come out of my weapon in slow-motion and fall to the ground about ten feet in front of me.

The guy kept shooting and then I would wake up. The nightmares were so bad I was afraid to go to sleep. I would stay up into the early morning hours watching television or surfing the internet until I would be so tired that I couldn't keep my eyes open.

My doctor suggested Ambien, a sleep aid. These worked really well to get me to sleep, but the pills made the dreams more vivid, making matters worse.

Another dream that repeated every few nights during this period was that I was in uniform again. I was walking at night through a large grassy field. It was a foggy nigh, the grass was littered with the bodies of the dead people that I responded to during my career.

I remember each one. I saw their faces and what they looked like when I arrived on scene. I still remember them all today.

I then began to have anxiety and panic attacks at work. I had to hide these negative emotions from my co-workers and subordinates. After every surgery, the doctors prescribed me opioid pain medications like Vicodin. Since I had no feeling in my feet, I never had pain, but they prescribed them anyway.

I knew they made me loopy, so I used them to take the edge off the anxiety attacks. At first. I only took one or two a day when I felt anxious. It soon became more than a dozen a day.

I continued to my job well even in addiction and I was promoted. I supervised every team in the office at one time or another. After a few years, I was promoted to manage a multi-jurisdictional narcotic task force in northern California. This happened to be the county where I grew up and lived. I was excited.

Each local jurisdiction would provide one or two police detectives to be assigned under my supervision. Every patrol officer's goal was to work on this task force: it was an elite group of men who worked extremely hard every day. My career was progressing well.

As my career was flourishing, my medical condition was deteriorating. It became difficult to safely handle my department issued handgun and machine gun. You may ask why didn't I just tell my supervisors, or just retire? I'm glad you asked that. In law enforcement, any sign of weakness is a career killer.

Everyone knew about my surgeries, but no one ever asked about the results or even the cause. This is because cops will never talk about illness or disease, it reminds them of their own mortality. Police officers must be fearless and brave, just like superheroes.

After years of cheating death, many believe they are invincible. When one is injured or dies in the line of duty, they are brought back to reality. Many officers work their shifts in dire pain from on-duty injuries because they do not want to appear weak or work while on strong pain medications even though it is against policy. Even more officers work through extreme emotional distress and depression because they are afraid to seek out help that may cause them to appear weak.

If an officer seeks psychological help, they are ostracized. No officer will work with them. Seeking help is the kiss of death.

Due to all my surgeries and the deterioration of my nerves and muscles, my feet became deformed. I have no movement in my ankles, I walk flat footed. I require a brace on each leg to walk normally. Without these braces, I am unable to stand in one spot for more than a few seconds. I have no balance; I must hold onto something to stand in one spot.

At one point my doctor wanted to remove my right foot so I could walk steadier with a prosthetic. I begged them not to take my foot. Thank God, they did not take it.

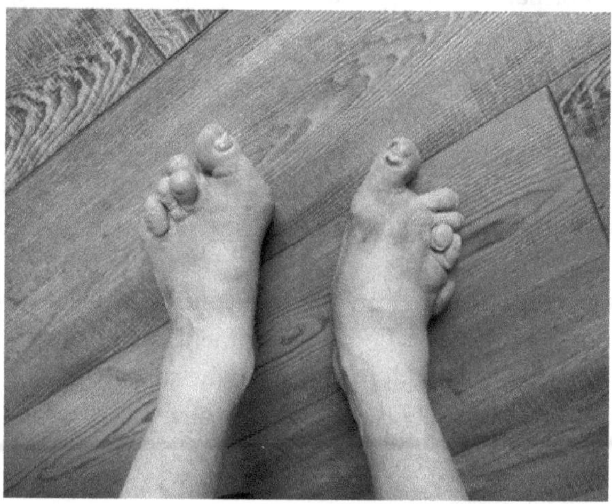

In 2008, with all this going on, my mom passed away at eight-five-years old. My father was devastated especially after fifty-nine years of marriage. I loved my mom and had a difficult time mourning her death.

I thought my dad would be mad at me if I grieved too much. I was not able to display emotion. To this day I have not mourned my mother's death.

In 2010, my youngest daughter was having pain in her abdominal area; she was twenty-two-years old. She was diagnosed with tumors on her liver. One tumor wrapped around an artery. The doctor told us this was serious.

They referred us to University of California, Los Angeles Medical Center to do the surgery. The complicated surgery gave her a fifty percent chance of surviving the surgery. The first step was to do a biopsy of the liver to determine the type of tumor. If it were cancerous, surgery was required, if not it could wait.

This put me in a downward spiral of depression. This was the same daughter who had the bone marrow surgery. She had my DNA. In my mind I thought that this was all my fault. I was defective and now because she has my DNA, she could possibly die.

These were false conclusions, but when you have a depressed state of mind to begin with, you sink even deeper into depression. That's Satan's goal, to bring us to a where there is no return.

My daughter wanted to think about what she wanted to do. She was handling it better than I was. But of course, I could not let anyone know what was going on in my head.

It was not more than a few weeks later I was parked on a dark frontage road trying to decide the best way to kill myself, because there were so many things going through my mind. I had this image of an incident my stepdaughter went through. I do not want to describe it here, but it was that incident that made me think twice about committing suicide.

Looking back now, I believe it was the Holy Spirit of God that brought this vision into my mind so that I would think twice about committing suicide. I could not do it. The next few months were a nightmare.

As I look back in memory, this time was a fog. I recall some things but not others. This is common in PTSD, but it also could be the opioids. I had lost all hope.

I was being attacked from all fronts. First, I was attacked by the degeneration of my strength. This degeneration made me lose hope for future health and a long life. I was no longer that strong cop that I had been for the last 25 years.

Second, I was emotionally devastated because I blamed myself for my daughter's tumors because of my flawed DNA.

And lastly, the negative emotions from PTSD were consuming me; I felt like I was losing the battle. PTSD had the upper hand. Now adding the problem of the opioid addiction, I did not know how to move forward. I thought I was going crazy.

My wife saw the changes in me and begged me to seek professional help. But I was too prideful. I was strong, I could fix whatever this was on my own. I wish I should have listened to her.

During the three or four months after my daughter's diagnosis, I made a lot of poor decisions that eventually sent me to prison. It took me years to figure out how I got myself so deep into that bad situation. I discovered that I had used counterproductive coping mechanisms to deal with my pain. I did not believe in God at that point.

I knew I was sinning but did not understand the consequences of my sin. I did not know how easy it was to be forgiven. My self-destructive behavior was from my sin. I would sin more trying to make myself feel better, but I was only sabotaging myself.

I was acting as my own god. I had no need for my true creator. I was a cop! I could do it myself!

My biggest sin was listening to someone I thought was a friend, who later stabbed me in the back. I do not blame him. I made all the decisions in my life. All my decisions were egged on by Satan. Satan, the god of this world influences our behavior.

We make our own decisions but are influenced by the king of all liars. I stole drugs out of the secure evidence room and gave it to this guy who needed the money for back taxes. A month later, I was arrested and sent to county jail.

I bailed out a few days later. This was my darkest hour, but it is always darkest before the dawn. I did not know how God was moving in my life.

PART 2: HOW I SURVIVED

God began His mighty work in my life a few days after I got home. My first blessing occurred one evening sitting in my house depressed, not knowing what to do. There was a knock on the door. I looked out and saw it was a uniformed officer knocking. I thought, "What more can go wrong?"

I opened the door and saw it was a man named Nick Turkovich who I had worked with years before. He stopped by to check up on me. As we talked, he told me about his experience with PTSD. And then told me what God had done in his life. Testimonies are powerful.

He planted the seed. He gave me the name and number of a police psychologist who was an expert in law enforcement PTSD. He was a retired cop and knew what officers go through. His name was Doctor Joel Fay. He was able to stabilize my emotions and taught me about PTSD and how to control my emotions.

Three days later, Nick's department ordered him to cut off all contact with me. My chief ordered all my co-workers to stop any and all contact with me. I felt abandoned by the men with whom I had been through so much. I had spent more time with my co-workers than my own family.

While out on bail I was an emotional wreck—a basket case. The stress and anxiety were indescribable.

A few days later in the evening, the telephone rang, I answered it. This was a call that would change my life. The caller identified himself as Pastor Jeff Kenney from New Hope International Church. A friend of my father who knew what was going on and told Pastor Jeff about me and what was happening.

At this time in my life, I did not believe in God. Pastor Jeff was loving and compassionate. He asked how I was doing and described his church. He offered his counseling services, but I politely declined. He invited me to church on Sunday.

I told him that I would think about it. I really had no intention of going to church. He asked if he could pray for me. I told him, "Sure." I didn't know it at the time, but he prayed the sinner's prayer.

When he finished, he asked if I accepted Jesus Christ as my Lord and Savior. Not wanting to be rude, I said "yes." He then invited me to come by the church anytime to talk and hung up. I went and joined my wife on the couch.

I felt strange, I somehow felt better, at peace. It was like a heavy weight was lifted off my shoulders. My wife sensed something; she asked me what I was feeling. I could not explain the feeling to her.

She was raised in a Catholic home and believed in God. But due to my beliefs, she did not talk to me about it. We talked about the call; she suggested that maybe it was God that was missing from my life.

She insisted that we go to church the upcoming Sunday. My mind was telling me that this feeling was unreal, but my heart was telling me to try and go to the church. We decided to go to Pastor Jeff's church next Sunday.

The next Sunday we went to New Hope International Church. The only times that I went to church I saw the people dress up. So, I dressed up. When we went into the church, we saw a wide variety of people, everyone was dressed casually. I saw many people in shorts, baseball hats, and some had lots of tattoos.

At that time, I still judged people. From my experiences, people with lots of tattoos were usually criminals. I know better now, most cops have tattoos today. We were greeted very warmly. Everyone greeted us with hugs, I do not believe they even knew who I was or what I had done.

They were so loving, I felt at home there. Pastor Jeff's sermon was awesome and uplifting. We continued to go every week.

I felt more comfortable there than anywhere before. I bought a Bible and began to read it. I also joined a men's group. I was experiencing some internal peace; however, I was still on the fence regarding believing in an all-powerful and loving God.

I read the Bible. I didn't understand too much of it. But the more I studied, the more God was revealed to me.

Pastor Jeff taught me how to pray. During one Sunday sermon, Pastor Jeff stopped the sermon and asked the congregation to pray for the healing of my daughter. They did. I cried a lot that day.

About a week later, I went with my daughter to have her biopsy. The hospital was great; they had an emergency backup team waiting in surgery in case of any problems. It went well, all glory to God.

About two weeks later we went to the doctor to get the results. The doctor told us that he had to do another scan. My daughter did the scan and we returned later that day to get the results.

The doctor placed two scans up on a lite panel. He pointed to one scan that showed the tumors. He then pointed to the new scan that showed no tumors. The liver showed no tumors! The doctor said the biopsy showed normal liver tissue.

The doctor could not explain it. I became very angry believing they misdiagnosed her illness. He showed us a second opinion from the UCLA Medical Center that gave the same diagnosis. It then hit me like a ton of bricks! God had healed her tumors. At that time, I felt a feeling that I cannot describe, of warmth, peace, love, and joy. I wish that I could describe it more accurately. I finally believed that there was a true living God! I have no doubt that God exists, and He is a loving compassionate God.

I began to study the Bible and attended weekly Bible studies. I decided to be baptized. The day of my baptism was one of the best days of my life. Just before getting into the pool; my daughter joined me and was also baptized. We were baptized together.

I later pled guilty to the charges. I was taken into custody and sent to a county jail. Because I was a police officer, they housed me in a suicide cell for my protection because inmates hate cops. The jail cell was about six feet by eight feet with a metal toilet and sink combination, and a small table in the room. There was a large window that allowed the correctional officer to make sure I did not harm myself, however, this allowed for no privacy to go to the bathroom. The lights stayed on 24/7. The mattress was the thickness of a yoga mat.

I was only let out of the cell once every three days to shower and have one hour to go outside. It was December and very cold. They provided no warm clothing. But even in jail God is good.

A bright spot was that in the next cell was another police officer who had committed spousal battery. We were allowed to go outside together. I got to speak with someone who knew "my language." "Outside" was the roof of the building in a half-court basketball court. Other inmates were in the other half-court separated by fencing.

I knew a few of the correctional officers from working together on cases. They gave me newspapers, encouraging words, and sometimes good food. Some officers were very rude and tried to humiliate you, others were kind and compassionate. One female officer let me use her personal Bible.

I learned so much by talking with inmates about a wide variety of issues while out on the roof. Some told me of their childhood, sexual abuse, abandonment, parent's drug addiction, as well as their own addictions. I saw that the judicial system is based primarily on punitive actions, not mercy or compassion. This was just the beginning of my education into why people do the things they do, good or bad.

I was in that county jail for nine months. I was later sentenced to fourteen years in prison. I was taken to the Federal prison in Fort Worth, Texas, even though my probation officer promised us that I would remain here in California.

Being sent far away from my family made it difficult for them to visit. I was angry, but God knows what He is doing. He has a plan and purpose for each of us.

On the first day there, I met an ex-sheriff out of Louisiana who had been transferred from another prison to Fort Worth. He had also received a long sentence for a drug crime. He was the nicest guy I have ever met. We became friends.

While helping him with an appeal, I saw that his claim of innocence was, in fact, true. I saw no evidence that he ever sold any drug. I met four other ex-police officers there. Two of them had questionable convictions. I did not know there were so many cops in prison, mostly because of stupid mistakes.

I worked at the prison's chapel with two other officers. Tyndale Seminary and Bible College came to the chapel and taught seminary courses. I took the classes and eventually earned my Master's Degree in Theology and Christian Counseling. I believe that God had a plan for me to go to seminary and meet the people I met. God directs our steps!

I was still suffering from severe PTSD symptoms. Nightmares and anxiety attacks bothered me daily. I went to weekly counseling sessions.

The psychologist who saw me was in training. She was very nice but not equipped to deal with PTSD. We talked for countless hours. She taught coping techniques, but no healing occurred.

One day, the prison chaplain called me into his office to meet someone. He introduced me to a new inmate named Ruben Palomares. Ruben was an ex-police officer from Los Angeles PD. He had been in prison for thirteen years. He had been in a minimum-security prison camp where a correctional officer had violated a policy. The administration wanted Ruben to testify against the officer, but Ruben refused. As a penalty for not testifying, Ruben was sent up to a higher security level prison. I believe God ordained our meeting.

Ruben would change my life. When we spoke, he told me about the critical incidents that led him to prison. He described some on-duty shootings where he was shot several times. Another time he described, he was forced to shoot and kill a guy who shot him. This trauma caused several addictions that led him to criminal behavior and a 20-year prison sentence.

While in county jail, a pastor from a local church came and helped him heal from the PTSD. The pastor taught him many scriptures related to

Jesus' healing ministry. Ruben introduced me to the ministry of "Elijah House." They specialize in healing the soul and spirit, they call this process "Inner Healing."

I read the book series "The Transformation Series" by Paula and John Sandford. I read all their books and had the chaplain order their DVDs. Ruben led me through the process that healed him. Ruben helped me through the steps and prayers.

In about four months I was free of PTSD symptoms. God healed me emotionally and spiritually. I identified each traumatic incident and my sinful responses that put me in an oppressed state. Ruben also showed me how to study the Bible with the intention on healing. Anyone can study the Bible from an academic standpoint, but we need to study with our hearts open to fully understand God's word.

The chaplain eventually allowed us to informally counsel other inmates who were suffering from negative life experiences. God worked wonders with them all. God knew what he was doing and orchestrated all the events that took place so that Ruben could come and show me how God heals. My experience in a federal prison was positive because of how God worked in the lives of the inmates there. We counseled together for several months.

The prison then sent him back to a minimum-security camp to finish out his sentence. I stayed in Fort Worth and counseled several inmates on my own. As I counseled, I modified the process so that it could be done without the help of anyone else and I added and removed some steps as I deemed necessary; I call it a "Christ-Centered" approach to healing of PTSD. Secular counseling focuses on the client's will, our approach focuses on a biblical approach. God's will, not ours.

After almost three years, I was transferred to a minimum-security prison.

But as I look back, I see God's fingerprints all over my pain. If things did not happen the way they had, my daughter would never have been healed. I would never made Jesus my Lord and Savior. I would have gone to hell. My family would have never been saved. I believe that if I weren't caught and arrested, I would be dead right now by suicide or opioid overdose.

Nevertheless, I missed so many things in my family's life. Both my daughters and one son got married and had children while I was in prison. It was a dream of mine to walk my girls down the aisle. My father passed away and I was not allowed to go to the funeral. Four grand children were born. I have only seen them a few times. My wife had to endure the loneliness and hardship of dealing with all the family problems by herself.

I missed my family so much. This will sound strange but if God were to come to me and allow me a "do-over," to go back and not have to have been arrested and go to prison, I would refuse the offer. The hardship and pain of all the things I endured brought me closer to God. I am a changed person.

God changed me from the inside out. I no longer hate people. I am patient, kind, and compassionate. I no longer hate myself. I no longer have pity on myself for my disease. I value my family and every minute I spend with them. I am content with who I am, what I have, and I know that God will provide for all my needs.

I am not defined by my mistakes or my past. I am defined by who God says I am. This is my story—my testimony. I left out many blessings that God provided me and my family due to space. God is GREAT! If you have strayed from God, or never knew Him, go to Him now and be blessed and healed!

CHAPTER 2

TRAUMA: EVERYONE HAS EXPERIENCED IT

"Be gracious to me, O LORD, for I am in distress; my eye is wasted from grief; my soul and my body also. For my life is spent with sorrow, and my years with sighing; my strength fails because of my iniquity, and my bones waste away."

Psalm 31:9-10

If God has led you to read this book, you have suffered from an overwhelming life event and are in need of healing. I placed these chapters in an order that is logical and practical. Please do not jump sections or chapters unless you are doing a review. To begin healing, it is important to understand what trauma is and how it affects our mind, body, and soul.

WHAT IS TRAUMA

The word "trauma" is derived from the Greek word meaning "wound." An individual who goes through a traumatic event is wounded. Just as in a physical injury like a deep cut, internal wounds need proper care in order to heal. Just as a cut that is not properly cleaned and dressed gets infected, wounds to the heart, if not treated, can become infected with anger, depression, and bitterness. Just as we feel pain from a physical injury, our emotional wounds can be devastating. The pain we feel from a traumatic incident can be Post-Traumatic Stress Disorder (PTSD).

When we talk about PTSD, we normally focus on military combat veterans, first responders, victim of terror attacks, victims of crime, etc. But emotional trauma is a much larger issue that affects almost every person on earth. Some consider emotional trauma a public health issue.

If we think about trauma and the variations of traumatic incidents, we can recognize that more people die from domestic violence each year than soldiers in Iraq or Afghanistan. In the United States, more women are likely to suffer from domestic violence than are diagnosed with breast cancer. Firearms kill twice as many children as cancer. And opioid addiction kills more people than firearms. Studies by the Center of Disease Control and Prevention has shown that one in five Americans was sexually abused as a child; one in four beaten by a parent, and one fourth grew up with an alcoholic relative.[2]

We must then consider the collateral damage within the families of a wounded person. Children today are exposed to many situations that may very well emotionally scar them. Kids growing up today are exposed to violent Internet and television content, cyber bullies, school shootings, and abusive parents. In areas where poverty and unemployment are issues, our children navigate violent gangs, shootings, drug dealers, inferior schools, alcohol or drug addicted family member(s), abandonment, all of which are breeding grounds for PTSD. Very few children go unscathed.

Another group of people who are Susceptible to PTSD are on the front lines are our first responders. The men and women that protect and rescue us from evil. First responders include: police, fire department personnel, ambulance personnel, and emergency room hospital workers. First responders witness the worst Satan has to offer. They respond to calls of people in need that most of us could never imagine.

They protect society and patrol the line between good and evil. Victimization, death, and destruction are witnessed on a daily basis. There appears to be no effort to protect these brave and selfless individuals.

We must also realize that civilians will also be exposed to overwhelming and difficult life events, as well as traumatic ones. As a society, we must

---

[2] the website of the CDC, several different articles, accessed 6/10/17, www.CDC.gov,

place more emphasis on our healing. If we do not, more people will be hurt. Hurt people hurt people.

Trauma is not new. It all began in the Garden of Eden with the first sin of Adam and Eve. Their act of disobedience caused God to curse the earth. Prior to this sin, there was no pain, no sorrow, guilt, or shame. This first sin, called the "fall of man" everything changed.

The curse included that all women would suffer pain during child birth, and she would always desire to rule over her husband but will not. God also cursed the ground of the earth so that man would never be satisfied with his work all the days of his life, and finally their sin resulted in spiritual and physical death. The consequences of sin are huge.

To add to the couple's problems, God evicted them from the garden, never allowed to return. As occurs to most families where PTSD has affected someone, their trauma was passed down to their children. Their oldest son Cain murdered his brother Abel in a jealous rage. This is referred to as generational trauma.

King David was affected by PTSD. David fought many battles and was said to have killed thousands of men. The Psalms that were written by David describes his sorrow, anxiety, and emotional pain. His emotional trauma infiltrated his family. One of his sons died due to David's sin. Another son raped his step-sister, one killed the other, and one attempted to take over David's throne by force. We can see that David's sin and emotional trauma caused his family to be dysfunctional.

Another biblical character named Job suffered the loss of all ten of his children on one day. He lost all his wealth, and few days later he was struck with a horrible disease. These are just a few of the biblical figures that endured great trials and loss. All made it through their trials better than before.

We see people suffering from trauma every day. The news often goes into graphic detail and plays extended coverage of tragedies. Some will experience secondary trauma just by watching the news unfold on television.

We know about PTSD in combat veterans but we do not associate it with the heavy burden carried by people who suffer through overwhelming life events such as the death of a spouse or loved one, divorce, diagnosis of a disease, miscarriage, abandonment, or loss of a job. All these events break the spirit—break the heart.

Wounds to the heart are invisible. A broken heart causes more damage than a broken arm (Proverbs 15:13 & 17:22). A wounded heart is difficult to heal without supernatural help.

Overwhelming life events leave a hole in your heart. The hole is made deeper by abandonment, humiliation, betrayal, not being allowed a voice, and having a constant feeling of insecurity. The hole is made wider by the sinful practices we use to cope with the pain with which we suffer.

For those who have suffered a traumatic event, or an overwhelming life event, family and friends often notice personality changes. Wounded people act differently than they did prior to the incident. Their personality does not change as much as their behavior. Due to the pain, they have modified their behavior in an effort to reduce their pain. The modified behavior is a coping mechanism that often goes against God's will.

Common coping mechanisms are normally sinful. Wounded people often make sinful judgments, have sinful expectancies, make sinful inner vows, and deny their wounds. This sinful behavior causes inner turmoil that negatively affects behavior, relationships, and inner peace. Denying a wound takes tremendous energy as the wounded person tries to function normally while coping with the memory and negative emotions from the wound. Anger, bitterness, guilt, and shame keep them in a cycle of oppression to their wounds.

As we remain stuck in our pain, trauma becomes engrained in worldview. The pain rules over our thoughts, emotions, and behavior. In an effort to lessen the pain, we seek out shortcuts to healing. We seek out activities that takes our mind off the pain. The problem lies in the type of activities we choose. Some include alcohol or substance use, pornography, gambling, under/overeating, excessive shopping, cutting, or dangerous sexual behavior, just to name a few.

These activities tend to cause more pain because they isolate us from others. Our pain infiltrates into every relationship we have. Trauma affects our moral compass and keeps us in habitual sin. We see things different than before. Our worldview changes into that of a victim's mentality. Psychiatrists cannot "heal" victims of abuse, war, abandonment, or any other overwhelming life event. What happened cannot be undone. Medication can only numb the pain, but cannot heal. That same medication can also cause more problems with physical reactions or overdose. It is only God that can heal the brokenhearted.

The results of trauma are different for everyone. The affects can be mild, moderate, or severe depending on the resilience of the individual. Resilience factors include:

- Positive support system
- Spiritual / religious beliefs
- Culture
- Age
- Education
- Gender
- Prior history of trauma
- Temperament
- Severity of traumatic event
- Life experience

PTSD AND TRAUMA

PTSD is considered an anxiety disorder. PTSD develops in response to extreme psychological and emotional distress caused by an overwhelming life event. It can result from a single traumatic event or multiple events like those experienced in war or in police officers. Symptoms can manifest within, days, weeks, months, or even years after exposure.

There are two types of anxiety disorders: Acute Stress Disorder (ASD) and Chronic or Complex PTSD. ASD normally results from an exposure of a single traumatic event where symptoms develop within days or weeks and only lasts for two to thirty days. Chronic PTSD is cumulative and lasts much longer and is more intense.

The Diagnostic and Statistical Manual of Mental Disorders, fifth edition (DSM-5) describes PTSD as:

"The automatic dysphoric cognitive essential feature is the development of characteristic symptoms following a psychological traumatic event that is generally outside the range of usual human experience. The characteristic symptoms involve re-experiencing the traumatic event; numbing the responsiveness to, or reduced involvement with the external world; and a variety of symptoms."[3]

Trauma results from an event outside the range of the normal human experience. Outside the normal life experience can be any event that causes emotional distress. Distress can manifest itself as fear, hopelessness, horror, despair, or grief. Types of events can include:

- Loss of a loved one
- Divorce
- Abandonment
- Loss of a job
- Childhood neglect
- Spousal abuse
- Childhood abuse both physical and sexual
- Serious vehicle collision
- Natural disaster
- Victim of a crime
- War
- Mass shootings
- Betrayal
- Terrorist attack
- Diagnosis of a serious illness
- Suicide of a loved one
- Financial loss
- Loss of a dream
- Arrest or incarceration
- Victim of a rape
- Victim of bullying or stalking
- The threat of any of the above

[3] Diagnostic and Statistical Manual of Mental Disorders, American Psychiatric Association, American Psychiatric Publishing, p. 225

Anyone can suffer secondary trauma by witnessing any of the above events or being subjected in some way to the incident. Most at risk are:

- Police officers
- Ambulance drivers
- Fire department personnel
- Paramedics
- Emergency relief workers
- Media
- Mental health workers
- Clergy or missionaries
- Emergency hospital workers
- Child protective services workers
- Families of a traumatized person

An individual can re-experience the traumatic event in vivid detail through intrusive thoughts, nightmares, and flashbacks. These symptoms are intense traumatic memories that intrude into the person's mind over and over again causing distress. These thoughts can be as intense as the original trauma.

Symptoms of ASD and PTSD include:

- Intrusive thoughts
- Flashbacks
- Nightmares
- Anxiety attacks
- Disassociation with the event
- Unable to recall trauma
- Isolation
- Feeling no emotion
- Unable to control emotions
- Constant state of fear
- Hyper-vigilance
- Loss of interest in activities
- Sleep difficulties—either too much or not enough
- Difficulty concentrating
- Exaggerated startle response
- Low self-worth
- Anger at God
- Suicidal ideation

- Mood swings
- Feelings of helplessness/hopelessness
- Impairment of judgment
- Panic attacks

God often brings these intrusive thoughts to memory; not to bring pain, but to help bring closure to the trauma by creating stress. This stress is meant to motivate a conscious resolution to trauma. For me, I experienced flashbacks and nightmares almost daily. They were so vivid that it seemed real. I thought I was going crazy and did not understand what was happening.

The flashbacks were so horrific that I was afraid to go to sleep. I Began to take opioids to take the edge off the intrusive thoughts and Ambien to force myself to sleep. I soon became addicted to the medications which caused even more distress.

When we look at the above symptoms, we can see the debilitating effects that can cause hopelessness and suicidal ideation. These symptoms are not visible to the ordinary observer. Most victims put on a mask attempting to cover up their secret world of pain. The hiding of continued trauma is a double-edged sword because it causes continued suffering while also not letting those around the victim help.

While the mask might hide the trauma on one side, on the other the wounds are invisible, so no one will know they exist. But if no one knows the trauma exists, no one can help. This coping mechanism often leads victims to believe no one cares.

I saw a quote from an unknown veteran in a book written by Dr. Joel Fay that said, "I sometimes wish I had lost an arm or leg during combat so that people could see my injury, maybe then they would understand what I'm going through." This is exactly how most of us who are in pain to trauma feel. Satan uses our trauma to discourage us, to break us down, and keep us in bondage to our sinful responses and the lies. We are blessed to have a healer in Jesus Christ who through His crucifixion took our pain, sorrows, sin, and afflictions. By His death and resurrection, we are healed.

PHYSIOLOGICAL EFFECTS OF TRAUMA

When God was designing mankind, He created humans to survive and defend ourselves in a variety of dangerous situations. God created within us an alarm system that interprets danger and then automatically responds to the danger. Trauma affects how our brain processes information and interprets and stores the event we experienced. Trauma often overrides the alarm system. It disrupts how the information is processed. Trauma over-stimulates the nervous system which causes the alarm to go off and arousal levels to increase.

People who have been traumatized often have re-occurring intrusive thoughts. It is these thoughts that set off the alarm, even when there is no present danger. Over-stimulation occurs causing the arousal levels to be chronically high. This constant state of arousal can have a serious impact on the human body. Effects include anger, rage, hyper-vigilance, sleep disturbances, guilt, detachment, shame, or depression.

Remember our bodies were not designed to experience trauma. God created a perfect world. Trauma first occurred after the fall.

God is our creator, unique in design, purposeful in its creation. Our brain and nervous system may be God's greatest creation. Their most important job is to ensure our survival, even under the most severe conditions. A normal brain has two halves. The left side is analytical, it is logical and rational, it gives us the ability to read, write, and speak. It holds our beliefs, values, and expectations.

The right side is spontaneous, emotional, non-verbal, and allows us to dream. It stores memories as pictures, but most importantly, it is the alarm center of the brain.

The limbic system is a part of the brain that controls emotions and formulates memories. There are three parts of the limbic system: the hippocampus, the amygdala, and the hypothalamus.

The Brain on Trauma

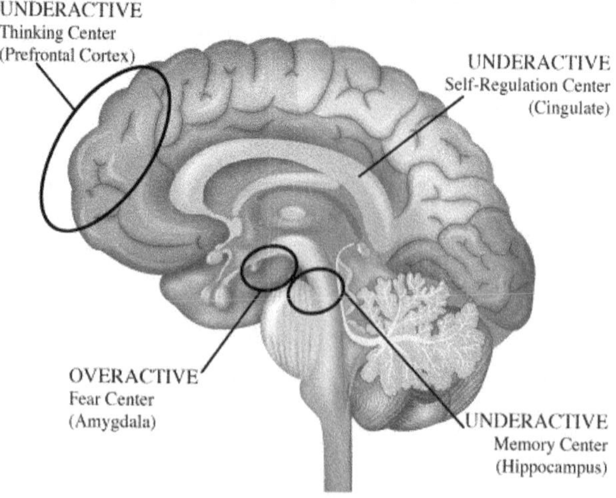

The Hippocampus

The hippocampus takes sensations and ideas that are in the mind at the present time and converts them to long-term memory. During intense stress, the hippocampus can shut down so that the short-term memory (present memory) does not get stored into long-term memory. This shutdown is why people do not remember some details of an extremely stressful event.

The hippocampus is analytical and calms down that part of the brain when danger is over. All unresolved experiences are stored in the hippocampus. Any event can trigger and activate an involuntary replay.

The Amygdala

The amygdala evaluates incoming stimuli to determine danger. It is the alarm center of the brain—the early warning system that, when necessary, prepares the body emotionally and physically for danger. It is the emotional part of the brain and therefore does not know how to reason. The amygdala deals with feelings, emotions, and memories of all things that present a danger. This memory of danger is learned from our childhood. If a trusted parent placed you in a dangerous situation with abuse, the amygdala would remember and set off alarms if that same person approaches. It remembers what you are afraid of.

The amygdala is always monitoring the areas around us. When you watch television, your eyes are focused on the television, but the amygdala scans the other parts of your visual field that you do not pay attention to. Even during sleep, it monitors sensory information for any sign of threat. The amygdala prepares us for the "fight, flight, or freeze" response.

The Hypothalamus

The hypothalamus receives information from the body such as heart rate, blood pressure, sounds, smells, and sight. It then regulates the body's organs and nervous system for potential danger. When the amygdala senses danger, it sends a message to the hippocampus to prepare the body for an emergency. This emergency alarm is done by the body's release of neurohormones including adrenaline that raises the heart rate, increases breathing, and tenses muscles to get ready for the fight, flight, or freeze response. Our brain then takes over. Our right brain creates memories in vivid detail. The entire event is being burnt into memory so that we will know how to react in the event that a similar situation occurs in the future.

The limbic system is overwhelmed preparing the body to react to the threat. At the same time the right brain (amygdala) continues to take in sensory information from the perceived danger or threat. Because of this overload, the memory sometimes remains in the short-term memory part of the brain. The memories never get transferred to the long-term memory area.

Since these memories remain in the present or short-term area, victims cannot recall some details of the incident. And because these memories are lodged in the limbic area of the brain, they continue to be brought up involuntarily, thus the intrusive memories, flashbacks, and nightmares. The limbic system sounds the danger alarm each time the memory is replayed.

With each flashback, the brain once again prepares the body for an emergency. The trauma is over, but the mind continues to send out distress signals. These repeated distress signals cause us to be in a constant state of hyperarousal. In combat or police work, this hyperarousal is a good thing. But where no threat exists, hyperarousal causes harm to the body, soul, and spirit.

Effects of Stress on the Body

Studies have shown that during stress there is a slight increase in the excretion of cortisol. Cortisol increases blood sugar, suppresses the immune system, and is responsible for the digestion of proteins, fats, and carbohydrates. This change in cortisol levels, as well as other hormones, causes a weak immune system. Excessive cortisol levels put us at risk for developing many illnesses including:

- Diabetes
- Depression
- Arthritis
- Sinus issues
- Anxiety
- Heart disease
- Migraine headaches
- Lack of concentration
- Suicidal ideation
- Autoimmune disease
- High blood pressure
- Changes in sleep patterns
- Body aches and pains
- Cancer

A study conducted by the Harvard Medical School found that trauma can affect your future health. The study focused specifically on children and childhood trauma. This study suggests that PTSD affects five to ten percent of the general population. PTSD is especially common in women, almost twice as many than in men. It is clear that past overwhelming life events can affect your present health. Beyond the illness listed above, traumatic events trigger emotional and even physical reactions that make victims more prone to a variety of health conditions including: heart attack, stroke, obesity, diabetes, and cancer.

The research shows that people who are exposed to traumatic incidents or overwhelming life events normally use poor coping mechanisms to escape their intrusive thoughts and memories. Common coping mechanisms that are considered risky behavior would be excessive use of alcohol, drugs, or even over eating, just to name a few.[4]

[4] Andrea Roberts, "Adverse Childhood Experiences in Particular, are Linked to Chronic Health Conditions." *Harvard Health Publishing* (blog) Harvard Medical School, Feb 12, 2021, https://www.health.harvard.edu/diseases-and-conditions/past-trauma-may-haunt-your-future-health

PTSD AS A SPIRITUAL DISORDER

PTSD is a spiritual disorder. N. Duncan Sinclair, in his book, *"Horrific Traumatica: A Pastoral Response to the Post Traumatic Stress Disorder"* tells us, "PTSD creates havoc at all levels of who we are. Chronic fatigue, sleeplessness, gastric disturbances, uncontrolled blood pressure are all exacerbated by the spiritual disturbances of PTSD.

When we speak of the loss of hope, we are speaking of a diseased heart. When we speak of loss of intimacy, we are speaking of chronic pain. When we speak of loss of peacefulness, we are speaking of chronic hyper-alertness.

It is within this framework that we conclude PTSD is a spiritual disorder not because the 'person is not right with God' or that 'God is not right with the person.' It is a spiritual disorder because the person who experiences the full impact of PTSD has been impoverished by the loss of a series of vital spiritual attributes that are essential to living a full life."[5]

This spiritual disorder is orchestrated by Satan who influences and encourages our sinful responses to the trauma. Trauma affects who we believe we are; it affects our self-identity.

We all see ourselves differently. Most of us believe ourselves to be kind, compassionate, strong, rational, and in control. We often lie to ourselves about who we are; we do not like to hear or see the truth. When we go through trauma, someone betrays us, someone does something to second-guess who we are, our optimism begins to crumble.

When a traumatic incident or an overwhelming life event occurs, we constantly think about our situation, almost driving us crazy. We want to see the rationale behind our pain. When we cannot find it, we sink into a deeper pain. The pain often drives us into despair, addictive activities, or compulsive behavior as quick fixes. Quick fixes never work. They even drive us into a cycle of trauma.

Trauma is a wounding of the heart. It is not the traumatic event that wounds us. It is our sinful response to the wound that causes us pain. If not

---

[5] N. Duncan Sinclair, *Horrific Traumatica: A Pastoral Response to Post-Traumatic Stress* (New York: Hawthorn Pastoral Press, 1993), 66

dealt with properly, we remain in a cycle of pain due to our sin. Some of the ways we remain in, our trauma include:

- We minimize our responsibility in the event
- We deny our responsibility altogether
- We blame others (like Adam and Eve)
- We minimize our actions after the incident
- We harden our hearts with anger and bitterness
- We refuse to forgive others
- We seek revenge that controls our lives
- We do not seek forgiveness from those we harmed
- We internalize our emotions
- We judge others for who they are
- We make inner vows obstructing us from God's will
- We isolate ourselves from others stewing on our anger
- We seek out quick fixes like alcohol, drugs, or other
- Addictive behavior.

Triggers

We also remain in our trauma through intrusive memories and flashbacks. These memories are often triggered by something that reminds us of the event. A trigger can be a sound, smell, taste, a geographical location, or any stimulus associated with the original experience that puts us back into the trauma via the flashback.

A trigger can activate a memory so dramatically that the adrenal glands become aroused and activates the body's fight, flight, or freeze responses.

It is possible for a flashback to retraumatize the victim because it seems so real. We can hear it, see it, and smell it as if it were happening all over again. One of the triggers for me that set off an anxiety attack was approaching a railroad crossing. As I drove up to a crossing, I would feel my heart beating faster. I would often experience a flashback of one particular female victim that was struck by a train at a crossing.

She had been walking next to the tracks and somehow was struck by the locomotive. The train was traveling over sixty mph. I will spare you the gruesome details. This vision is burned in my mind. I went through these anxiety attacks for fifteen years.

My sinful response to this incident was a belief that if God existed, He was not a good God. After I reflected on it, I went back and repented for my unbelief and anger against God. We are allowed to question God, but it is when we accuse God of being bad, it becomes a sin. When I came home, I found that my anxiety around the railroad tracks had been healed. He did it for me, and He will do it for you too.

Once a trigger has been identified, many victims go out of their way to avoid the thing that triggers them. If there is more than one trigger, the person often isolates themselves from the world due to the fear of having intrusive and frightful thoughts.

Researchers have found that those who try to suppress their triggers by avoidance, and who suppress intrusive scary thoughts, memories, and dreams end up experiencing more severe symptoms. In avoiding triggers and suppressing thoughts, victims suffer more frequent manifestations that go beyond the actual trauma and involve thoughts of suicide, aggression, violence, and other life-threatening events.[6] Some re-experience the event through life-like nightmares. These dreams seem so real because they are vivid. They feel the same fear, anger, grief, and helplessness as they experienced during the original incident. Some are afraid to go to sleep and develop insomnia. People who live with the pain of a broken heart often replay the event over and over again in their minds. These thoughts prevent a good nights' sleep and which can lead to other more serious problems.

The Bible talks about this fear and its medicine. Proverbs 3:24-26 says, "If you lie down, you will not be afraid; when you lie down, your sleep will be sweet. Do not be afraid of sudden terror or of the ruin of the wicked, when it comes, for the LORD will be your confidence and will keep your foot from being caught."

Byproducts of Trauma

There are several byproducts of trauma. When we are in pain because of a wounding, we tend to focus on our emotions. If we are angry, we focus that anger on the person we perceived hurt us or the system that allowed this to happen. The frustrations on normal situations may erupt in uncontrolled anger.

---

[6] **J.W. Pennebaker and R.S. Campbell** "The Effects of Writing about Traumatic Experience," Clinical Quarterly, 9 (2): 17 2000, 19-21

We become angry even at insignificant events. We not only harbor anger at the person who harmed us but we also are angry at ourselves or God for allowing this pain to happen. God created within us the ability to become angry. It is a God-given emotion. But God did not intend us to hold onto our anger. The Bible teaches, "Be angry and do not sin; do not let the sun to go down on your anger, and give no opportunity to the Devil" (Ephesians 4:26). God is telling us to deal with our anger prior to the sun going down. In other words, don't hold onto your anger. Uncontrolled anger is a sin and allows Satan the opportunity to oppress you. But this is not how it works in the world, most of us allow anger to control our behavior. Uncontrolled anger leads to rage, bitterness, depression, helplessness, and suicidal thoughts. When we stay in anger, we are in habitual sin. Habitual sin separates us from God and keeps us in our pain.

Like anger, depression is a complex blend of thoughts (I'm no good; I'm a failure; I'm ugly). Coping mechanisms like isolating oneself, substance use, inactivity, oversleeping and emotions such as anger, shame, guilt, and unforgiveness are breeding grounds for depression, A person who is in a depressed state will interpret every life event in a negative light. This negativity will cause a deeper depression. Depression is not God's will for us. Guilt occurs when we feel bad about something that we did or did not do. God created us with the emotion of guilt, which is designed for correcting us when we do something wrong. Guilt forces us to make amends for our wrong doing.

But uncontrolled guilt can be overwhelming. We often keep our guilt in secret so that no one will find out what we did because we fear the condemnation of others. Guilt causes us to withdraw from others and avoid the activities we once enjoyed. No one wants to feel guilty, so they try to escape these feelings with sinful behavior like alcohol, drugs, or excessive gambling. It is this sinful behavior that begins the downward spiral into hopelessness.

We must forgive ourselves. If we do not forgive ourselves, we place ourselves above God. This is also sin. God has forgiven us. There is no longer condemnation for our mistakes (Romans 8:1).

Guilt often results in shame from something we did wrong. Shame results from who we believe ourselves to be. Shame comes from a negative self-worth that is influenced by Satan. If we believe we are no good or flawed, we feel ashamed for who we are. Shame is a form of self-punishment that makes us feel inferior, embarrassed, and inadequate.

Shame is self-centered. it is a very powerful emotion because it involves negative critical judgments of ourselves that lead to feelings of humiliation and low self-worth. Shame leads to isolation, depression, hopelessness, and suicidal tendencies. Shame overrides who God says we are.

God says we are loved, we are His children and are wonderfully made. Shame is not God's will for you. Feeling shame leads to sinful behavior. Wounded people often try to cope with pain by using defensive coping mechanisms. Defense mechanisms are a form of self-protection. This is a learned behavior through difficult and painful situations and by watching our parents.

Problems arise when our default defense mechanisms are not aligned with God's will. Poor defense mechanisms result in sinful behavior. Defense mechanisms that are most common and lead us into sinful behavior include: unforgiveness, bitter root judgments, bitter root expectancies, and inner vows. These will all be explained in detail later. Man's response to the pain of trauma or emotional wounding is either to deny the pain or to suppress it. Society's response to wounded people is to increase their self-esteem. This is based on the belief that if you love yourself everything will be fine. Psychologists call this a client-centered or person-centered counseling. The focus is on the person; God is left out of the equation.

A psychologist's and psychiatrist's plan often are to prescribe medications that tend to numb the person's feelings and pain, then sit down and discuss the events in their lives for countless hours, days, weeks, months, and years. This plan will never lead to healing. I believe that psychologists and psychiatrists have valuable purpose for those with chemical imbalance in the brain and those persons who need immediate interdiction. But I also believe that true healing will not occur without God.

Secular and Christian Counseling

Secular counseling will only teach wounded people how to make it through the day with proper coping skills. God created humans and will only heal through a spiritual component. Christian counselors understand this principle. Trauma and overwhelming life events wound the heart. It is not the initial incident that keeps us in long-term pain, it is our sinful response to the trauma that keeps us in a cycle of pain oppressed by our sin.

God created humans in His image with feelings and emotions. Each emotion has its purpose. It is when we use our emotions in ways that God never intended that we stay in our pain. If we follow what the Bible teaches us about our emotions and how to navigate trials in our lives, we remain in His will—the way we were designed to be. But when we go against God's will and plan for our lives, our pain is magnified.

For example, the emotion of anger: if a loyal friend betrays us, we become angry. The Bible teaches us that anger is a normal emotion and is permissible. God said, "Be angry but do not sin." So, we see it is alright to be angry; but don't hold onto your anger. God knows that when we harbor anger, it turns into bitterness and thoughts of revenge. These thoughts go against God's will and are sinful. Sin separates us from God, and being separated from God blocks us from God's healing and blessings.

God created our complex heart. Only God can heal what He created. It is our continual habitual sin that prevents our healing. He may heal while you are still in sin, but the separation is an obstacle to healing.

If we rely on a person-centered approach to healing, we will never heal because the heart is deceitful above all things, and desperately sick (Jeremiah 17:9). It is only a Christ-Centered approach that restores our relationship with God. Once restored, the healing begins.

Diagnosing the effects of trauma is not difficult. Determining our sinful response to our wounding is much like a doctor who diagnoses and illness. The doctor examines the patient and looks at the symptoms that the patient exhibits.

For example: a person with a deep cut to the skin complains of swelling, fever, and pain. These are the symptoms. The doctor examines the wound and diagnoses an infection. The infection is the resultant problem.

Although the initial issue is the cut, a response solely to that issue would be insufficient to heal the wound because an infection developed. The wound caused a certain amount of pain, but the infection caused substantially longer-lasting pain. In order to heal the wound, stop the pain, and return the patient as they were created, the doctor prescribes antibiotics, regular cleaning and dressing changes. This is the treatment. After time, the wound is healed.

The same is true with emotional and spiritual wounds. The symptoms are observable, objective manifestations that tell us that something is wrong. The symptoms are not the problem. The problem is the initial incident and our sinful response. The symptoms are a result of improper wound care.

The reason that you purchased this book is because you noticed that the symptoms were a warning that something is wrong. The treatment to combat the symptoms must be Christ-Centered. For example: a person might exhibit signs of bitterness and anger (symptoms). After self-examination, we learn that a friend betrayed them (cause/problem). The patient holds unforgiveness and thoughts of vengeance (sinful response).

The Bible prescribes a treatment that we should forgive the offender, repentance, and renouncing the will for vengeance (treatment). The treatment cleanses the wound and promotes healing. Continual vigilance with cleansing prevents further infections.

There is hope for your healing. If you are reading this book, believe that it is God's will to heal you. It is not a coincidence that you got this book and began reading it. God wants you to be healed! If God is for you, no one can be against you (Romans 8:31).

CHAPTER 3

THE BIBLE TEACHES HEALING

All Scripture is breathed out by God and profitable for teaching, for reproof, for correction, and for training in righteousness, that the man of God may be complete, equipped for every good work" (2 Timothy 3:16-17). The heart was created by God and only God can heal a broken heart. Jesus Christ came to earth to heal the broken hearted—that's you and me! God wants to bless you. The Bible teaches that when you are in God's will you will become blessed and healed. The question then becomes; *What is God's will?*

Romans 12:2 says, "I appeal to you therefore, brothers, by the mercies of God, to present your bodies as a living sacrifice, holy and acceptable to God, which is your spiritual worship. *Do not be conformed to this world, but be transformed by the renewal of your mind, that by testing you may discern what is the will of God,* what is good and acceptable and perfect" (Emphasis mine).

The Apostle Paul is telling Christians that through conversion (rebirth), Christians will experience a change, a transformation. This transformation occurs when we do not follow the popular culture and manner of thinking that is in rebellion against God, or the world, and instead follow the teachings of Jesus. When you follow Jesus, you will have a new worldview and will learn God's will. The Word of God will reveal His will for your life.

Before we begin, I want to make something clear: this is not a book on biblical doctrine. I do not intend this to be a theological study. My intention is to teach in plain English the scriptures in the Bible that I believe are important to healing our trauma and pain from life's overwhelming events. I will only discuss a few of the texts that teach the gospel and God's law and principles that bring blessing and healing. I will make every effort to simplify these scriptures.

There are still many mysteries in the Bible. There are many people who interpret the text to suit their ideology. Some scriptures are still hotly debated by theologians, so do not be discouraged if you have difficulty understanding certain texts.

If there is a text that you do not understand, pray and ask the Holy Spirit to reveal it to you. When you come to a point where you are having difficulty, keep reading. Scripture will often reveal its meaning in the next chapter. So, do not blindly believe anyone's interpretation of scripture. Not even my opinion. Rely only on the Holy Spirit to reveal it to you.

All below interpretations are my own. They are just overviews of concepts and principles in the Bible that relate to emotional, spiritual, and physical healing. My primary goal is to make you want to study the scripture in greater depth and detail.

I tried to define every theological term in the listed text. It is of great benefit to purchase a Bible dictionary to help you in your studies. I also recommend that you have your Bible ready as you continue to read this book to read the scriptures before and after the listed texts.

Do not be afraid to write in your Bible. Feel free to underline or highlight texts that touch your heart or pertain to healing. Your Bible may have a different interpretation than the one I am quoting from. Don't worry, it will turn out the same at the end. I am using the "English Standard Version" (ESV) to supply the scripture quoted. I believe this to be a plain and simple and true interpretation of the original text. I suggest if you are going out to purchase a Bible, get a "Study Bible." Study Bibles have notes at the bottom of each page that helps you interpret the scriptures. But remember, those notes are just the personal interpretation of the publisher. Just because the note shows the text to mean something, it doesn't make it fact.

There are many interpretations and styles of Bibles. In my opinion, the easiest to understand is the New Living Translation (NLT). I like the English

Standard Version (ESV). The difference is in the translation from the original text. No matter which type, the meaning is the same.

As we become more mature in our faith, we learn God's purpose and plan for our lives and begin to live in His will. As I grew in my faith, I was freed from my spiritual bondage. I know that there are many others who have placed themselves in a self-imposed prison due to their habitual sin. The devil has them living defeated lives, slaves to anger, bitterness, guilt, and shame. They feel helpless and often hopeless, because they are oppressed by their habitual unrepented sin.

Even seasoned Christians can be led astray by Satan's lies. Living apart from God will prevent us from living the abundant life that a close loving relationship with Jesus Christ will bring. The word of God will change your life.

As you prepare to begin the healing process, you must understand the biblical principles the Bible teaches. The most important component is learning and understanding who you are in Christ and who God says you are. Without the knowledge and understanding of God's word you will not heal or mature in your Christian life.

As we go through scriptures in Bible, I want to touch on significant events, concepts, principles, and interesting tidbits that every Christian should know. The listed scriptures are important to fully understand who God is and what Jesus has done for us.

One of God's great gifts to us is His Word, the Bible. This incredible book is not only a history book that details the origins of life, but a "user's manual" for us to live according to His will. The Bible is the best-selling book in history. It will become the most important book in your life.

The Bible tells us what we need to know about life and how to obtain eternal life with God in heaven. It instructs us on what God desires for our lives and gives us a biblical worldview or perspective. A worldview is the basic assumptions a person believes about life and the world. It is based on religion, gender, life experience, culture, race, and or socioeconomical status. The Bible strengthens us with this worldview. Its gives us hope through times of difficulty that all of us go through. God's truth changes our lives, gives us hope, peace, and joy.

The Bible is the inerrant word of God. God uses the Bible to reveal Himself to His creation. The books were written by forty different authors over a 1,500-year span. The authors came from every walk of life including: doctors, fishermen, kings, peasants, poets, and scholars. Each author was inspired by God's Holy Spirit to document what God wanted them to write.

Simply put, God wrote the Bible using man as a tool (2 Timothy 3:16). Despite a timeframe of 1,500 years, the composition and theme show remarkable complexity and cohesiveness. It is truly amazing. Volumes of books have been written on the divine inspiration of the Bible, its inerrancy and authority, as well as its subject matter.

In a nutshell, the Old Testament is an account of creation, the first sin, the beginning of civilization, the flood, God's dealing with mankind, the establishment of the nation of Israel, God's dealing with the Israelites, the need for a savior, and the prophecy of the coming Messiah—Jesus Christ. The Old Testament sets up the New Testament. Both are interwoven.

The New Testament is comprised of twenty-seven books, there are four divisions; the four Gospels, the Book of Acts, the Epistles, and the Book of Revelation. These books describe the conception, birth, life, ministry, death, and resurrection of Jesus Christ.

We can trust that the Bible is true and accurate because it is the most scrutinized book in history. The Bible has been corroborated through archaeology, science, and by the fulfillment of biblical prophecy. Hundreds of prophecies that were made thousands of years ago have come true with amazing accuracy. No fault has been found.

The Bible gives us the history of the heavens and Earth, and the human race. It explains why mankind needs a savior and how God provided that savior in His son Jesus Christ.

Bible history include accounts of war, famine, and overcoming trauma and adversities. There are stories of Satan, demons and angels, dysfunctional families, kings and queens, giants, adultery, love poems, and divine miracles. Each story is better than the last. The more we read, the more we learn about God's mercy and grace.

The Bible is a book that needs to be studied. Each time you read it you will discover something that you never saw in the past. Many times, you will discover a scripture that applies directly to the current trial that you are going through. When you open the Bible and read it, you will learn what great promises and gifts God has for those who love Him. The Bible will change your life, it changed mine.

I suggest you begin with the Gospel of John. Gospel means "good news." The Apostle John explains the Gospel of Christ. After finishing John, read the Old Testament beginning with Genesis.

Before you begin, pray and ask the Holy Spirit to give you clear understanding on how to apply the scripture to your life. I recommend that you read each chapter two times.

Ask yourself if this scripture applies to you. What does it mean to you? What does this teach about God? Is there a lesson to learn? And how does this apply to what you are going through right now?

Every book of the Bible has a message. There is a reason that God put it in there. There are spiritual laws and principles God wants us to understand. Everyone should read the entire Bible throughout each year. It's just a few chapters each day.

When reading, take your time. It is better to understand the text. If there are scriptures that you do not understand, do not get frustrated, learned theologians dispute scripture. Ask the Holy Spirit to reveal the meaning to you. Wait quietly and listen for what God has to say. The Word of God will change your life!

God's will is that you be healed. Knowing the promises of God and believing in them, as well as understanding who God is, and who you are in Christ is instrumental in your healing. This section lays out the scriptures relating to healing. As you build your relationship with God, healing becomes more intense. Let's begin the study. God bless you.

WHY CREATION VS. EVOLUTION AFFECTS YOUR HEALING

Before we dive into the scripture, it is very important that you believe that the Bible is the true and accurate Word of God. Christians believe in God, but most do not believe that everything in the Bible is the true Word of

God. They pick and choose which scriptures they believe are true. We cannot say one scripture is true but another is not. We must believe that everything in the Bible is true in order to grow in our faith and trust in Jesus. One of the main arguments I often hear from people is that they believe the Bible, except for the story of creation. They believe in evolution rather than creation. We have all been taught in school that man evolved from monkeys. This is not what God teaches. I believe that it takes more faith to believe in evolution than it takes to believe in creation.

I will briefly show you why there is more than enough evidence to prove creationism. Below is a brief overview of my take on the controversy. If this subject interests you, there are many books out there written by scientists who now believe in creation.

Evolution

Charles Darwin is the Father of Theory of Evolution. In his 1859 book, *The Origin of Species*, Darwin theorizes that life on Earth began with a single-celled organism 3.8 billion years ago. This single-celled organism spontaneously sprang to life, before there was life. He believes that this cell came to life from non-living chemicals. The cell was then able to reproduce itself, subsequently changing itself into every life form on the planet. This was supposed to have occurred billions of years ago.

The theory is that this one cell changed by genetic mutations. This allowed the organism to slowly improve and reproduce. Over these billions of years, this one cell that came from nothing produced all living things.

In this theory every living thing on earth like fish, trees, birds, grass, flowers, snakes, rats, elephants, and human beings all came from this one cell. This makes the trees in front of your house your distant relative. This theory is not backed by any evidence. Even so, some scientists have demonstrated great faith in this theory and teach it as if it were fact.

Let's imagine that this theory is correct and evolution is how we were all created. The question comes up, where did this single-cell organism come from? How did it come to life and form? How did a living thing come from nothing?

It appears to me that there are three options that may answer these questions. The first option is that the entire universe always existed. The second option is that the universe was created by someone or something. The third option is that the universe created itself.

We know from science that nothing cannot create something. Something must first exist before it can create something. In order to explain this, some scientists came up with the "Big Bang Theory."

Basically, this theory says that in the beginning there was nothing. At some point in history there was an explosion that resulted in bringing nothing into something that existed. For this theory to be true, we have to have something before there can be an explosion. If there is nothing, how can it explode?

The Big Bang theory cannot be considered until we can prove that there was something to explode. Science is not exact. Experiments and potential evidence must be evaluated and interpreted. This is all done by fallible individuals with a non-Christian worldview. Interpretations can be stretched to make any theory plausible.

In 2011, there was a BBC documentary called *What Happened Before the Big Bang?* Doctor Michio Kaku, Professor of Theoretical Physics at City University, New York spoke about getting something from nothing. He said, "I think there are two kinds of nothing. First there is something I call absolute nothing: no equations, no space, no time, no anything that the human can conceive of, just nothing. Then there is the vacuum which is nothing but the absence of matter."

What? If there is a vacuum, where is the vacuum coming from? Dr. Michio has no evidence to support his theory of two nothings. He obviously has faith in his theory. Because he is a scientist, people believe him blindly.
Now let's assume that the big bang did occur. It caused an explosion that brought Earth, planets, stars, sun, moon, land, and water on Earth into existence. Now where did life come from? An explosion requires chemicals, there is no life in chemicals. Where did this single-celled living organisms come from?

Creation of a living organism requires design and craftsmanship so complex that even today is the world's most advanced scientific laboratories we are unable to create a living cell. Scientists have been working decades on this very theory. Never has any scientist succeeded in creating life through chemicals or explosions.

PROOF OF THE BIBLE'S TRUTH

The last theory is that of creation by a designer. Neither I, nor anyone else can prove that God exists. Evolution and creation have the same issue, no proof on either side.

We must look at the evidence presented. The facts herein have been summarized just to make a point for further research. Entire books are written on this subject. Check for yourself.

The Bible has been proven historically accurate. Throughout the world since the beginning of time, man struggled to figure out how Earth fit into the heavens. Ancient scientists had many theories.

The Romans believed that there was a God that held up Earth in his hands. Many believed that Earth was flat. The book of Job is thought to be the oldest book of the Bible. Some believe it was written prior to 1,500 B.C. We do not know who wrote it, but we do know God inspired the writer to make it the accurate word of God.

Job 26:7 says, "He [God] stretches out the north over the void and hangs the earth on nothing." This was written in 1,500 B.C. The earth sits in its orbit by nothing. The Romans were the most educated people of their time and they thought that their false god Atlas held up the earth with his hands.

The Book of Isaiah was written in about 750 B.C. The author is the prophet of God. Isaiah made many predictions—all came true. For example, Chapter forty describes God's greatness. Isaiah knew that Earth was not flat.

Isaiah 40:22 says, "It is He [God] who sits above the circle of the earth, and its inhabitants are like grasshoppers; who stretches out the heavens like a curtain . . ."

Most scientists believed that the earth was flat in the third century A.D. It wasn't widely believed the earth was round until the 15th century. Isaiah wrote that in 750 B.C. How did Isaiah know that the earth was round? God the creator of the universe told him.

Archaeology has also proven the accuracy of the Bible. In 1925, researchers found the Nuzi Tablets near the Tiger River, these date back to about 1,800

B.C. These tablets confirm the historicity of the ancient customs practiced at the time of Abraham, before Israel's slavery in Egypt. The tablets confirm social practices and customs that are described in the Bible.

Tablets found in 1922 in the ancient city of Ur in southern Sumer date back to about 1,600 B.C., the same time that Abraham walked the earth. One tablet has the name "Abram." This was Abraham's name prior to when God changed it. This is a very strong argument for the reliability of the Bible as a historical text.

There are umpteen examples of various archaeological artifacts that prove the Bible's reliability. There are also many books published detailing all this evidence that include the numerous artifacts found in those ancient cities proving the Bible accurate.

In addition, there are medical bits of wisdom in the Bible. One example has to do with the practice of circumcision. Genesis 17:12 says, "For the generations to come every male among you who is eight days old must be circumcised . . ."

Circumcision is a sign of the covenant between God and the Israelites (Genesis 17:11). The Bible does not provide a reason for this to be done on the eighth day of life. Medical science has determined on the eighth day of life is the best time for surgery because the newborn's blood has vitamin "K" present as well as a large amount of the element "prothrombin" which is required for blood clotting. Surgery conducted any earlier would most likely cause the baby to bleed to death. Today, babies are given a shot of vitamin K prior to circumcision to promote the clotting of blood.[7]

The Bible contains hundreds of prophecies regarding things to come. The fulfillment of prophecy presents the strongest case for reliability for the Bible.

There are over 300 prophecies regarding the birth of Jesus, His life, death, and resurrection documented in the Old Testament. Sixty are major prophesies and 260 are ramifications of prophecy. All were made over 400 years before the birth of Christ. Jesus Christ fulfilled every single one of them, perfectly and accurately as foretold.

---

[7] Bert Thompson, "Why the Eighth Day," *Bible Apologetics – A Daily Devotional* (blog), Bible Apologetics, December 28, 2020, https://bibleapologetics.org/circumcision-why-the-eight-day/

The Bible gives us an accurate account about the origin of mankind. The first chapter of Genesis details God's creation of the heavens and the earth (Genesis 1:1-2). We must then assume that prior to creation there was nothing but God.

Hebrews 11:3 says that everything was created by the Word of God. God spoke it and it was done. The universe was made from things not visible. God spoke into creation living land creatures such as livestock, lions, tigers, elephants and things that creep on the ground like insects, snakes, and worms.

All things were created according to their kinds (verses 24-25). God then said, "Let us make man in our image, after our likeness" (Genesis 1:26). God created male and female. God blessed them and said, "Be fruitful and multiply and fill the earth and subdue it and have dominion over the fish of the sea and over the birds of the heavens and over every living thing that moves on the earth" (Genesis 1:27-28).

Man was created in God's likeness. He created mankind with intelligence, emotions, the ability to make moral decisions, have relationships, and best of all He created man to live in complete fellowship with Him forever. There was no death in the Garden of Eden. But as we will learn, Adam messed that all up for everyone.

Age of The Earth

One of the biggest debates is: What is the age of the earth? Is it billions of years old as evolutionists theorize or is it only thousands of years old as the Bible testifies?

When I went to school in the sixties and seventies, we were taught that the earth was billions of years old and that man evolved from monkeys. I spent all my life believing this teaching.

Now, based on my studies and much prayer, it is my opinion that the earth is between 8,000 and 12,000 years old. Most biblical scholars estimate the earth at around 4,000 to 5,000 years old based upon the Bible's genealogies. I like to give some wiggle room and add some for God adding age to the world prior to creation of man. Most modern scientists believe the earth is about 4.6 billion years old. This is a huge difference; both cannot be right. Before I begin to explain my stance, remember that evolutionists believe that all living things originated from one single-celled organisms. The most important part of their theory is based on time, lots of it. In order to have this theory make sense, they must give an age of billions of years. Without billions of years, evolution could not happen.

In the 1950's, scientists believed the earth was only two billion years old. Now its 4.6 billion. Time is so very important to the evolutionist. We must understand that scientists are under a lot of pressure to prove their theories.

Many scientists are funded through grants. The way they get funded is by being published.[8] Scientists are then considered for further funding for their research. If no evidence of their theory is found, funding stops and so does their paychecks. You can see the potential for bias and even misrepresentation of evidence.

In a 2003, Discovery Channel documentary called *Walking With Cavemen*, an unknown scientist admitted, "The thing about science is that there isn't just one truth. Everything is interpretation, and in this case, if you were to gather every piece of fossil evidence on which interpretations about early humans [evolution] are based, it would fit quite easily into one small car."

I have to admit that the church is also biased. However, their agenda is not financially driven. This is not a great debate within the church. We know that many Christians in the church do not fully believe in the truth of the Bible. This non-belief makes for an unhealthy Christian. You cannot pick and choose the parts of the Bible that you want to believe and not believe. This makes God out to be a liar.

There are two ways to determine the earth's age. The Bible or science. Many people choose science. Most people believe that science is black and white. Science is indisputable. As we can see, science is assumptions and interpretations driven by the scientist's worldview or bias.

The Bible gives an eyewitness account from the God that created all things. God created the earth and all living things with some age. If God created the earth with no age, plants would just be seeds, there would be no food for the first human to eat, no garden to take care of. If this is true, then

---

[7] Kelsey Piper, "Can a new approach to funding scientific research unlock innovation?" Vox, December 18, 2021, https://www.vox.com/future-perfect/2021/12/18/22838746/biomedicine-science-grants-arc-institute

wouldn't God have created the rocks, mountains, and all things with the same age? So, to be fair to both sides, I believe the earth to be 8,000 to 12,000 years old.

Now let's go to the evidence. According to *National Geographic Magazine* Volume 113, the oldest living thing on earth is the Bristlecone Pine Tree. A study of the growth rings shows an age of about 4,000-years old. Several other neighboring trees were found to also be about 4,000-years old.[9] There is no evidence of any trees of a generation prior to those now growing. Incidentally, the flood is the story of Noah was about 4,500 years ago.

In order to date the age of Earth, scientists use rocks and other substances to come to a range date. Some of the scientific dating methods rely on radioactivity. It involved the decay of unstable or radioactive elements into stable, non-radioactive elements. This can make for many possible errors and misinterpretations because everything depends on a constant decay rate. There is no way to be confident that the decay rate remains consistent.[10]

The Institution for Creation Research and the Creation Research Society entered into a joint project called *Radioisotopes and the Age of the Earth* or RATE. An eight-year study found that the earth had experienced periods of greatly accelerated decay in the past.[11] This means that a rock formed 100 years ago could be dated at a billion years old.

---

[9] *Encyclopedia Britannia Online*, s.v. "The Bristlecone Pine, Oldest Living Thing," accessed 7/5/2023, https://www.britannica.com/plant/bristlecone-pine

[10] "Radioisotopes and the Age of the Earth," accessed July 20, 2015, www.irc.org/rate

[11] "Radioisotopes and the Age of the Earth," accessed July 20, 2015, www.irc.org/rate

There have been documented dating errors like the one researchers made in Hawaii.[12] A volcano known to have erupted in about 1,800 A.D. and initiated the formation of rock from the lava. Researchers dated that rock at three billion years old. RATE team research found other dating errors based on different dating technique. Their research is posted on their web site—www.icr.org.

A Young Earth

What evidence is there on the biblical worldview side? We only have the Bible. Just because God created the earth about 8,000 to 12,000 years ago does not mean that everything will date back to that time. God created everything including all the chemical elements and compounds necessary to sustain life on earth. In Genesis we see that God created all living things with apparent age or appearance of age. The plants, trees, fish, animals, Adam and Eve had some age in them.

God created Adam and Eve and placed them in the Garden of Eden. Since man is a living creature requiring food, these plants and trees must have been created with fruit already on the branches. If they had no fruit and the plants were just sprouting, Adam and Eve would have no food to eat. They were created as vegetarians. Adam and Eve must have been created with age because they could talk, work, and reason.

There is a lot we do not know about how much time passed after God created the universe, it is reasonable to conclude that God created the universe to be fully functional, a complete wonderfully functioning mechanism. God is sovereign and almighty. His miracle of creation was done to show His glory.

There are many more examples like these. More knowledgeable people than I have written on questions about DNA, the gap theory, evidence of a worldwide flood, Noah's Ark, and carbon-14. Please do the research, it will answer lots of questions and build your faith and trust in Jesus.

The theory of evolution cannot be substantiated. It is only assumed. Evolutionists base their theory on time and only positive mutations. History has shown that genetic mutations are for the most part, only detrimental to

---

[12] J. Cohen, "Our Genes Aren't Us," *Discover Magazine*, EDITION 1994, 78-84

organisms in their survival and future reproduction. However, there are some cases that could have positive impact on the organism.

Think about how wonderfully complicated the human body is. Google how the eye works, how the ear works, how our immune system works, or how complicated our nervous system is. Can all these systems generate from one single-celled organism?

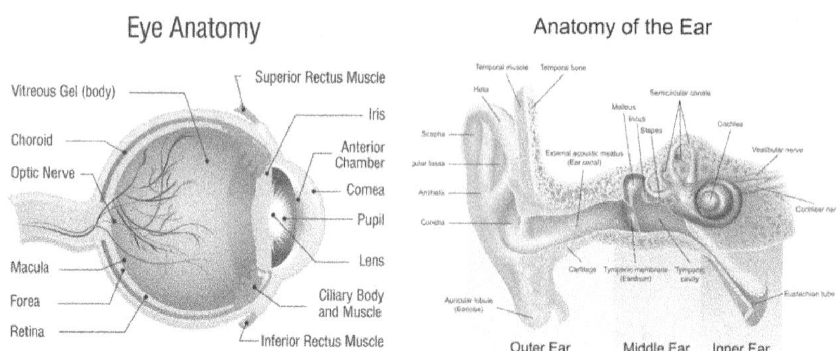

Also, it's difficult to accept that this single-celled organism morphed into a fish; a fish to a frog; a frog to a lizard; a lizard into a monkey; and a monkey into a human being. For fun, let's assume that the lizard developed into the first monkey. Did it develop into a male or female monkey? It is the first and only monkey. How could it reproduce to survive?

The very first of all these mutated creatures would have all died off. For this theory to be true there would have to have been a second lizard undergoing the same random positive mutations as the first lizard, EXCEPT that the second lizard would have to mutate into the opposite sex of the first so that both monkeys, male and female could mate and reproduce. Just think about the odds of this happening, not only with one creature, but thousands of times with every living creature on earth. Even with a hundred billion years this scenario is highly unlikely.

I believe the Bombardier Beetle is a good example of a complex trait that is difficult to explain via evolution.

This innocent-looking one-inch-long beetle seems defenseless to predators. These tiny beetles are anything but defenseless. Bombardier Beetles have two chambers that store hydrogen peroxide and hydroquinone. These chemicals would explode if mixed together in a laboratory, but somehow the beetle was designed with an inhibitor substance that blocks the explosive reaction.

When challenged, the beetle exerts muscular tension to move the chemicals to a compartment called "the explosion chamber." Muscular tension shoots out the chemicals at its enemies at a scalding 212 degrees. How did this trait evolve without killing the beetle off with its own chemicals? God must have given this beetle a self-defense mechanism.

Bombardier Beetles

Lastly, the dinosaur. Scientists have uncovered hundreds of dinosaur fossils identifying many different species of the animal. Scientists date then back to millions of years ago. How do Christians explain this? I have already shed a bit of light on the current dating methods and their errors.

The Bible describes huge creatures that were very powerful. We believe dinosaurs roamed the earth with man. There is a beautiful church in Northern England called the Carlisle Cathedral. One of its bishops that died in 1496 A.D. is buried in the church.

The tomb of Bishop Bell is in the center of the church. There is a brass inlay surrounding the tomb. The brass was engraved with medieval etchings over 500 years ago. The etchings depict animals such as dogs, a fish, an eel and what looks remarkably like two dinosaurs. Experts have identified these to look like Sauropod dinosaurs.

Evolutionists want us to believe that dinosaurs are millions of years old. This tomb is just over 500 years old. Five-hundred years ago no one had found any dinosaur fossils nor studied anything similar to dinosaurs. Fossils had not been found until the 1800s.[13]

How would the people of that time know what a dinosaur looked like unless they saw renderings or drawings from their forefathers. History records accounts of people encountering huge beasts that they called dragons around the time before the flood of Noah.[14] You decide what to believe.

Again, there is so much information available presenting evidence on both sides. I just want to provide food for thought. I encourage you to research evolution and creation yourself and ask the Holy Spirit to help you decide.

Who is the God that Heals Us?

> *"This says the LORD, your redeemer, who formed you from the womb; I am the LORD, who made all things, who alone stretched out the heavens, who spread out the earth by Himself…" (Isaiah 44:24).*

God exists. "The fool says in his heart, there is no God" (Psalm 14:1). God reveals Himself through the Bible. He created all we see. Thus, there is no excuse not to believe in an almighty sovereign God, creator of all things.

---

[13] "Dinosaurs," last modified June 29, 2023, accessed May 3, 2020, https://www.hsitory.com/topics/pre-history/dinosaurs-an-introduction

[14] Mark Hardwood, "Elephants in the room" Creation Magazine, Volume 36 No. 2 2014, 35-37

Second Corinthians 4:5 says that Satan has blinded the minds of unbelievers to keep them from seeing the truth of God. God reveals Himself to us through His Holy Spirit and allows us to comprehend the will of God (1 Corinthians 2:10-11).

The Bible says that God is a spirit. John 4:24 says, God is a spirit, and those who worship Him must worship in spirit and truth. As a spirit, God is a living God. God has many names. But He himself revealed His name as "YAHWEH." This is thought to mean: "I am who I am" (Exodus 3:14). Whenever you see the word "LORD" in lower case capital letters, it means God's true name—YAHWEH.

Even though God is a spirit, He has a personal nature, He is our Creator and our Heavenly Father. Matthew 5:45 says we should pray for those who are against you so that, "... you may be sons of your father who is in heaven."

Scriptures portray God as a real person who gave Himself in a reciprocal relationship with man. God has many attributes, some include:

- God is eternal—He is the Alpha and Omega, the beginning and the end. God exists endlessly. He never came into existence. He was not born or created. He is endlessly self-existent (Psalm 90:2). This is a difficult concept to understand but God always was and always will be
- God is love—God is love (1 John 4:8) God loved the world (John 3:16). Love consists of warmth and affection and correction if necessary. A loving father corrects his children because he loves them not because he hates (Hebrews 12: 6-11).
- God is omnipotent—God is all powerful and able to do all things. One of His names is God Almighty (Genesis 17:1). God's power is unlimited.
- God is omnipresent—God is everywhere at all times (Psalm 139:7-11). There is no place on earth or heaven that the presence of God is not.
- God is omniscience—God is all knowing. He knows all things, there is nothing he does not know, there is nothing that He can't learn.
- God is Holy—God cannot sin (James 1:13). God hates sin. God cannot lie (Titus 1:2). God is good, God is light, God is righteous (Psalm 11:7). Holy means sinless or separated from sin.

- God is sovereign—God is supreme. He controls the universe as He wills. God is in complete control of all things in heaven and on earth.
- God is truth—God has revealed Himself truthfully. God is reliable, faithful, fair and consistent.
- God is one—There is only one true God. Only one God is revealed in the Bible.
- God is perfect—He does everything right. It is a privilege and honor to know Him and to walk with Him.

Jesus Christ's Ministry was about Healing

> *"He [Jesus] Himself bore our sins in His body on the tree, that we might die to sin and live to righteousness. By His wounds you have been healed" (1 Peter 2:24).*

As Christians we must always remember that physical illness, emotional illness, sorrow, and death came as the result of Adam's sin. Sickness is simply part of the curse after the fall. The good news is that God sent His son to redeem us from the curse by His death on the cross. The prophet Isaiah received revelation from God regarding Christ's mission on earth.

Isaiah 61:1-3 says, "The Spirit of God is upon Me [Christ], because the LORD has anointed Me to bring good news to the poor; He has sent Me to blind up [heal] the brokenhearted, to proclaim liberty to the captives, and the opening of the prison to those who are bound [spiritually oppressed] . . . to comfort all who mourn; to grant to those who mourn in Zion—to give them a beautiful headdress instead of ashes, the oil of gladness instead of mourning, the garment of praise instead of a faint spirit; that they may be called oaks of righteousness . . . "Isaiah explained the meaning in relation to our healing of Jesus' work on the cross in Isaiah 53:4-5, "Surely He [Jesus] has borne our grief and carried our sorrows; yet we esteemed Him stricken, smitten by God, and afflicted. But He was wounded for our transgressions; He was crushed for our iniquities; upon Him was the chastisement that brought us peace, and with His strips (wounds from whipping) we are healed."

These passages tell us that through Jesus' beating, murder, and resurrection, we are healed of physical, emotional, and spiritual illness. Jesus paid the ransom for us. His beating and death was supposed to be our punishment for sin, but He took upon Him the ill effects of the fall; He defeated Satan and freed us from Satanic oppression.

During Jesus' short ministry He focused on healing and teaching. He healed all those brought to Him. The gospels record 414 distinct instances of physical and emotional healing. God created man with a physical body (flesh), a soul (mind, thoughts, and emotions), and a spirit (1 Thessalonians 5:23).

This unity cannot be separated.

Christianity and physical/emotional health are inextricably intertwined. The spiritual component cannot be denied. Secular counseling does not accept the spiritual component as of any importance. This is why there is no healing with a secular method of focusing on the person. The Christ-Centered approach focuses on Jesus. Jesus is our physician. Utilizing a spiritual component promotes healing.

When we look at Jesus' healing ministry, we see that it is God's will to heal the sick; physically, emotionally, and spiritually. God did not create mankind to have illness, sorrow, or grief. This is a result of the fallen world. It is Satan's will for us to be sick and live defeated lives because he hates God. God heals people because He loves them with an unconditional love that we could never comprehend.

How do we heal physical illness for ourselves or others? We must remain in fellowship with God. When we are in fellowship with Him, He hears our prayers. The scriptures teach that God does not listen to those with unrepented sin, but He hears the prayers of the righteous. We need to pray in faith believing that if it is in God's will He will heal.

We must pray with a sincere heart. We must pray that no matter what happens, God will be glorified. God answers prayers, but we must remember that God is sovereign. Even though it is His will to heal all of His children, it may be that His plan is that a person's illness is being used as part of His plan. If His plan depends on this illness, He may not allow healing.

We see this in Second Corinthians chapter twelve where Paul tells the church in Corinth that he has been inflicted with a "Thorn in the Flesh."

We do not know what He meant with a thorn in the flesh. Some theologians believe Paul had a recurrent physical illness and others believe that it was a constant harassment by Satan. Paul asked God for healing, God refused to heal Paul. God said, "My grace is sufficient for you, for My power is made perfect in weakness." (2 Corinthians 12:9).

God had a plan and purpose for Paul, His plan included this affliction. Our prayers should include a phrase similar to "if it be Your will" or "I want Your will to be done in my life, whatever happens, healing or not." Remember, " . . . we know that for those who love God all things work together for good, for those who are called according to His purpose" (Romans 8:28). If God chooses not to heal, you can be assured that God will make something good out of the circumstances.

In respect to healing and prayer, it is very important to understand that God has a plan for every person. We may never understand His complete plan, but we need to know that His plans supersede our plans. We see very little of God's plan and purpose for our life, while God sees it all; from the beginning to the end. If He chooses not to heal, we must trust that there is some higher purpose for our affliction.

God often uses trials or illness to draw us to Him, it is in difficult times that we seek God. We never seem to look for Him when times are good. God is always there to help provide us with the strength to endure.

It is many people's testimony, as well as my own, that trials bring us closer to God. In my life I did not believe there was a loving God. As you, I am chosen, God waited as long as He could for me to repent of my sins. I did not respond. He allowed trials in my life.

I chose the sinful way out, and I came to prison. He chose us before the foundations of the world. I was going to be a Christian the easy way, or the hard way. Unfortunately, most of us are like me and choose the hard way.

In my case, God allowed a neuro-muscular disease into my life. This led me to many surgeries and severe emotional distress, yet I did not humble myself. Then, I began to suffer symptoms of PTSD that led me to an opioid addiction, I still refused to humble myself before God. God knew how to get at me, He allowed my daughter to have liver tumors with a negative prognosis. I still didn't submit.

I finally tapped out looking at a long prison sentence, I humbled myself before my Lord. I am not saying God orchestrated these afflictions, but He allowed it for my good and the good of God's kingdom. God healed my daughter, and later He healed me.

Psalm 119:67, 71 says." "Before I was afflicted, I went astray, but now I keep your word."

Through our suffering we grow in our faith. Jesus Christ had and still has a healing ministry. We must keep the faith and trust in Him, and when you do not see immediate healing, keep trusting and know that God has a plan. Romans 8:28 says, "And we know that for those who love God all things work together for good, for those who are called according to His purpose." Jesus is the great physician; it is His will to heal. Remember sin blocks our healing. Restore your relationship with Him today and pray for healing.

God's Will Is That You Be Healed

> *"Do not be conformed to this world, but be transformed by the renewal of your mind, that by testing you may discern what is the will of God" (Romans 12:2).*

In order to live the life of a mature spiritual Christian and obtain the blessing and healing that continual sanctification brings, we must know and follow God's will. In Paul's letter to the church in Colossae, he tells the church, "... we have not ceased to pray for you, asking that you may be filled with the knowledge of His [God] will in all spiritual wisdom and understanding, so as to walk in a manner worthy of the Lord fully pleasing to Him, bearing fruit in every good work and increasing in the knowledge of God" (Colossians 1:9-10).

Paul is telling us not to be happy with the things of this world. Christians should have an intimate relationship with God in praise and worship. God transforms our minds which leads to a Christian worldview. That is the will of God. Our continued fellowship with God and following the leading of the Holy Spirit aligns us with God's will.

God's will is twofold. The "general" will of God is found through biblical scripture. The Bible gives us clear direction in all facets of our life on earth. For example, the Ten Commandments are simple rules to follow that obeys God's will. God's general will provide guidelines on how to live our lives and how to treat others.

God also has a "specific" will that is directed towards a specific person. We learn God's general will by studying he Bible. We learn God's specific will by listening to the Holy Spirit. Through a loving relationship with our triune God, we hear the Holy Spirit's voice who will lead us and reveal what He deems important for us to know about God's plan and purpose for our lives. John 16:13-15 says, "When the Spirit of Truth [Holy Spirit] comes, He will guide you into all truth, for He will not speak on His own authority, but whatever He hears He will speak, and He will declare to you the things that are to come. He will glorify Me [Jesus], for He will take what is mine and declare it to you. All that the Father has is Mine and declare it to you."

The Holy Spirit will reveal all things necessary to live a life that reflects the will of God. The Holy Spirit will place God's plan in your heart when you are ready to receive it. Through the Holy Spirit we have direct access to our creator instantaneously, no 'waiting in line' or 'on hold' on the phone, and no prerecorded messages! We can tell Him anything, any secret; we can ask him anything. He will not judge. Walk in the Holy Spirit and the will of God will be provided to you.

In relation to healing, it is God's will to heal you. The Book of Deuteronomy provides us some of God's laws. Moses wrote these laws down in the final years of his life, so the Israelites would forever know them.

Moses said, ". . . He [God] will love you, bless you, multiply you. He will also bless the fruit of your ground, your grain and your wine and your oil, the increase of your herds and the young of your flock in the land that He swore to your fathers to give you. You shall be blessed above all peoples. There shall not be male or female barren among you or your livestock. And the LORD will take away from you all sickness, and none of the evil diseases of Egypt, which you know, He will inflict on you, but He will lay them on all that hate you" (Deuteronomy 7:13-15).

This is God' will for you today. This is a promise from God to you. Believe in God's word.

The New Covenant Promises Healing

> *" . . . He [Jesus] is the mediator of a new covenant, so that those who are called may receive the promised eternal inheritance . . ." (Hebrews 9 :19).*

During the Old Testament times, God dealt with the Israelites based on the Mosaic Covenant. The Word "covenant" means an arrangement made by one party. The other party can accept it or reject it, but it cannot be altered. The law was intended and instituted to keep people righteous, however, no one could keep all the laws. But what the law did, was to show us that none of us is without sin, and we are all in need of a savior. God sent Jesus to put an end to these burdensome rules.

In Jeremiah 31:30-34, God told the Prophet Jeremiah that in the future God would make new covenant with the nation of Israel. God would place the law in their hearts and not on stone tablets like the Ten Commandments. Through this new covenant, God will forgive people's sins. This was prophesied 600 years before Jesus' birth. The new covenant would be established by Jesus' work on the cross.

Ezekiel 36:25-26 tells us that God will cleanse the Israelites and give them a new heart to replace their heart of stone (sinful heart), and give them the Holy Spirit to be with them always. This new covenant would include all people, not just Jews (Romans 11:11-24).

Any promise from God made to the Jews is applicable to all of us. The night before Jesus' death was the annual Passover celebration. It was a Thursday night. Jesus was having Passover dinner with His disciples. It was to be their last meal together.

This is known as "The Last Supper."

Mark tells us what occurred at this first communion, "And as they were eating, He [Jesus] took bread, and after blessing it broke it and gave it to them [disciples], and said, 'Take, this is My body.' And He took a cup, and when He had given thanks He gave it to them, and they drank of it. And He said to them. 'This is My blood of the covenant, which is poured out for many.'" (Mark 14: 22-24).

Luke 22:17-20 adds, "And He [Jesus] took the bread, and when He had given thanks He broke it and gave it to them, saying, 'This is my body, which is given to you. Do this in remembrance of Me.' And likewise the cup after they had eaten, saying, 'This cup that is poured out for you is the new covenant in My blood.'"

The broken bread symbolizes Jesus' body that was broken upon the cross. The cup of wine represents His blood that was shed on that cross. Interestingly Jesus says, " . . . which is given for you . . . " and " . . . that is poured out for many." He is referring to his sacrifice as a gift to you, as well as mankind.

The blood shed by Jesus cleanses us from our sins (1 John 4:7-10). God considers us no longer guilty of sin, we are adopted into God's family with the same inheritance as Jesus. We belong to God and will live with Him forever in heaven.

In the Old Testament, Jews believed (and still believe today) that the only way to heaven was to follow the 613 statutes of the law. But through Jesus Christ's sacrifice on the cross, the "law" no longer rules over us. We are freed from the stress of making sure we follow rules. Our only "law" is to love God and one another (Matthew 22:37-39). Romans 7:6 says, "But now we are released from the law, having died to that which held us captive, so that we serve a new way of the Spirit, and not the old way of the written code."

This new way is the Holy Spirit who is placed in the hearts of those who are saved to love God and one another.

Christians are now under Jesus' law, the new covenant. Jesus tells us the law in Matthew 22:37-40, " . . . you shall love the Lord your God with all your heart and with all your soul and with all your mind, this is the great and first commandment. And a second is like it: You shall love your neighbor as yourself . . . "

Loving God and your neighbor replace all 613 Old Testament laws! Christianity is so simple; anyone can follow these two rules. This love will give us peace and joy that only belief in God can provide. Love conquers all. God is love!

UNDERSTANDING WHO GOD IS AND WHO YOU ARE IN CHRIST

The key to healing is understanding who God is, what Jesus Christ has done for you and who you are in Christ. It is important to understand the biblical principles and laws that must be followed to stay in God's will. This is not an in-depth study but an overview of God's divine plan for our lives. I suggest joining a Bible study from your local church in order to learn as much as you can about God's word.

Let's begin with some of the scriptures that relate to spiritual, emotional, and physical healing:

- "The LORD is a stronghold for the oppressed, a stronghold in times of trouble" (Psalm 9:9).
- " . . . weeping will tarry for the night, but joy comes in the morning" (Psalm 30:5).
- "When the righteous cry out for help, the LORD hears and delivers them out of all their troubles. The LORD is near to the brokenhearted and saves the crushed spirit. Many are the afflictions for the righteous, but the LORD delivers him out of them all" (Psalm 34:17-19).

This Psalm describes God's benefits to those who follow Him. Benefits include: forgiveness of sins, physical healing, emotional healing, spiritual healing, delivering you out of trials, and salvation.

- God provides us with love and mercy so that our youth is renewed (Psalm 103:1-5).
- "Obey God and He will heal your physical body" (Proverbs 3:5-8).
- "A gentle tongue [kindness] is the tree of life [source of life/wisdom], but perverseness [sin] breaks the spirit" (Proverbs 15:4).
- "A joyful heart is good medicine" (Proverbs 17:22).
- "A man's spirit will endure sickness, but a crushed spirit who can bear?" (Proverbs 18:14)
- "There is healing through fasting" (Isaiah 58:6-11).
- "Obey God and all will go good with you" (Jeremiah 7:23).
- "Sin no more and all will go well with you" (John 5:1-16).
- "Pray for one another's healing, you will be healed" (James 5:14).

We will begin our Bible study at the beginning of the Bible with the creation of mankind and go through to Christ's death on the cross:

1. God created man in His likeness (Genesis 1:26-27)
2. God created a man to be perfect
3. God created man intelligent with reasoning ability
4. God created man to be holy
5. God created man to have eternal life
6. God gave man authority over the entire earth

God created man in His image. Theologians believe that this refers to God's moral likeness having freedom of choice, intellectual faculties, in direct communication with God, free from sin, with eternal life. We believe these things because Genesis 5:3 says, "When Adam lived 130 years, he fathered a son in his own likeness, after his [Adam] image, and named him Seth." We are all made in the image of God. After the fall some of these characteristics went away.

The first sin on earth read Genesis 3:1-17

The first sin (the fall of man) caused loss of fellowship with God, resulting in spiritual death and physical death—consequences for sin. Sin brought guilt and shame into the world. Adam's sin transferred authority of the earth to Satan (Luke 4:5-7).

God created Adam and Eve without sin. This purity enabled them to be in complete fellowship with God. God gave them only one rule: do not eat from the tree of knowledge of good and evil. They were warned that if they ate from the tree, they would die. This was a spiritual death and later a physical death. I believe that God allowed Satan to tempt Eve to test the couple, to determine their obedience to Him. This scripture shows that God created us with freedom of choice as to whether we would voluntarily choose to obey God and serve Him or not. God did not create mankind to be a robot or an automation.

Satan tempted Eve the same way he tempts us today. Satan's lies tell us that forbidden fruit is sweet. As we all do, Eve rationalized that the fruit was good to look at and would be good to eat. She probably thought, "Why would a kind loving God withhold something so good from me?"

Satan played on her pride and ego. Satan suggested that if she ate the fruit she would be like God. Who wouldn't want to be like God? She ate and then gave some to Adam.

Adam knew better. God told Adam not to eat the fruit. The consequences of Adam's sin include:

- Guilt and shame entered the world
- Humans now suffered spiritual death: loss of fellowship with God
- Humans now suffered physical death. No longer would man live forever with God
- Childbirth would now be accompanied by pain. This suggests that God designed childbirth to be pain free.
- Dominion of the world was turned over to Satan.
- God cursed the ground of the Earth. Humans daily work would now be difficult and meaningless.
- Adam and Eve were banned from the garden.

Two important ramifications came from Adam and Eve's sin. The first was from that day forward, sin would forever be epigenetic, meaning trauma can leave a chemical mark on a person's genes, which can then be passed down to future generations. This means sin then entered the human DNA, passing it down to all future generations. So, Eve's sin affected Adam negatively and Adam's sin was imputed into all his ancestors. Everything we do impacts others. No sin can be kept private and all sin has consequences.

Second, sin, once committed, can never be undone. History cannot be changed. Confession and repentance will restore fellowship but does not erase the consequences of sin.

- The first blood sacrifice for atonement (Genesis 3:31)
- The penalty for sin is death (Roman 6:23)
- Without the shedding of blood there is no forgiveness of sin. (Hebrews 9:22)

Genesis 3:21 says that God made cloths from an animal so that Adam and Eve could cover themselves. This was the first animal sacrifice to "cover sin." The animal sacrifice meant that the animal was used as a substitute in place of the sinner. The sacrifice was to atone sin, to cover guilt and shame. This practice was only a temporary remedy.

Leviticus 1:1-17 talks about the atonement for sin prior to Jesus Christ. God developed a plan that when a person sinned, they were to offer an animal sacrifice in the form of a "burnt offering" to God. The animal that was to be sacrificed was to be an unblemished male sheep, goat, or bull. The animal was to take the place of the sinner. The sinner was to lay his/her hand on the head of the sacrificial animal to symbolize complete identification with the animal as his/her substitute. This was the forerunner to the sacrifice of Jesus Christ on the cross for all the world's sin.

The animal sacrifice was only temporary. Christ's perfect sacrifice was permanent. Deuteronomy chapter twenty-eight is an interesting and frightening chapter. Deuteronomy 28:1-14 lists all of God's blessings. These are the blessings He will give you when you trust and follow Him.

Deuteronomy 28:15-68 lists all the curses that God will put on you if you do not accept Him as Lord and savior. With the advent of Jesus Christ, those who accept Jesus as their Lord and savior cannot be cursed (Galatians 3:13). The list of curses applies only to non-believers.

What is important to understand about this chapter, is that it teaches that God uses physical illness and disease for His purposes. Additionally, we see that God can bring emotional problems such as madness or confusion (v 28) and can cause you to be oppressed continually (v 29) for His purpose. The reason I point this out is that God uses these as trials in our lives to draw us closer to Him. However, if we obey Him and place our trust in Jesus and make every effort to walk in the Holy Spirit, we stay in fellowship with God which brings us His blessings. Here are some examples of God's sovereignty:

- The potter and the clay (Jeremiah 29:11-15)
- The Book of Job. God is our creator, He has rights over His creation (Romans 9:19-24)
- God created everything for a purpose (Proverbs 16:4)
- Man makes his own plans, but God directs his steps (Proverbs 19:9, 19:21 & 10:14)
- All things work for the good for those who love God (Romans 8:28-29)

The above scriptures are important to understanding God's sovereignty. They are too in-depth to detail here, please read and meditate on the texts at your own leisure.

Merriam Webster defines Sovereign as: self-governing or having supreme power. God is the creator of all things and has supreme power over all His creations. Many theologians prefer to use the term "providence." Pastor Charles Stanley (CharlesStanley.com) defines Providence as God's continual involvement with all created things in such a way that he (1) keeps them existing and maintaining the properties with which he created them; (2) cooperates with created things in every action, directing their distinctive properties to cause them to act as they do; and (3) directs them to fulfill his purposes.

God directs all created things to act as they do; and that God directs His creation to fulfill His purpose.

Hebrews 1:3 says "He [Jesus] is the radiance of the glory of God and the exact imprint of His nature, and He upholds the universe by the word of His power." And Colossians 1:17 adds, "And He [Jesus] is before all things, and in Him all things hold together." It is God that keeps all created things existing.

God maintains Earth's stability and orbit in this universe, keeps the sun in the perfect distance from earth; any closer we would burn up, any further away we would freeze. Anything He created; He maintains for His purpose. Ephesians 1:11 says, "In Him [God] we have obtained an inheritance, having been predestined according to the purpose of Him who works all things according to the counsel of His will . . . " God directs all things according to His plan and purpose for the world and our individual lives. Nothing falls outside His providence.

We see that God is all powerful and sovereign. This text also brings up the issue of good and evil. It says that God creates good and calamity. Calamity is defined as: an extremely serious event fraught with terrible loss and affliction; a state if dire distress. God allows trials and affliction in our lives and sometimes even ordains them using Satan or evil people to accomplish His will. There is no scripture in the Bible that blames God for bringing evil into our situation. There are several scriptures similar to this one. However, it is important to understand that the evil deed is not done by God. He uses people who are already evil or Satan who is the "evil one" to fulfill His divine plan.

All people are sinners and have evil desires. God knows the hearts of all men. An example, of this is in the story of Israel's exodus from their enslavement in Egypt.

Exodus 4:21 says, " . . . I [God] will harden his [The Pharaoh's] heart so that he will not let people go." Here God says He will influence the Pharaoh's decision, but the Pharaoh already possessed rebellion as a non-believer with a hard heart. God used the Pharaoh's evil inclination to serve His purpose.

The Apostle Paul explains God's sovereignty in Romans 9:14-23, " . . . Is there injustice on God's part? By no means! For He [God] says to Moses, 'I will have mercy in whom I have mercy, and I will have compassion on whom I have compassion.' So then it depends not on human will or exertion, but on God, who has mercy.

The scripture says that God said to Pharaoh, "For this very purpose I have raised you up, that I might show my power in you, and that my name might be proclaimed in all the earth.' So then He has mercy on whomever He wills. You will say to me then, 'Why does He still find fault? For who can resist His will?' But who are you. O man to answer back to God? Will what is molded say to its molder, 'Why have you made me like this?' Has the potter no right over the clay, to make out of the same lump one vessel for honorable use and another for dishonorable use? What if God desiring to show wrath and make known His power, has endured with much patience vessels of wrath prepared for destruction, in order to make known the riches of His glory for vessels of mercy, which He has prepared beforehand for glory."

There is so much in this text to unpack, but the summary is that God created all things. God has the ultimate right to do what He wills with His creation. God has a purpose and plan for the world, the church, and every person on earth, whether they believe in Jesus Christ or not. He knows each person's heart. He knows who will follow Him and who will reject Him.

Paul was referring to the story of the potter and the clay in the Book of Jeremiah chapter eighteen. The prophet Jeremiah says that humans are the clay and God is the potter. He created us to His unique specifications. Everyone is special and wonderfully made. During our life, God molds and shapes us into what He sees as the end result.

And God created mankind with one trait in common, the freedom of choice to follow or reject Him. God sees the future. He knows who will accept Jesus as their Lord and Savior and who will not. If His creation chooses not to obey Him, He has the right to reshape and mold that person. We cannot say that this is unfair, because He is our creator.

"For You formed my inner parts; You knotted me together in my mother's womb. I praise You, for I am fearfully and wonderfully made" (Psalm 139:13).

He made us with a plan and purpose in mind. He will use each if us to bring His plan into perfection.

The Bible teaches that God does bring evil and destruction on people who are in judgment due to unbelief or sin. God often uses people, or allows Satan to use them to fulfill His plan and purpose with the intent to bring glory onto Him. God would never use good people to do evil things. God knows our hearts and knows what we are capable of doing.

The most evil deed in the history of the world was planned by God. It was God's divine plan of salvation for man that required a perfect sacrifice. That perfect sacrifice was the God/man Jesus Christ. In order to complete God's plan, God predestined all participants to fulfill their respective roles. Acts 2:23-24 says, " . . . this Jesus delivered up according to the definite plan and foreknowledge of God, you (the Jewish people) crucified and killed by the hands of lawless men."

The people God used to arrest and kill Jesus were not forced against their will to complete their conspiracy against the Son of God. Rather, God knew what their choices would be, He knew they would eagerly kill Jesus. Judas was a follower of Jesus but he was not a true disciple because we find out that Judas had been stealing money that was intended to help the poor. The religious elite (Pharisees) acted like holy people; however, they were arrogant, prideful, selfish, and power-hungry. God weaved all these people together to achieve His plan and purpose that Jesus should die for the sins of all men.

This was a bittersweet event; Jesus suffered for our sins and was crucified so that our sin debt could be paid—that we would be forgiven. If God's plan had failed, we would have never received the gift of salvation. God used what was bad for Jesus to be great and wonderful for all mankind. Proverbs 16:4 says, "The Lord has made everything for its purpose, even the wicked for the day of trouble."

The Bible teaches that God is involved in every aspect of our lives. When we examine our pain and suffering, we must understand that God is involved in our pain. There is no such thing as "luck" or "coincidence." God is in charge and in control. Proverbs 16:9 says, "The heart of a man plans his way, but the Lord establishes his steps."

Why does God need to be so intimately involved with our lives? Proverbs 16:25 says, "There is a way that seems right to a man, but its end is the way to death."

God knows that all humans have a heart for evil. He loves us so much that He gave His only son Jesus, not wanting anyone to perish in hell. Christians can rejoice because God chose them for salvation. All things that happen in your life is part of God's plan.

We can be assured that all things work for the good for those who love God. Be comforted knowing that God is right there in your trial standing next to you, and if necessary, carrying you. Even though it may not seem fair, trust in God's plan, God wants best for you. When you make it through your trial you will be able to see that God was there making you stronger, building your faith, providing you with inner peace, joy, and contentment.

WHY THE GOSPEL OF SALVATION IS ESSENTIAL TO HEALING

The gospel is one of the most important things to understand about Jesus. Jesus provides us salvation as a free gift to those who ask. When you understand the meaning of the gospel, of what Jesus has done for you, and how God sees you, your healing will begin.

Theologians have given certain terms to the steps of salvation. The order of salvation is a list of events in chronological order that God ordains to obtain salvation in our lives. This does not need to be memorized, but it should be understood by every Christian. The list of events called the order of salvation are:

1. **Election**: God chooses who will be saved
2. **The Gospel Call**: we must hear the gospel and respond

3. **Regeneration**: born again or saved
4. **Conversion**: faith and repentance
5 **Justification**: not guilty of sin and right legal standing with God
6. **Adoption**: we become a member of God's family
7. **Sanctification**: walk in the Holy Spirit set apart of God
8. **Perseverance:** enduring trials and remaining in faith
9. **Death**: physical death
10. **Glorification**: receiving our resurrection body in heaven

Election

There are several passages in the New Testament that clearly teach the doctrine of election. Romans 8:28-30 says, "And we know that for those who love God all things work together for good, for those who are called according to His [God] purpose. For those whom He foreknew He also predestined to be conformed to the image of His Son, in order that He [Jesus] might be the first born among many brothers (fellow Christian). And those whom He (God) predestined, He also called, and those whose He called He also justified, and those whom He justified He also glorified."

Predestination is a broad term that means "to decide beforehand." Paul said those who love God have been called by Him. God foreknew who He was going to choose to be saved. And by being saved, they would be conformed to the image of His Son Jesus. And those God chose to give salvation; God forgave their sins and found them not guilty of sin. Those who He forgave, He gave them everlasting life in heaven.

In Romans 9:10-13 Paul provides an example of election from the Old Testament, " . . . when Rebekah had conceived children by one man, our forefather Isaac, though they were not yet born and done nothing either good or bad—in order that God's purpose of election might continue, not because of works [good deeds] but because of Him who calls—she was told, 'The older would serve the younger." As it is written, "Jacob I [God] loved, but Esau I hated."

Paul is referring to Genesis chapter twenty-five, the story of Isaac and Rebekah. Rebekah was pregnant with twins. Before their birth, God told her that the older would serve the younger. In those days, the firstborn son had a preeminent place in the family and was the heir to the father's estate. When the twins were born, Esau came out first, he was the older brother, then Jacob was born.

God chose Jacob to be the father of the men who would lead the twelve tribes of Israel. By ancient tradition it should have been Esau. But God chose Jacob in this important role for the Nation of Israel. Esau would later be the father of the Edomite Nation (Genesis 26: 24). The Israelites and the Edomites had a stormy relationship, though Jacob and Esau reconciled, the two nations were enemies.

Paul adds more in his letter to the Ephesians 1:4-6 " . . . even as He [God] chose us in Him before the foundation of the world, that we should be holy and blameless before Him. In love He predestined us for adoption as sons through Jesus Christ, according to the purpose of His will, to the praise of His glorious grace with which He has blessed us in beloved."

Paul could not make it any clearer, God chose who are now and will be Christians to be with Him in heaven. Paul also says that God decided for us to receive salvation even before God formed the earth. Think about that! Before the earth was created, God chose you to be forgiven and spend eternity with Him in heaven. God decided to adopt you as His child before you were born. There are more scriptures that teach this but I will only touch on two or more.

The Bible's teaching cannot get any clearer on the doctrine of election. Every person who believes and trusts in Jesus was called to be a Christian and through God's grace provided them salvation. We may never learn how or why God chose us or what His decision-making process was, but we can be assured that once someone becomes a Christian, God made that decision before He created the universe. God chose us because He has a plan for our lives, no one can thwart His plans. He has mission on this earth for each us.

What is that mission? That's the question that can only be answered by drawing closer to God.

Arguments against the doctrine of election are that if election were true, humans have no free will to choose the gospel. This would make us a robot or subhuman with no freedom of choice. We are created in God's image; He has allowed us to make genuine choices that affect our lives. And Paul tells us that we have no excuse, Romans 1:19-23 says, "For what can be known about God is plain to them [non-believers], because God has shown it to them. For His invisible attributes, namely, His eternal power and divine nature, have been clearly perceived, ever since the creation of the world, in the things that have been made. So they are without excuse, for although they knew God, they did not honor Him as God or give thanks to Him, but they became futile in their thinking and their foolish hearts darkened. Claiming to be wise, they became fools . . . "

Non-believers do not know God because their hearts are darkened. Who darkened them? We are not sure. It is either God or Satan or maybe God using Satan as His agent. The bottom line is that God is the creator, He can do as He pleases.

If you chose to accept the doctrine of election, it has significant practical application to your healing and well-being. It is an awesome feeling to know that God chose you to be with Him in heaven. Even after what you have done or what you have not done, God knew beforehand and still chose you for salvation.

How do you know if you are chosen for salvation? I believe that you have been chosen by God. If God put it in your heart to seek Him, you have been chosen. This process can be influenced by someone asking you to go to church, coming upon a Christian radio or television show, suffering through a trial or traumatic incident, or someone placing this book in your grasp.

Maybe you're feeling guilty for some poor decisions you've made and you're seeking forgiveness from a Savior. If this sounds familiar, God is calling you. It is now your responsibility to accept Jesus as your Lord and Savior to begin your healing.

The Gospel Call

The second of the ten steps to salvation is the gospel call. God chose you. Now what? In order to respond to the gospel call, you must hear the gospel. Romans 10:14 says, "How are they to believe in Him [Jesus] of whom they have not heard?"

In Romans 8:30 Paul tells us that our calling is an act of God. "Those from He predestined [elected] He also called; and those He called He also justified; and those whom He justified He also glorified." We see that it is God the Father that calls you based on His election of you. Paul lays out the order in which our salvation occurs.

This calling is like a court summons. You are summoned by God to receive the gospel. How are we called? Second Thessalonians says,

"But we ought always give thanks to God for you, brothers beloved by the Lord, because God chose you as the first fruits [from the beginning] to be saved, through sanctification by the Spirit and belief in the truth [gospel]. To this He called you through our gospel, so that you may obtain the glory of our Lord Jesus Christ."

For all those whom God chose, He called them to hear the gospel. But for those who are not called to Him, they cannot hear it. Some would debate this but in Second Corinthians 4:3-4 it says, "And even if our gospel is veiled, it is veiled only to those who are perishing [non-believers]. In their case the god of this world [Satan] has blinded the minds of the unbelievers to keep them from seeing the light of the gospel of the glory of Christ who is the image of God."

We see that when the Gospel is preached, some respond to the call and some do not. Hearing and even believing in the Gospel is not enough for salvation. Those who are saved have faith in and trust in Jesus. Even the demons believe that Jesus is the Son of God and fear Him (James 2:19). However, the demons do not trust Jesus as their Lord and Savior. Therefore, they have no salvation.

What is the Gospel? The good news of the Gospel is simple. The Gospel has three elements. All Christians should have a basic understanding of the gospel. The three basic elements are:

1. Every human being is a sinner.
    a. "For there is no distinction, for all have sinned and fall short of the glory of God" (Romans 3:23).
    b. "... for we have already charged that all, both Jews and Greeks [non-Jew], are under sin, as it is written: "None is righteous, no, not one; no one understands; no one seeks for God. All have turned aside, together they have become worthless; no one does good, not even one. Their throat is an open grave; they use their tongues to deceive. The venom of asps is under their lips. Their mouth is full of curses and bitterness. Their feet are swift to shed blood; in their paths are ruin and misery,

and the way of peace they have not known. There is no fear [reverence] of God before their eyes" (Romans 3:9-18).

2. The penalty for sin is death.
   a. "For the wages of sin is death . . . " (Romans 6:23)
   b. " . . . death spread to all men because all sinned . . . " (Romans 5:12)
3. Jesus Christ died to pay the penalty for our sins.
   a. " . . . God shows His love for us in that while we were still sinners, Christ died for us. Since, therefore, we have now been justified by His blood, how much more shall we be saved by Him from the wrath of God. For if while we were enemies we were reconciled to God by the death of His Son, much more now that we are reconciled, shall we be saved by His life" (Romans 5:8-10).
   b. "He [Jesus] is the propitiation for our sins, and not for ours only but also for the sins of the whole world" (1 John 2:2).

Propitiation means "atoning sacrifice." In the Old Testament, God allowed the Israelites to sacrifice animals in payment for their sins. This payment was required yearly: it was only a temporary atonement. The animal sacrifice was the forerunner to Jesus Christ and His work on the cross. Through Jesus' sacrifice, all the sins of the world are forgiven forever with one perfect sacrifice.

Understanding these three elements alone cannot provide salvation, we must confess and repent of our sins and place our trust in our Lord and Savior Jesus Christ. You can do this by praying the below prayer.

Father,
I come to You today to confess that I am a sinner. I repent of my sins. I want to make Jesus Christ my Lord and Savior. I believe that He died for my sins. Through His death and resurrection, I am forgiven. Thank You for loving me, calling me, and forgiving me.
In Jesus' name I pray, Amen

Regeneration

Upon accepting the gospel call, we go through a process of regeneration. Regeneration is an act of God that imparts a new spiritual life to us. We are born again. This is described in Ezekiel 36:25-27, "I [God] will sprinkle clean water on you [baptism], and you shall be clean from all your uncleanliness [sins], and from all your idols I will cleanse you. And I will give you a new heart, and a new Spirit I will put within you. And I will remove the heart of stone from your flesh and give you a heart of flesh. And I will put My Spirit within you, and cause you to walk in My statutes and be careful to obey My rules."

There is no need to do anything but accept God's calling. God does all the work. Accepting of the gospel and regeneration occur simultaneously and instantaneously. This occurs even before we are able to have faith and trust in God. God through His Holy Spirit awakens our new spiritual life.

Fruits of this event can be seen immediately but will be more evident over time. As our heart changes, so does our behavior. You will know true regeneration by the fruit that comes forth. You will believe and begin to trust Jesus; you will look at sin from God's perspective. You will love more, and you will feel the peace that only Jesus can bring.

What type of Christian are you? What type of Christian do you want to be?

Conversion

After regeneration we go through a process called conversion. Conversion is our willing response to God's call in the preaching of the gospel where we sincerely repent of our sins and place our trust in Jesus Christ for our salvation. This involves a conscious decision to make Jesus your Lord and Savior. This is called 'saving faith.'

Faith in Jesus is that through His death and resurrection we are forgiven and have eternal life in heaven. Faith and repentance work together. For true conversion you must repent your sins.

Repent means to turn away from your sinful behavior. There must be a sincere heartfelt sorrow for sin. You must make a commitment to turn away from your sin and work in obedience to God. True repentance is from the heart, when there is a change of heart in reference to sin, the repentant person's life is changed profoundly. You go from not producing fruit to producing the fruit of the Spirit.

Repentance for sin is a lifelong process. It is not a one-time come-to-Jesus event. We must out our faith and trust in Jesus every single day. Trusting God is important.

Trusting is not easy. Trust comes from a relationship between two parties. I supervised a team of agents that served a lot of search warrants. We trained all the time; some smaller law enforcement agencies asked us to do their high-risk arrest or search warrant service. The primary objective is to safely apprehend a suspected dangerous person and/or to safely enter the residence of a dangerous person who a judge authorized a search.

This is one of the most dangerous activities in law enforcement. The team needs to be close-knit and work together well. Communication, teamwork, and trust are vital requirements of members. Lone wolves are not wanted. If there is no trust, there is no cohesion.

Trust comes from spending time together, communication, and working as a team. This often requires hundreds of hours of training, and working together. As we build trust, our anxiety goes down.

The same principle applies to trusting our heavenly Father. It is through spending time with Jesus that our trust is built up. How can we do that? Study the Bible, pray, and spend time with other Christians. Listen to other believer's testimonies on what God has done in their lives.

The more time you spend with Him, the more trust is built up. As we learn that we can trust God with all our needs, our anxiety and fear levels go down. Our trust in God is the foundation of a peaceful and joyful life in Christ. Trust brings spiritual maturity that produces good fruit. This is referred to walking in the Holy Spirit.

Justification

At the moment that you have sincere repentance and place your trust in Jesus, you are justified.

Romans 3:28 says, "For we hold that one is justified by faith apart from the works of the law [following rules or doing good deeds]." Faith is an action on our part.

Justification is an act of God alone. Justification is a legal declaration of God who considers our sins forgiven because of the work of His Son Jesus Christ. Through His death and resurrection, God declares us "not guilty" of sin; past, present, and future. God forgave our sins and will never bring them up to us again. The legal declaration is not due to anything we did to earn our forgiveness. It is through the grace of God that we are justified. Romans 3:22-26 says, " . . . for there is no distinction, for all have sinned and fall short of the glory of God, and are justified by His grace as a gift, through the redemption that is in Christ Jesus, whom God put forward as a propitiation by His blood, to be received by faith. This was to show God's righteousness because in His divine forbearance He had passed over former sins, it was to show His righteousness at the present time, so that He might be just and the justifier of the one who has faith in Jesus."

Romans 5:15-17 adds, "But the free gift [forgiveness/salvation] is not like the trespass. For if many died through one man's [Adam] trespass, much more have the grace of God and the free gift by the grace of another—Jesus Christ abounded for many. And the free gift is not like the results of that one man's sin. For the judgment following one trespass brought condemnation, but the free gift following many trespasses brought justification."

The grace of God means "unmerited favor." We are unable to earn favor with God. The only way to receive His favor is through His abundant grace. This takes all the pressure off of us who strive to do good and have performance anxiety over everything we do trying to make sure we please God. Christians should not have stress, God gives us grace because He loves us. The only thing we must do is to repent our sins and make
Jesus our Lord and Savior. What could be easier?

Adoption

You have been called through God's election, you have accepted the gospel call, you received a new spiritual life, and through sincere repentance and trust in Jesus you have been declared not guilty of sin. Now, you are adopted into God's family. John 1:12 says, "But to all that did receive Him [Jesus], who believed in His name, He gave the right to become children of God."

Romans 8:14-17 says, "For all who are led by the Spirit of God are sons of God. For you did not receive the spirit of slavery to fall back into fear, but you have received the Spirit of adoption as sons, by whom we cry, "Abba [daddy] Father!" The Spirit Himself bears witness with our spirit that we are children of God, and if children, then heirs—heirs of God and fellow heirs with Christ, provided we suffer with Him in order that we may also be glorified with Him."

Galatians 3:26 adds, " . . . for in Jesus Christ you are all sons of God, through faith."

1 John 3:1-2 adds, "See what kind of love the Father has given to us, that we should be called children of God, and so we are."

Adoption is an act of God where those He justified, He made members of His family. We are sons and daughters of God, our Father. This makes Jesus our older brother. As children of God, we receive full benefits and privileges as Jesus. Being a child of God makes us co-heirs with Jesus to a great inheritance in heaven. Being a joint heir means we receive all that Jesus receives.

Galatians 4:6-7 says, "And because you are sons, God has sent the Spirit of His Son into our hearts, crying "Abba Father!" So you are no longer a slave, but a son, and if a son, then an heir through God."

Ephesians 3:6 adds, "This mystery is that the Gentiles [Non-Jews] are fellow heirs, members of the same body, and partakers of the promise in Jesus Christ through the gospel."

First Peter 1:3-5 adds, "Blessed be God and Father of our Lord Jesus Christ! According to His great mercy, He has caused us to be born again to a living hope through the resurrection of Jesus Christ from the dead, and to an inheritance that is imperishable, undefiled, and unfading, kept in heaven for you, who by God's power are being guarded through faith for a salvation ready to be revealed in the last time."

What is our inheritance? Our inheritance includes: the gift of the Holy Spirit, entrance into the royal family who will reign with Jesus, forgiveness of sins, eternal life in heaven, and many other blessings that will boggle your mind.

Sanctification

As a child of God, we must continually strive for our ongoing sanctification. Sanctification is a continual progressive work where man and God work together in an effort to live our earthy lives free from sin, and through this work we become more in the likeness of Jesus Christ. We will never be free from sin until our sanctification is completed in our glorification when we receive our resurrected bodies in heaven.

In order to be free from sin, we must understand that through regeneration we are dead to our sin. Romans 6:1-11 says, "What shall we say then? Are we to continue in sin that our grace may abound? By no means! How can we who died [regeneration] to sin still live in it? Do you not know that all of us who have been baptized into His [Jesus] death? We are buried therefore with Him by baptism into death, in order that, just as Christ was raised from the dead by the glory of the Father, we too might walk in newness of life. For if we have been united with Him in death like His, we shall certainly be united with Him in a resurrection like His. We know that our old self was crucified with Him in order that the body of sin might be brought to nothing, so that we would no longer be enslaved to sin. For one who has died has been set free from sin. Now if we have died with Christ, we believe that we will also live with Him. We know that Christ, being raised from the dead, will never die again; death no longer has dominion over Him. The death He died to sin, once and for all, but the life He lives, He lives to God. So you also must consider yourselves dead to sin and alive to God in Christ Jesus."

Romans 6:17-18 says, "But thanks be to God, that you who were once slaves of sin have become obedient from the heart to the standard of teaching to which you were committed, and having been set free from sin, have become slaves of righteousness." Second Corinthians 5:17 adds, "Therefore, if anyone is in Christ, he is a new creation. The old has passed away; behold, the new has come."

Through Jesus' death and resurrection, our old self has died and a new person has been resurrected. We are dead to our previous sins of our life. We are no longer a slave to that sin, but a slave to Jesus to do His will. We will always sin, but with the power of the Holy Spirit, sin will not control our behavior. As we sin less, we become sanctified.

Freedom from sin is a free gift from God through Jesus' work on the cross. Hebrews 10:14 says, "For by a single offering [Jesus' crucifixion] He [Jesus] has perfected for all time those who are being sanctified."

Hebrews says "to those being sanctified," this shows it is a continual process throughout our Christian life. Our sanctification is ongoing as we walk in the Holy Spirit and do God's will. When we receive our resurrection bodies, our sanctification will be complete. We will then be free of sin forever.

Sanctification is a collaborative effort but with God doing most of the work.

Our role in this process is minimal but very important to our healing. We must obey God and walk in the Holy Spirit. First Thessalonians 4:3 says, "For this is the will of God, your sanctification."

Perseverance

Perseverance, often referred to as "perseverance of the saints," means that Christians who truly give their lives to Jesus are born again and will persevere as Christians until Christ's return. Christians can be assured that they will not lose their salvation.

Many Christians lose their peace and blessing because they are not assured of their salvation; they doubt. Jesus assures us in John 10:27-29, "My sheep [followers] hear My voice and I know them, and they follow Me. I give them eternal life, and they will never perish, and no one will snatch them out of My hand. My Father, who has given them to Me, is greater than all, and no one is able to snatch them out of the Father's hand."

Jesus clearly says, "no one" will take Christians away from His care. ALL who follow Jesus will never die and will enter heaven. Those who are truly born again will persevere to the end. Ephesians 1:13-14 says, "In Him [Jesus] you also, when you heard the word of truth, the gospel of your salvation, and believed in Him, were sealed with the promised Holy Spirit, who is guarantee of our inheritance until we acquire possession of it, to the praise of His glory."

God guarantees that if you possess the Holy Spirit, you will receive your inheritance in heaven. In Paul's letter to the Philippians, he says "And I am sure that He who began a good work in you will bring it to completion at the day of Jesus Christ" (v. 1:6).

Paul is writing to believers telling them that those who have placed their trust in Jesus will persevere until Christ's second coming. Jesus said, " . . . those who endure to the end will be saved" (Matthew 10:22).

What about those who do not fully give their lives over to Jesus? The Bible teaches that if you do not make Jesus your Lord and Savior, you will not partake of God's inheritance promised to only believers. Jesus warned His disciples about fakers in Matthew 7:21-23, "Not everyone who says to Me,

'Lord, Lord,' will enter the kingdom of heaven, but the one who does the will of My Father who is in heaven. On that day many will say to me, 'Lord, Lord, did we not prophesy on Your name, and cast out demons in Your name?' And then I will say to them, 'I never knew you; depart from Me. You workers of lawlessness.'"

Jesus is referring to His second coming when He will judge non-believers at the White Throne Judgment. Jesus says that there will be people who claim to follow Him but they never gave their full trust in Him. He knows people's hearts. These people were not saved due to their lack of faith. The lack of faith makes them fall away from Christianity.

There are many people who fall away when trials come into their lives. They do not have the strength to persevere through these trials. Only Jesus can give us the strength needed to persevere.

Death

What happens when we die? Earlier we discussed that the penalty for sin is death. Through Jesus' death and resurrection, death no longer applies to Christians. Physical death is a result of a fallen sinful world. God has chosen to allow Satan to reign on this earth until Christ's return and final judgment. On the new heaven and earth there will be no more sin, no more death. First Corinthians 15:24-26 says, "Then comes the end, when He [Jesus] delivers the kingdom of God the Father after destroying every rule and every authority and power [classes of angels and demons]. For He must reign until He has put all His enemies under His feet. The last enemy to be destroyed is death."

Jesus' enemy is death itself. Until that time, humans will experience physical death as a result of this fallen world controlled by Satan. Christians and non-Christians alike will experience death from disease, aging, natural disasters, and more. Suffering will still occur for Christians as a result of Adam's sin, sinful living and the consequence of sin.

While Paul was in prison and he did not know if he was going to live or die, he wrote, "For me to live is Christ, and to die is gain. If I am to live in the flesh, that means fruitful labor [doing God's work] for me. Yet which I shall choose I cannot tell. I am hard pressed between the two. My desire is to depart and be with Christ, for that is better" (Philippians 1:21-23).

What Paul is saying that to be in heaven with Jesus is better than to live in this sinful world. He would rather experience physical death and to be in heaven with Jesus. This applies to the physical death of all Christians. When a family member dies, we mourn.

Mourning is good, however, if our loved one is Christian, we should thank God and praise Him for the blessing of our loved one's life. We are assured that our loved one is in heaven with Jesus. In heaven we will live with our Savior Jesus Christ. First Thessalonians 5:9-10 says, "For God has not destined us for wrath, but to obtain salvation through our Lord Jesus Christ, who died for us so that whether we are awake [alive] or asleep [dead] we might live with Him."

The physical death of a non-believer is a different story. A non-believer is not "saved" so there is no salvation available to them. Remember, the penalty for sin is death, both spiritual and physical. A non-believer is not "born again" therefore not in the family of God. There is no inheritance to those not in the family. Only those who believe in Jesus Christ are written in God's Book of Life. If they do not believe, they are going to hell. This contradicts many people's argument when they say, "I'm a good person, God sees that and will allow me into heaven." I used this many times before my conversion. There are no second chances. Paul gives us an indication of how bad hell is by saying, in Romans 9:1-3, "I am speaking the truth in Christ—I am not lying; my conscience bears me witness in the Holy Spirit—that I have great sorrow and unceasing anguish in my heart! For I could wish that I myself were accursed and cut off from Christ for the sake of my brothers, my kinsmen according to the flesh."

Paul here is speaking about the Jews who will not believe in Jesus. Paul said he would rather be cursed and sent to hell in substitution of his Jewish brothers who are going to hell for unbelief. He understood how bad hell is and that he wished that no one suffered this penalty.

Based on this scripture, we learn that when Christians die, their spirit goes immediately to heaven in God's presence where they remain until they receive their new glorified bodies.

If there is doubt, Jesus reassures us in Like 23:43. Here Jesus has been nailed to the Cross. With Him were two criminals. One of them acknowledges that Jesus is Lord and Savior. Jesus says, "Truly I say to you today you will be with me in Paradise." This shows that the one criminal redeemed himself by believing that Jesus was Lord. Upon his death, he would be with Jesus in Paradise or heaven.

Therefore, Christians need not fear death for family or ourselves. Paul said it best when he said, "my desire is to depart and be with Christ" and that he would rather be away from the body and at home with the Lord.

Glorification

The last step in the order of salvation is the glorification of our dead bodies. When we experience physical death, our spirits go to the temporary heaven; our bodies are either buried or cremated. The Bible teaches that our dead bodies will be resurrected when Jesus Christ returns and raise our bodies up from the dead. This is also called "the redemption of our bodies." Romans 8:23 says, " . . . we wait eagerly for adoption as sons, the redemption of our bodies." The act of Jesus redeeming our bodies is called "glorification."

Romans 8:30 says, "And those whom He [God] predestined He also called, and those whom He called He also justified, and those whom He justified He also glorified."

Glorification will occur when Jesus returns to Earth for His church and raises all the believers who have died. Our bodies will be reunited with our spirit in heaven. We will have glorious new and perfect bodies. Bodies that will never age, a body just like Jesus (Romans 8:17).

The day of Jesus' return to earth is only known by the Father. It will be a victorious day for all Christians. On that day when our bodies are raised and glorified, we will experience total victory over sin and over death. God's divine plan for redemption will be complete.

First Thessalonians 4:14-17 says, "For since we believe that Jesus died and rose again, even so, through Jesus, God will bring with Him those who have fallen asleep [died]. For this we declare to you by a word from the Lord, that we who are alive, who are left until the coming of the Lord, will not precede those who have fallen asleep. For the Lord Himself will descend from heaven, with a cry of command, with the voice of an archangel, and with the sound of a trumpet of God. And the dead in Christ will rise first. Then we who are alive, who are left, will be caught up together with them in the clouds to meet the Lord in the air, and so we will always be with the Lord."

Paul describes our glorified bodies in First Corinthians 15:42-45, "So is it with the resurrection of the dead. What is sown is perishable; what is raised is imperishable. It is sown in dishonor; it is raised in glory. It is sown in weakness; it is raised in power. It is sown a natural body; it is raised a spiritual body. If there is a natural body, there is also a spiritual body. Thus, it is written, the first man Adam became a living being, the last Adam became a life-giving spirit. But it is not the spiritual that is first but the natural, and then the spiritual."

Paul describes our glorified bodies as imperishable, powerful, and spiritual and best of all in the image of Jesus Christ. First Corinthians 15:51-54 goes to say, "Behold I [Paul] tell you a mystery. We shall not all sleep, but we all shall be changed, in a moment, in the twinkling of an eye, at the last trumpet. For the trumpet will sound, and the dead will be raised imperishable, and we shall be changed.For this perishable body must put on the imperishable, and this mortal body must put on immortality. When the perishable puts on immortality then shall come to pass the saying that is written: 'Death is swallowed up in victory." Paul is describing the "rapture." This is when Jesus returns and raises all the dead Christians first, then in a moment, takes up all the living Christians. All those taken up to heaven will be changed to their glorified bodies. The time of the rapture is not known by anyone but God the Father.

All this will happen in the blink of an eye. How fast is that? I'm not sure, but it sounds fast.

Our new bodies will be imperishable, they will never age, be stricken with disease, nor will they wear out. We will be perfect, just like Jesus. Some people do not believe that we will have a body in heaven. But the above scriptures prove that we will have some sort of physical body. We do not know what type of body, but there will be a body for our spirit to reside.
I do not believe that we will have a body made of flesh and blood because Paul has told us, "Flesh and blood cannot inherit the kingdom of God" (1 Corinthians 15:50). Paul says we will be changed, I don't know how, but I'm looking forward to find out.

THE SIGNIFICANCE OF THE VIRGIN BIRTH TO HEALING

The Book of Luke describes how the birth of Jesus came about. Mary, a virgin, was engaged to be married to a man named Joseph. The Angel Gabriel was assigned to tell Mary that she was chosen by God to give birth to the Son of God. Isaiah foretold this event in chapter nine. This was to be a union between deity and humanity. Jesus is fully God and was fully human at the same time.

Jesus' birth was a miracle of the Holy Spirit. Mary conceived a child by the Holy Spirit. The birth of Jesus resulted in a person that was fully human and fully God—a God-man. Jesus was fully God with all the power that God possesses as well as fully human being born of mortal flesh and blood. All in one person, yet all separate.

The theological term for this is "the Hypostatic Union." Jesus Christ incarnate is Jesus the God-man. Incarnate means "endowed with a human body."

The incarnation of Jesus means that the Son of God, who is God, took on humanity at His Virgin birth (John 1:14). Jesus had the same attributes and power as He had while in heaven.

Jesus is called both the "Son of God" and the "Son of Man." Son of Man refers to His human attributes. This is very important to understand. We need a God-man to atone for our sins to heal and restore our relationship with God.

Remember how an animal sacrifice cleansed us of our sins in the Old Testament? The shedding blood of a perfect lamb was the price paid to God for a person's sin. Imagine how many millions of animals lost their lives for these sacrifices. This was required once a year.

God had a better plan. The problem for God was that a perfect human sacrifice could not be found. There was no one without sin. God could not just send Jesus down to earth and kill him because Jesus was a spirit could not die. God needed a perfect human being to be the people's sacrifice.

Jesus was sent to be that sacrificial lamb. He devised His divine plan to place Jesus in a human body because a body of flesh and blood can die. The sacrifice of a sinless person was the only way it could be an effective payment for the sins of the world (1 John 2:2). Jesus' death satisfied the righteous demands of God, and through His death and resurrection, we have been redeemed.

The word redeem in Greek is translated as "one who is purchased" as in a slave market purchase. When we are redeemed we are no longer a slave to our sinful ways, we are reconciled to God. Reconciled means a "restored relationship." We change from an enemy of God to a member of His family. The passion or suffering of Jesus Christ was necessary for our redemption. On the night before His crucifixion Jesus endured great emotional stress knowing what was to come. On Friday, the day of His crucifixion, Jesus endured beatings so severe that the Bible tells us that afterwards He was unrecognizable (Isaiah 52:14).

He was whipped, scourged and verbally humiliated. Scourging is being struck with a whip that has had either pieces of bone or metal tied to its end. This was designed to inflict the most possible pain on its victim by ripping open the victim's skin and tearing the muscle tissue. It is difficult to imagine that pain and suffering Jesus went through that day.

Jesus was then forced to carry the wooden cross beam on which He would be hung. Roman soldiers paraded Him over two miles to the place He was to be crucified. The weight of this cross beam is estimated to be over thirty pounds and would have been difficult to carry being about six feet long. Remember, He is God. He could have stopped the torture at any time and killed those who were beating Him. But because of His great love for humanity. He followed through with His Father's plan.

Crucifixion is a horrible means of death. The place where Jesus was crucified was called "Golgotha." This means "place of the skull" in Aramaic. The rock formations apparently looked like a skull. At this place there would be pre-dug holes in the ground where long poles would be placed.

Jesus carried the cross beam that was to be affixed to the longer poles and inserted into the holes. Jesus would have been stripped naked and nailed this wooden cross. Roman executioners would drive seven-inch nails through Jesus' wrists and ankles. The nails had a large head so that the body would not slide off the nail. Death through crucifixion was a slow horrific death.

It often would take up to three days to die hanging from the cross. Soldiers would often break the victim's legs to hasten death. While hanging in the crucified position, breathing is labored, the victim would have to push up on their legs to take the pressure off the chest to prevent asphyxiation.

We read about Jesus' murder in the gospels of Matthew, Mark, Luke, and John. Each tells the same story with slight variations. These differences are minor, each wrote as the Holy Spirit prompted placing significance on different points. We must read all these gospels in order to obtain a clear view of the entire event. The result of Christ' s pain and suffering was so those who believe in Jesus are forgiven and healed. Isaiah 53:4-5 says, "Surely He [Jesus] has borne our grief and carried our sorrows; yet we esteemed Him stricken, smitten by God, and afflicted. But He was wounded for our transgressions [sinful thoughts]; He was crushed for our iniquities [sins]; upon Him was the chastisement [punishment] that brought us peace, and with His strips [beatings and pain] we are healed."

Isaiah is predicting Jesus' pain and suffering and explaining that the people of that time believed that Jesus was being punished for His own sins, but this was far from the truth. Jesus suffered vicariously for the sins of all people and through His pain and suffering and death we are forgiven and healed spiritually, emotionally, and physically.

Romans 5:17 says, "For if, because of one man's [Adam] trespass [sin], death reigned through that one man, much more will those who receive the abundance of grace and the free gifts of righteousness reign in life through the one man Jesus Christ."

God counts us righteous as He Himself is (Psalm 35:24, 35:28). This righteousness is based on Jesus' death and resurrection. Jesus was the propitiation to satisfy God's wrath against us for sin. Propitiation means to appease or to pay for. God required a payment for sin. Jesus paid that ransom by substituting Himself so that we would not be put to death. Jesus' sacrifice was for all people of the earth (1 John 2:2). Romans 5:19 adds, "For as by one man's [Adam] disobedience the many were sinners, so by the one man's [Jesus] obedience that many were made righteous."

Romans 5:8-11 explains, " . . . God shows His love for us in that while we were still sinners, Christ died for us. Since, therefore, we have now been justified by His blood [death], much more shall we be saved by Him from the wrath of God. For if while we were enemies we were reconciled to God by the death of His Son, much more now that we are reconciled, shall we be saved by His life. More than that, we also rejoice in God through our Lord Jesus Christ through whom we now have received reconciliation."

God's divine plan was to sacrifice Jesus, the God-man who died as a substitution for us. Because of His death and resurrection, we are forgiven. Our relationship with God has been reconciled and we are now members of His royal family. This is a free gift from God. We are required to do nothing but believe in His Son Jesus.

Union with Jesus Christ, if you believe and trust in Jesus, means that God the Father considers you the same as His Son Jesus. We have a union with Jesus, this union is a term that summarizes our relationship with Jesus that secures our salvation. The Bible uses the term "in Christ," Jesus is in us, and we are in Him.

Once we have secured our salvation, you have died with Christ, been buried with Him, and resurrected with Him. Colossians 2:12 says, " . . . having been buried with Him in baptism, in which you were also raised with Him through faith in the powerful working of God, who raised Him from the dead."

We see that through our faith we died with Him, were buried with Him, a new person has been resurrected, as well as a new nature. Through this sequence of events, the Holy Spirit begins good work in your character. You are dead to the old sinful way of life and you are a new creation to serve

God. Second Corinthians 5:17 says, "Therefore, if anyone is in Christ, he is a new creation. The old has passed away; behold the new has come."

We begin a new life "in Christ." Ephesians 1:7-14 says, "In Him [Jesus] we have redemption through His blood, the forgiveness of our trespasses, according to the riches of His [God] grace, which He lavished upon us, in all wisdom and insight making known to us the mystery of His will, according to His purpose, which He set forth in Christ as a plan for fullness of time to unite all things in Him, things in heaven and things on earth. In Him we have obtained an inheritance, having been predestined according to the purpose of Him who works all things according to the council of His will, so that we who were the first to hope in Christ might be to the praise of His glory. In Him you also, when you heard the word of truth, the gospel of your salvation, and believe in Him, were sealed with the promised Holy Spirit, who is the guarantee of our inheritance until we acquire possession of it, to the praise of His glory."

We see that the term "in Christ" refers to every stage of being born again that includes: salvation, regeneration, and justification. Because of this process, our lives are inseparable by our connection to Jesus. You are in Christ, and Christ is in you. Paul tells us in Galatians 2:20, "I have been crucified with Christ who lives in me. And the life I now live in the flesh I live by faith in the Son of God, who loved me and gave Himself for me."
And Jesus tells us in John 15:5, "I am the vine, you are the branches. Whoever abides in Me and I in him, he it is that bears much fruit, for apart from Me you can do nothing."

THE FRUIT OF THE HOLY SPIRIT PROMISES HEALING

When we are born again, God gives us His Holy Spirit. The Holy Spirit is a free gift to all Christians. These are some scriptures describing the Holy Spirit.

- The Holy Spirit is a gift from God (John 14:25, Luke 3:16, 14:25, Romans 5:5)
- The Holy Spirit renews you (Titus 3:4-8, Acts 11:16)
- The Holy Spirit helps your weakness (John 8: 26-27)
- The Holy Spirit will teach you all things (John 14:26, 1 Corinthians 2:12)

The Holy Spirit is the third person of the trinity. The Holy Spirit is a spirit and fully God with all the Father's attributes. The Holy Spirit is given to us to guide us through life's difficult times, to protect us from evil, and to convict us when we sin. It is important to learn to listen to the voice of the Holy Spirit and follow His instructions.

This will take time to discern, but is well worth it. When we listen to the guiding of the Holy Spirit it is called "walking in the Holy Spirit." When we walking in the Spirit we will see positive changes in our thoughts, actions, and emotions. Others will also notice the positive fruit that you will exhibit as you follow in God's will. Walking in the Spirit will begin the process of healing. The fruit of the Spirit is described in Galatians 5:16-25. With the indwelling of the Holy Spirit, every new Christian receives a new heart. Why? Because of the fall of man "the heart is deceitful above all things and desperately sick" (Jeremiah 17:9). Paul reminds us that no one does good, not even one person, and no one seeks God (Romans 3:11-12). God replaces our old hardened heart of stone with a compassionate heart of flesh and fills us with the Holy Spirit (Ezekiel 36:26).

Being in Christ with the Holy Spirit living in us, our nature and character structure is changed. We slowly learn God's will and our wants and needs change from the focus on ourselves to our focus on God. The Holy Spirit changes us from the inside out. We choose to turn away from sin and the worldly way of life, this is the sanctification process. We walk in the power of the Holy Spirit, we no longer carry out the desires of the flesh (Galatians 5:16).

Following the Holy Spirit's prompting, our mind is renewed to be in sync with God's will for our lives (Romans 12:2-3). Our mind, will, and emotions are transformed from what the world wants us to believe and think, to believing the Holy Spirit. Our character begins to produce the fruit of the Spirit: Love, joy, peace, patience, kindness, and self-control. As we walk in the Holy Spirit our relationship with God grows, after time we no longer want to do the sinful things of the past, those sins that controlled us, not because it is against God's rules, but because we love Him and do not want to disappoint Him.

How do we know if we are walking in the Holy Spirit? First, take an honest look at your life. Paul describes a person who is not led by the Holy Spirit, "The works of the flesh are evident sexual immorality, impurity, sensuality, idolatry, sorcery, enmities, strife, orgies, and things like these" (Galatians 5:19-21).

Everything in the Bible comes down to just one thing: LOVE!

First John 4:11-21 says, "Beloved, if God so loved us, we also ought to love one another. No one has ever seen God; if we love one another, God abides in us and His love is perfect in us. By this we know that we abide in Him and He in us, because He has given of His Spirit. And we have seen and testify that the father has sent His Son to be the Savior of the world. Whoever confesses that Jesus is the Son of God, God abides in Him, and he in God. So we have to come to know and to believe the love that God has for us. God is love, and whoever abides in love abides in God, and God abides in him. By this is love perfect with us, so that we may have confidence for the day of judgment, because as He is so also we are in this world. There is no fear in love, but perfect love casts out fear. For fear has to do with punishment, and whoever fears has not been perfected in love. We love because He first loved us. If anyone says, 'I love God,' and hates his brother, he is a liar; for he who does not love his brother whom he has seen cannot love God, whom he has not seen. And this commandment we have from Him, whoever loves God must also love his brother."

If we love one another:

- We cannot be angry at a friend
- We cannot gossip about a friend
- We cannot steal or cheat a friend
- We cannot abandon a friend
- We must forgive a friend
- We must not be jealous of a friend
- We cannot place ourselves above a friend

As we walk in the Holy spirit, our mind will be transformed to the mind of Christ (1 Corinthians 2:16). Love will begin to permeate our hearts, we will experience the peace and joy only loving relationship with Jesus Christ will bring (Romans 15:13).

REALIZING WHO SATAN IS AND HIS GOAL TO KEEP YOU BROKEN

Here are the scriptures relating to Satan:

- Satan was God's greatest angel (Ezekiel 28:11-19)
- Satan's fall was due to pride (Isaiah 14: 12-17)
- Satan was banished to earth and took a third of the angels with him (Revelation 12:4)
- Satan is looking for someone to oppress (1 Peter 5:8)
- Sin opens the door to Satan (Ephesians 4:26-27)
- Satan blinds the minds of non-believers to the gospel (2 Corinthians 4:3-4)
- Satan can disguise himself as an angel of light (2 Corinthians 11:14)

In his letter to the church in Ephesus, Paul tells them that they are in a constant spiritual battle. The battle is not with humans but with Satan and his demons. Satan is a created being. His name was Lucifer and he was a beautiful guardian cherub.

A cherub was assigned to guard the holiness of God. The Bible says that Lucifer was created perfect with wisdom and beauty. Lucifer was filled with pride and became corrupted because of his pride.

Isaiah 14:12-17 tells us that Lucifer sinned by his arrogance, pride, and conceit. He wanted to be like God, to be God. Arrogance and pride are sins. Due to these sins, God took away his angel status and banished Lucifer down to the earth. Satan had a huge following of the other angels, Lucifer took one third of all the angels in heaven with him to the earth. These fallen angels are now called demons. Lucifer is now called Satan or the devil.
Because of this, Satan hates God and all His followers. In an effort to get back at God he attacks believers with the fierceness of a dragon (Revelation 12:3), or a roaring lion seeking someone to devour (1 Peter 5:8). Satan can adapt himself to any situation and can even appear as an angel to fool believers and trick them into believing his lies (2 Corinthians 11:14). Satan is not all-knowing like God, but is skilled at predicting human behavior. He has studied humans for thousands of years and knows our weaknesses and how best to defeat us.

Satan's primary goal is to prevent as many people as possible from knowing God. He blinds the minds on non-believers so that when they hear the gospel, they will not understand it and reject it (2 Corinthians 4:4). Our human tendency is to be self-centered. Satan uses this and promotes power, sex, influence, wealth, and status. All the things that world reveres. God made Adam ruler of the earth, but due to his sin, authority was given to Satan. Satan is the god of this world.

In relation to believers, his goal is to make us ineffective by trying to get us to go back to worldly living and habitual sin. Once in habitual sin, we become slaves to that sin, thus slaves to Satan. His goal here is to damage our relationship with God. He does this by trying to make us believe that we are no good, not loved, or that our sin is so bad that God will never forgive us. He tries to instill fear in our hearts so that we cannot spread the gospel fearing that others will call us names like "Bible thumpers" or "Wackos."

Satan can see when we are in emotional pain, his goal is to keep us in pain for as long as possible and then blame God for our pain. Lastly, he tempts us into all sorts of sinful behavior. He knows our individual weaknesses and exploits them.

DISCOVER GOD'S PLAN AND PURPOSE IN YOUR PAIN

The below scriptures talk about our trials:

1. God tells us to rejoice in our trials (Romans 5:1-5)
2. God uses those in trials to do His will (1 Corinthians 1:26-30)
3. God allows trials. When we go through a trial, we are then able to comfort others who are also going through trials (2 Corinthians 1:3-7)
4. Trials produce steadfastness (James 1:2-4)
5. God disciplines those He loves (Hebrews 12:7-11)
6. The vine and the vine dresser (John 15:1-11)

Trials in our lives are important and even necessary. You may not agree, but it is true. When times are good, we do not seek God; we do not grow. We only grow by going through difficult times. When we go through a traumatic event or an overwhelming life event, we cannot see the growth through the pain, but it is these trials that prepare us to fulfill God's purpose and plan for our life.

Trials grow our spiritual muscles. When we workout in a gym, we use heavy weight to build muscle. It is the heavy weight during proper exercise that cause small tears in the muscle. These tears cause pain and soreness. These tears are traumatic to the muscle. As the muscle heals, these tears cause the muscle to grow larger and stronger. Stronger muscles allow us to accommodate heavier weight. The muscle is stronger because of the trauma it endured. No pain, no gain.

During difficult times we feel pain and it is through this pain that our spiritual muscles grow stronger. Along with new strength we develop endurance, perseverance, and wisdom. Whether we like it or not, Jesus warned us that we will all experience tough times in our lives (John 16:33). But it is through Jesus that we overcome our pain.

God will never give us more that we can handle, He knows how much pain is necessary for repentance and growth. Each trial brings different opportunities for growth, every failure a learning opportunity. You are not the person you are today if it were not for the difficult experiences you endured in your life. If you look back on these trials you will be able to see God's fingerprints all over your pain.

Generational Sin Keeps Us Broken

Here are scriptures about generational sin:

1. Relating to generational sin (Deuteronomy 4:40, 5:29, 12:28, & 30:19-20)
2. Countering generational sin (Ezekiel 18: 14-20, Galatians 3:13, Romans 5:6-11)

Some of us live in our pain from the trauma and overwhelming life events that are a part of a cycle of generational sin. Studies have shown that children who grew up with abusive or alcoholic parents tend to follow their parent's modeling and themselves become abusive alcoholics. In Deuteronomy 5:9-10, God tells the Israelites, "You shall not bow down or serve them [idols]; for I the Lord your God am a jealous God, visiting the iniquity of the fathers on the children to the third and fourth generation of those who hate me, but showing steadfast love to thousands of those who love Me and keep My commandments."

An idol is anything you place before God. An idol can be your job, family, sports, making money, alcohol or drugs, or any activity you place above God.

In Deuteronomy 30:19-20, God says, " . . . I have set before you life and death, blessing and curse. Therefore, choose life, that you and your offspring may live, loving the LORD your God, obeying His voice, and holding fast to Him, for He is your life and length of days . . . "

God gives his people choice: choose him or not. Follow God and be blessed, or disobey God and be cursed. All curses are listed in Deuteronomy 28:15-68. Some include: diseases, inflammation, fever, madness, blindness, confusion of the mind, oppression, and that you will always be victimized. God's blessings are listed in 28:1-14. Some examples include: your children will be blessed, your enemies will be defeated, your work will be blessed, you will prosper, and you will have money to lend, these are just a few. If you place your trust in Jesus, He will give you a long life and you and your family will prosper (verse 4:40).

How does this personal history affect us? According to scripture, if our parents or grandparents worshipped idols or were in habitual sin, we could be cursed. This is a problem because we do not know what our ancestors did.

Sometimes it is easy to determine if there is a generational curse on a family. If you honestly look at your family's history and answer questions like: Does your family have good jobs? Is there alcoholism or drug use in the family back generations? Is your family healthy both physically and emotionally? Does everyone in your family seem to have bad luck? History of depression or suicide? Do you see blessings in your family history? Is there constant drama in your family like arguing or fighting? Does your family possess joy? When you answer these questions you may identify familial sin.

After you have completed this spiritual assessment of the issues that you struggle with, I recommend talking with a parent or blood family member to get a truthful family history. This isn't always easy because there may be family secrets that would like to be left secret. Try to speak with family in private. Explain your struggles open and honestly. Do not blame or accuse, just seek the truth. If no family is available, pray the sample prayer in the appendix asking the Holy Spirit to reveal generational sins of your ancestors.

For example, let's say you are struggling with a gambling addiction. Addiction causes turmoil in your life and you do not understand why this stronghold is so difficult to overcome. A stronghold is anything that has power over you. More on strongholds later.

Your gambling has caused severe financial losses to your family. You talk with your father and confess your struggles with gambling. He tells you that there is a history of gambling within the family. He has an issue with it, as well as his father. The cause of your stronghold is generational.

Satan and his minions have been watching human beings for thousands of years. They have extensive records on all people, including you. They know all your family secrets, and are waiting for an opportune time to use them against you. As you get deeper into your secret sin, Satan will try to convince you that you have it under control. It is his goal to keep you in sin separated from God and in pain.

Generational sin is real, do not dismiss it as a possible issue in your life. However, it is very easy to break this cycle of sin by trusting in Jesus Christ today.

Ezekiel chapter eighteen explains that even if your father is an unrepentant sinner, an abusive person, a non-believer, or worse, if you make Jesus your Lord and Savior, the curse is broken, Ezekiel 18:20-22 says, "The soul who sins shall die. The Son [or daughter] shall not suffer for the iniquity [sin] of the father [or mother], nor the father suffer for the inequality of the son. The righteousness of the righteous shall be upon himself, and the wickedness of the wicked shall be upon himself but if a wicked person turns away from all his sins that he has committed and keeps all My [God] statues and does what is just and right, he shall surely live, not die. None of the transgressions that he has committed shall be remembered against him; for the righteousness that he has done he shall live."

When we place our trust in Jesus, He took on the curse that was intended for us.

Galatians 3:13 says, "Christ redeemed us from the curse of the law by becoming a curse for us—for it is written, 'Cursed is everyone who is hanged on a tree . . .'"

Jesus died for us while we are still sinners. Thus, we are saved from the wrath of God. Through His crucifixion we are reconciled to the Father, the curse is removed. If you have not fully trusted in Jesus and believe that your family may be in a cycle of unrepented sin, place your trust in Jesus or re-affirm your trust in Him if you have fallen away, and break that cycle now. Give your children new hope for their future, it is up to you. In the appendix there is a prayer to renounce generational curses. If you have placed your trust in Jesus and are living a Christian lifestyle, there is no need to pray this prayer, however, when you pray this prayer out loud, you not only make Satan aware that you belong to Jesus but you reaffirm your commitment to God.

The Holy Spirt will bring to mind the unrepented sins of your ancestors when God believes you are able to handle the information. As issues come to mind, write them down on a notepad. Think about the things you wrote. Do they apply to your life? Is there a pattern in your life? Take a few days and think about the issues raised. If you have siblings, speak with them about these issues. When you're ready, use the sample prayer in the appendix to renounce and repent for generational sins. These are just sample prayers. Modify them to fit your needs. Each issue brought to mind must be renounced separately. This is a good time to reaffirm Jesus as your Lord and Savior.

Just as generational sin can negatively affect your life, ancestors who have sowed good behavior can bring you generational blessings that have a positive impact in your life. The law of reaping and sowing applies to future generations also. If you want your descendants to be blessed, change your behavior today. Stay in God's will, be generous and kind, you and your descendants will reap the blessings.

This was just an overview of the scriptures related to your salvation and healing. I highly recommend that you spend some time in the Bible every day. Choose a time during the day when you will not be interrupted by anyone. Turn off the television and the phone for just thirty minutes. Pray prior to opening the Bible and ask God to help you understand the scriptures and how to apply them to your life; How does this scripture relate to me? And to show you how to apply it to your healing.

UNDERSTANDING SIN IS THE CULPRIT THAT KEEPS US BROKEN

"... there is no health in my bones because of my sin" (Psalm 38:3-6).

Sin means "missing the mark." Sin is rebellion against God. Sin disrupts our relationship with God, it takes us out of fellowship with Him. Missing the mark suggests that there was a correct mark or target and we missed it. The target would be doing God's will or doing the right thing. The Apostle John defines sin as "lawlessness" (1 John 3:4). Sin can also be defined as a lack of conformity to God's moral standards.

Every person on earth is a descendant of Adam and Eve. Adam's sin corrupted all his descendants. We all have the tendency to lie, cheat, and steal. If you say that you have never committed any of these sins, you lie. Sin is engrained in us from birth. If you are a parent, you know that when you tell your child to not do something, they will do it.

When my daughters were young, about two and six, I used to make them a special breakfast if they were good. I would bake chocolate chip cookies from scratch. I would under cook them so that they would be soft and chewy. Disclaimer: I know this was not a nutritious breakfast, I'm sorry!

One day after baking this special 'breakfast,' I left the cookies to cool a bit and left the room. When I returned, I saw a couple of the cookies missing. I looked at the girls and saw chocolate all over their mouths and fingers. I asked them who took the cookies. They both said, "I don't know." They denied eating the cookies. At this age I had taught them right from wrong and not to lie, but they still denied it.

We also see this pattern in how children play games. They always cheat. I lost a lot of games of checkers until I realized they cheat.

These are all symptoms of a fallen world. It is our nature, we are created with the knowledge of right and wrong, it's written on our hearts. Children know when they push another child down that it is wrong to hurt them, we also know that helping others is good. But what do we do most of? Self-serving activities! We often choose to sin and ignore our conscience. Romans 2:15 says, " . . . and the work of the law is written on our hearts, while their conscience also bears witness, and their conflicting thoughts accuse or even excuse them . . . "

Everyone has a sinful nature, even the Apostle Paul wrestled with sin, and he was chosen by God to write a large portion of the New Testament and to spread the gospel. Romans 7:15-20 says, "For I [Paul] do not understand my own actions. For I do not do what I want, but I do the very thing I hate. Now if I do what I do not want, I agree with the law, that it is good. So it is no longer I that do it, but the sin that dwells within me. For I know that nothing good dwells in me, that is, in my flesh. For I have the desire to do what is right, but not the ability to carry it out. For I do not do the good I want but the evil I do not want, it is no longer I who do it, but the sin that dwells within me."

This inherent nature is a difficult concept to grab a hold of. We all believe ourselves to be good people. But this is according to what the world believes is "good." Inside us, we all have the capacity to do evil. This can be remedied through a personal relationship with Jesus Christ.

The consequences of Adam's sin is our spiritual death and separation from God. This loss of fellowship develops unwanted character traits such as pride, self-reliance, anxiety, shame, a broken spirit, and the most serious consequence is that unrepented sin opens the door for Satan to get a foothold in our beliefs and behaviors. This foothold often develops into a stronghold that oppresses us and steals our joy. Strongholds influence us to go against the will of God, they keep us in habitual sin.

A stronghold causes us to entertain thoughts of self-pity, self-righteousness, isolation, and encourage addictive behavior. Our fleshly worldview causes us to live our life to our own happiness with no regard for others. We serve ourselves, not God. When we turn away from God, our world becomes a mess. God is our only source of peace, love, joy, wisdom, and contentment. We were created to be in God's presence, to love Him, and live with Him in peace.

In order to restore our relationship with God we must acknowledge our sins and repent from them. First John 1:5-10 says, "This is the message we have heard from Him [Jesus] to proclaim to you, that God is light [good] and in Him there is no darkness [evil] at all. If we say we have fellowship with Him while we walk in darkness, we lie and do not practice the truth. But if we walk in the light, and He is in the light, we have fellowship with one another, and the blood of Jesus His Son cleanses us from all sin. If we say we have no sin, we deceive ourselves, and the truth is not in us. If we confess our sins, He is faithful to forgive us our sins and to cleanse us from all unrighteousness. If we say we have not sinned, we make Him a liar, and His word is not in us."

When we confess our sins and trust in Jesus, we are born again, a spiritual rebirth. We now serve God, not Satan. Rebirth restores our relationship with God, He forgives us our sins, past present, and future. Yet still, Christians are locked in a spiritual battle. Paul warns of this spiritual battle in Ephesians 6:12, "For we do not wrestle against flesh and blood, but against rulers, against authorities, against the cosmic powers over this present darkness, against the spiritual forces of evil in heavenly places."

Our enemies are Satan, his demons, the current society influenced by them and our fleshly desires. The Bible refers to this evil culture as "the world." Satan is at war with God; he despises what God represents and he hates all who follow Him.

Satan's goal is to get Christians to sin, resulting in losing fellowship with God, thus making them ineffective. When non-believers see a Christian's sin and act like everyone else, they have no testimony. They do not make others want to be Christians through their behavior, nor please God. God can use Satan as His agent to do many things, God can use Satan to test our faith (1 Peter 1:6-7). God can use Satan to teach us something (1 Peter 4:12-13 & 5:8), or to bring us closer to Him and deepen our trust and love for Him. Satan can tempt us to sin in many ways such as a peer or societal structure that pressure us to conform to the ways of the world. Satan encourages us to be prideful which becomes a catalyst to most sins.

Proverbs 16:18 tells us, "Pride goes before destruction and a haughty spirit before a fall."

The more prideful one is, the more difficult it is to resist sin, especially if one is influential or in power. Power breeds corruption. Pride is being self-centered, having a large ego, or arrogant. In a society influenced by Satan, often called the "world," these character traits are encouraged and even revered. This type of behavior is displayed for all of us to see in the reality television world.

We see that people who cause problems and drama make for great ratings which encourages others to act out in response and be even more outrageous. Rarely we see nice gracious people on these shows that always do the right thing. Why do we enjoy watching these shows? It is our fallen nature! Pride separated us from God; a prideful person cannot get close to God (Psalm 138:6).

Idolatry and envy are additional tactics that Satan can use to destroy an effective Christian. Unfortunately, too many people are consumed by lust for material possessions. We should be focused on heavenly things. We can see that Satan's job is not too difficult.

Most people envy someone, we envy the lifestyle of the rich and famous, sports stars, and people in power. Envy can eat us up and cause severe depression. Envy can drive us to seek financial gains whether from legal or illegal sources. We focus on money, not God, idolatry is anything we place before God. Idols can be money, possession, people, jobs, hobbies, or even church. We cannot serve both God and money (Matthew 6:24).

First Timothy 6:10 says, "For the love of money is the root of all kinds of evils. It is through this craving that some have wandered away from the faith and pierced themselves with many pangs."

Money in itself is not evil, it is the love of money that can lead to all sorts of problems. No one should ever be ashamed of having money or being wealthy. But if money is their ultimate goal and it is placed before the worship of God, then there is a good chance that the love of money will make you turn away from the Lord.

When we die, money will do us no good. Jesus tells us in Matthew 6:19-20, "Do not lay up for yourselves treasures [money/ possessions] on earth, where moth and rust destroy and where thieves break in and steal, but lay up for yourselves treasures in heaven [following God's will] where neither moth or rust destroys and where thieves do not break in and steal."

Jesus is telling us that we should not collect material possessions that are treasured by the world, but be led by the Holy Spirit and do God's will so you will be ensured that you will store up blessings in heaven.

Another way Satan tries to pull us away from God in through his lies and deceit. This is especially true when we go through trials in our lives, when we are at our lowest and go through times of difficulty—times of illness. One of his greatest lies is to convince us that there is an easy way out of our pain. He influences us to seek comfort in sinful activities like alcohol or drugs. He knows that substance abuse will destroy us as well as our families. He tricks us into going with the easy route instead of the difficult road that leads to long lasting healing.

Unrepented sin gives authority to Satan to harass us. When we walk in the Holy Spirit and are in fellowship with God. Satan has no right to attack. Satan can however still try his lies even though we are in fellowship with God.

When we hold unrepented sin in our lives, our fellowship is broken, we are separated from God. This opening gives Satan authority to begin his oppression. It happens slow at first, Satan gets into our minds with a toehold, then as he gets us to sin more, he enlarges his oppression to a foothold. Then when we are a slave to our sin, Satan makes this sinful activity into a stronghold. We will discuss strongholds later.

A perfect example of this release of authority is about traffic laws: when you are driving your car and following traffic laws, the police have no authority to stop you and give you a ticket. When you commit a traffic violation (sin), however, the police have the authority to stop you and write you a ticket.

When we follow God's laws, Satan has no right to oppress you, you are under the authority of God. The Book of Job teaches that God places a hedge of protection around you. But when you break God's laws, Satan has every right to begin his work in you.

What if we sin? First, let me say, we all sin, and always will, so do not stress. All you have to do to restore fellowship with God is to acknowledge your sin and repent and your relationship is restored.

SATAN'S LIES WILL DISRUPT OUR HEALING

Satan is the father of lies. We must be vigilant to his lies. For example: addiction impairs our judgment and uproots or self-control; this is when Satan does his best work. When we try to get our life straightened out, Satan tells us another lie by saying that our addiction is too strong or that God will never forgive us.

This is a lie! Sinful behavior as a response to our trauma are attempts to fill the voids and stop the pain. We are born with a God shaped hole is our heart. God put it there so that we will seek Him. Because of pride and arrogance, we deny God's existence. We then attempt to fill that hole with anything that may make us feel better, when we do this, we will never find the peace and joy we all seek. Only God can fill this hole in our hearts that will make us whole.

In order to heal and make ourselves whole, we must switch dependencies. We must switch to being dependent on God. We can and will overcome our addiction and afflictions with the help of Jesus who shed His blood for our sins so that we could be forgiven. Jesus' blood has the power to deliver us from our emotional pain, addictions and the power that sin has over us.

There is no trial, PTSD, or illness that we could ever experience that Jesus does not understand and been through Himself. Anything that we may go through in our lives is able to be overcome through Jesus' work on the cross.

If we know and believe that Jesus came to set us free by the truth of the gospel, why do we not believe when Jesus tells us that the truth will set us free? (John 8:32). Because Satan is working hard to blind our minds to reject Jesus.

We see this great example to deception in John 8:31-32, "So Jesus said to the Jews who had believed in Him. 'If you abide in my word, you are truly My disciples, and you will know the truth, and the truth will set you free.'" They [Jewish religious elite] answered Him, 'We are offspring of Abraham and have never been enslaved to anyone. How is that You say, you will become free?'"

It is funny that the Jewish elite made this statement to Jesus while they were being oppressed by Roman rule. They must have forgotten that the Israelites were enslaved for over 400 years by the Egyptians and for seventy-nine years by Babylonia. There are Jewish festivals that commemorate their release from slavery. But they said that they were never been enslaved to anyone. Satan is good at his job, he was also able to convince the Jews they had never been enslave to anyone.

Satan was also able to convince the Jews to murder Jesus for no reason. Satan does the same with us. We are a slave to our sinful behavior, but Satan lies to us making us believe that we do not have any issues, we have it all handled. Believing his lie keeps us in sinful behavior and locks us into our pain. Jesus told the Jews, "Truly, truly, I say to you, everyone who commits sin is a slave to sin" (John 8:34).

And Paul says, "... for whatever overcomes a person, to that he is enslaved" (2 Peter 2:19). It is only through the power of Jesus that we will be set free.

Unrepented sin soon becomes habitual sin. Unrepented habitual sin becomes a stronghold. A stronghold is a habitual way of thinking influenced by Satan that keeps us in a cycle of habitual sin. The habitual sin can have a life of its own and will affect every relationship in our lives. Strongholds keep us in bondage to Satan, they can become so engrained in us that we lose our free will, we are enslaved to our sin.

There are many strongholds including: unforgiveness, substance use and abuse, sexual perversion, physical or emotional abuse, racial or religious bias, and a works of the law mentality. This means that one is oppressed by the beliefs that doing good deeds brings you closer to God. The only way to destroy a stronghold is to trust in Jesus, confess and repent your sin, and renounce inner vows, unforgiveness, judgments, and expectancies.

Satan's lies can be very successful if we are not aware of his schemes. Some of the lies he uses to get us caught up in sin include making you think:

- Money or possessions will make you happy.
- Cheating on your spouse will bring sexual gratification and satisfy your lust.
- You are too smart to be caught up in your sin.
- There are no consequences to sin.
- Approval from certain people will make you liked, popular, or happy.
- Excessive consumption of food or alcohol will make you happy.
- If you were better looking or had some cosmetic surgery, you would be popular or happy.

To overcome a stronghold we must understand that Jesus' work on the cross set us free from Satan's oppression. The most difficult thing is to recognize the stronghold in your life. This can only be done by being brutally honest with yourself. Once stronghold has been determined, you simply confess and repent the root sin. Verbally declare that you have been set free of that stronghold.

Each stronghold must be dealt with separately. You may have several different strongholds that are causing you to live a defeated life. All sin will be forgiven through confession and repentance, except for the sin of unbelief. This is the unforgivable sin. The one who speaks against God will not be forgiven. Unbelief is the ultimate sin. Unbelief will reap judgment, however, judgment can be reversed at any time by believing and trusting in our Lord Jesus Christ.

We see that sin is an act of doing something or not doing something we should have done. A sin that is an act of our will is called a sin of commission. A sin that comes from something we should have done (but didn't) is called a sin of omission. An extreme example of a sin of omission is if you would see a person drowning in a pool, but you do nothing and walk away. This is a sin.

The Holy Spirit will convict us when we sin. One day I was walking across a parking lot. I saw an obese man in a wheelchair. He was struggling to move the wheelchair across the pavement. I walked by thinking I should help the man, but Satan was right there with his lies. The thought popped up in my mind, "The man should do this on his own so that he can lose some weight and get stronger."

As I walked past him, I felt the Holy Spirit telling me that I was wrong not to help. I felt guilt come over me. I did go back and helped the man get to where he was going. As it turned out, the man was very sick and had been for a long time, he was not in a wheelchair by his own choosing or by making bad choices. Not helping our fellow men/women is a sign of uncaring and arrogance. The conviction of the Holy Spirit like a constant nagging with a bit of guilt added to it. God gave us this conscience that the Holy Spirit works through to tell us we did wrong.

The key to winning the battle of the mind is knowing that we are all sinners. Then believe that Jesus overcame the power of sin, and as Christians, we have access to that power. We also need to know the schemes of the devil being aware of his lies. Lastly, that we must evaluate thoughts that try to get us to go against God's word. Is that thought confirmed by the word of God? If not, don't do it. If it is, go ahead with assurance. This way we can always have a clear conscience.

Taking the thoughts captive is difficult at first, but becomes easier the sore you do it. Soon it will become part of your decision-making process. Trust in Jesus and He will give you the strength to overcome sinful behavior.

MANKIND'S FIRST SIN AFFECTS OUR HEALING EVEN TODAY

When God created Adam and Eve, He gave them authority over all things on earth. God put them in the Garden of Eden to work it. I know what you are thinking, even Adam and Eve had to work for a living. God told them that they could eat the fruit of any tree from the garden except for the tree of the knowledge of good and evil. If they ate from that tree they would die.

Things were going well for this young couple. They were in perfect fellowship with God and they were naked and unashamed. They had dominion of the earth and everything on it. They had eternal life, all they could eat, and perfect weather. They had it all.

Satan and his demons had been banished to the earth due to their sin. Satan had no authority over the first people on earth. Adam had all authority.

In Genesis we read Satan approached Eve in the form of a serpent. You may ask why did Satan take the form of a snake? We do not know what Satan looks like but I would assume that God stripped Lucifer of his beauty. Maybe he has horns and is red in color? Who knows?

Eve was familiar with all the animals on the earth and in the garden. If Satan would have approached her in his true form, she would have been frightened. He took the form of something familiar to her, a snake. This is how he does his business; he approaches us in a similar fashion so that we will not fear him. Satan spoke to Eve; he is a master manipulator and made her feel comfortable.

Satan knows what type of approaches will work, he suggested that God was unfair and enforced too many rules. He suggested that God was trying to keep the couple down by implementing unnecessary rules. These comments made her think, why would God withhold the best fruit from them? Why would God not want them to be wise? Satan made her doubt God's words. Eve looked at the tree and saw that the fruit of this tree was good to the eyes and the taste buds. She thought that she wanted to be wise like God, so she took the fruit of the forbidden tree and ate it. She also gave some fruit to Adam who ate also, even though he knew better because God told him not to eat from the tree. Eve justified eating the fruit just like we justify our sinful behavior, we explain it away. The bottom line is that they disobeyed God, for Satan, mission accomplished.

Everything we do has repercussions, and sin has consequences. After they ate the fruit, their eyes were opened and they realized that they were naked, they immediately felt ashamed. The first sin brought shame into the world, they knew they disobeyed God. When God came into the garden, the couple hid from Him.

God is all-knowing, He knew what they had done and where they were. I'm sure that God was disappointed and sad over the sin. He called out to them, they came out of hiding. God asked them if they ate the fruit of the forbidden tree. They admitted that they had, Adam then blamed Eve. Does this sound familiar?

We all tend to blame others for the things we have done. Then Eve blamed the serpent. God hates sin, He knows that sin ruins our lives and separates us from himself. He had no choice but to discipline them for their disobedience. God cursed the serpent to crawl on the ground forever. He told Satan that he would be defeated by the soon to come Son of God.

God cursed all women in that childbirth would from now on be a painful experience and women would want to rule over their husbands, but their husbands would rule over them. God cursed the earth so that little would grow causing man to have to work very hard for every bit of food. As God warned, mankind would now experience both a physical and spiritual death, separation from God. This would affect all of Adam's descendants. This was the first and most impactful sin of all time.

Genesis 3:21 describes the first animal sacrifice to atone for sin. Since the couple was now ashamed to walk around naked, they required a covering. God made clothing from the skin of an animal to cloth them. God restored their fellowship with God by killing an animal, maybe even a lamb. This would have been the first death in this newly created world. God forgave them through this sacrifice, but sin has consequences, God ejected them out of the Garden of Eden. God placed a cherubim at the entrance to the garden to protect the garden from trespassers.

The ramification of Adam's sin affected the entire human race—all his descendants. Adam has to take the blame for this sin because Eve was deceived by Satan, but Adam knew better than to eat of the tree. God warned Adam, but Adam knowingly disobeyed God. We learn that our sin affects others: even the smallest sin can hurt your family. Adam's sin infected the entire human race (Romans 5:12-21). This event is known as "the fall of man."

The fall brought death into a perfect world, this was one of the darkest days in human history. Every person born into this world is born in sin imputed from Adam's sin.

Ephesians 2:3 says we are all by nature children of God's wrath. Every person sins, there is no one that does not sin. The theological term for this is "total depravity." We are born separated from God, spiritually dead. (Ephesians 2:1-3). The only remedy for this sin is to trust in the Lord Jesus Christ as your Lord and Savior.

If all that was not enough, Adam's sin gave Satan authority to rule over the earth. Satan is now the god of this world. But we need not worry because the true God is on the throne and in control. Satan can do nothing without God's permission.

Because Satan has been defeated by Jesus' work on the cross, when we follow God and walk in the Holy Spirit, evil cannot touch us (1 John 5:18). I know that I am not the only one who us going to kick Adam in the rear end when I get to heaven. I bet there will be waiting a long line to kick him.

BEWARE SIN'S CONSEQUENCES THAT THWART YOUR HEALING

We live in a sinful fallen world. We must always remember the sin we choose to partake in has consequences. When we sin, our sin separates us from God. He still loves us and watches over us, however, His blessing and healing are removed.

The Bible is the owner's manual to our life here on earth: our instruction manual. The Bible teaches us about the consequences of sin in many stories. The best is the story of King David, a man after God's own heart. David was chosen by God to be the future King of Israel at a very young age. God was with him throughout his life, he was blessed in all he did.

David was young when he defeated the giant Goliath. He married King Saul's daughter and went to work for King Saul. David fought battles with the Israelite army and was a mighty warrior who killed more of the enemy that King Saul. Saul was jealous and tried to kill David several times, but God was with David. David became king when Saul died during a battle.

It was fifteen years between when God anointed David to be king to when he became the King of Israel. Israel prospered under King David's leadership. The Lord was with him and David became greater and greater, the kingdom became more powerful.

This story is a must-read. The consequences of David's sins fell not only on him, but his offspring, and his kingdom, as well as the people residing in his kingdom. After David's sin, things were never the same, he went from peace to constant turmoil. David was a man after God's own heart (1 Samuel 13-14). A man chosen by God and filled with the Holy Spirit, but he was also a sinner and suffered the consequences of his sin.

We are all sinners, Jesus was the only sinless person on Earth. When we do sin, our Heavenly Father must discipline us for our sin. If God never punished people for their sins, this world would be an evil place.

Hebrews 12:4-11 says, "My sons, do not regard lightly the discipline of the Lord. For the Lord disciplines the one He loves, and chastises every son who He receives. It is for discipline that you have to endure. God is treating you as sons. For what son is there whom his father does not discipline? If you were left without discipline, in which all of us have participated, then you are illegitimate children and not sons. Besides this, we have had earthly fathers who disciplined us and we respected them. Shall we must more be subject to the Father of the spirits and live? For they disciplined us for a short time as it seemed best to them, but He disciplines us for our own good, that we may share in His holiness. For the moment all discipline seems painful rather than pleasant, but later it yields the peaceful fruit of righteousness to those who have been trained by it."

When we become a Christian, we are adopted into the family of God. God disciplines those he loves. Those who are parents understand that as a parent, we discipline our children for correction and education that teaches them that their poor behavior negatively affects their lives. Parents correct their children to protect them, not be mean to them. We do this because we want our children to succeed.

God has the same reason for His discipline of sinners. He is teaching us the right way to live and to be more in the likeness of His Son Jesus. Proper discipline will develop positive character traits or what the Bible refers to as good fruit.

Everything we do will result in some sort of consequences, for bad behavior we receive discipline, for good behavior we receive blessings.

Galatians 6:7-9 says, "Do not be deceived; God is not mocked, for whatever one sows, that will he also reap. For the one who sows to his own flesh will from the flesh reap corruption, but the one who sown to the Spirit will from the Spirit reap eternal life. And let us not grow weary of doing good, for in due season we will reap. If we do not give up."

The spiritual law of sowing and reaping comes into play every day. When we live our life selfishly, we reap judgment, but as we follow the Holy Spirit, we reap blessing and healing. We never knew when we will reap these consequences, good or bad. We seldom reap immediately; God is patient and gives us time to repent for poor behavior.

When you sin—and you will—you are blessed to have a loving, compassionate and merciful God who forgives your sins. God loves you even when you mess up. The worst thing we could do is to stay in our sin. Maybe it becomes a stronghold, or we just do not believe that God will forgive us. Either way He still loves us, we must restore the relationship that unrepented sin breaks.

God is our heavenly Father, just as those who are parents know, when a child does something to disappoint us, in example commit some pretty crime, we do not love them less but our relationship has been damaged. We do not abandon that child, they are our family, we love family unconditionally. When the child comes forward and acknowledges what they have done and makes an effort to make amends with restitution and makes an effort to change their behavior, our relationship is restored. The confession does not absolve them from the consequence of their behavior. That's a separate issue, and the only way that our children learn right from wrong. It is because we love them too much to allow them to go down the wrong road.

Our heavenly Father does the same thing. This should be of great comfort to all Christians, for when we make a mistake, our God is merciful and forgives us upon request. God knows our weakness and understands we are only human and we all make mistakes. He looks into our hearts. He knows our thoughts and intentions, when he sees our sincere effort to avoid sin. He forgives us and heals us.

THE NATURAL MAN VS. THE SPIRITUALLY-HEALED MAN

> *"Now may the God of Peace Himself sanctify you completely, and may your whole spirit and soul and body be kept blameless at the coming of our Lord Jesus Christ" (1 Thessalonians 5:23).*

In order to understand the Christ-Centered approach to healing, we need to know how God created human beings and understand God's original design for man and how the fall of Adam and Eve affects the human race.

Theologians debate whether man was created of two or three distinct parts. Some theologians believe in the "dichotomous" view, that man was created with two distinct parts, an immaterial part, the soul, and a material part, the body or flesh. The other view is the "trichotomous" view that is human we're created with body of flesh, soul, and a spirit. I believe the Bible teaches the trichotomous view, everything herein based upon the trichotomous view.

A human being has a physical body that relates to the world through our five senses. We have a soul that includes our mind, will, and emotions, and we have a spirit that is meant to have a union with God. We were originally created to be spiritually alive in perfect sync with God. As we see in figure one our spirit talks to and receives communication from God. We call this original focus the "innocent man."

With our spirit focused on God, our minds are directed to think godly thoughts that directs our will to do God's will that produces fruit of the Spirit (Galatians 5:22-23). Adam and Eve were created innocent. They had no sin.

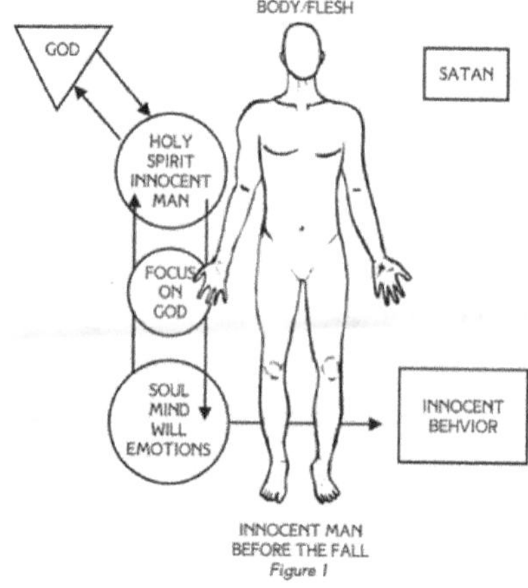

INNOCENT MAN BEFORE THE FALL
Figure 1

They did not look to other's significance they knew they were children of God and that God was taking care of them. They possessed a loving relationship with their heavenly Father, the creator of the heavens and Earth.

The Result of Sin: The Natural Man

Adam and Eve were originally created innocent in full union with God. They were put in charge of the Garden of Eden. God warned Adam that they could eat from any plant in the garden except from the tree of the knowledge of good and evil. God warned them that if he ate from this tree "you will surely die" (Genesis 2:17). What did Adam do? You're right; they ate of the forbidden tree.

Physical death was one result of their sin; but spiritual death came immediately. They were separated from God due to their sin. No more walks in the garden with God, no more sense of security or significance, only a realization of guilt and shame. They were cast out of the garden, their security and food source removed.

The effect of Adam's sin has been passed down through every generation since Adam. We all inherited this spiritual death, a separation from God. "Therefore, just as sin came into the world through one man, and death through sin, and so death spread to all men because all sinned" (Romans 5:12).

As we see in figure two, The Natural Man, our spirit has no access to God.

"The natural person does not accept the things of the Spirit of God, for they are folly to him, and he is not able to understand them because they are spiritually discerned" (1 Corinthians 2:14).

God has blocked our number. This lack of connection allows Satan access to harass us because by default we have given him the authority to do his will in our lives because the natural man has a spirit but not the Holy Spirit. Thus, the natural man is focused on self-gratification and focusing on self. The result is going against God's will. The separation from God allows Satan to rule in our mind and body. This results in unrest, hopelessness, and causes us to live in the flesh.

Galatians 5:19-21 says, "Now the works of the flesh are evident: sexual, immortality, impurity, sensuality, idolatry, sorcery, enmity, strife, jealously, fits of anger, rivalries, dissensions, division, envy, drunkenness, orgies, and things like these. I warn you as I warned you before, that those who do such things will not inherit the kingdom of God."

Living in the flesh tends to make us feel insignificant, inadequate, and full of doubt, with worry and stress. We seek significance or purpose through sin. We become our own god. The natural man will not be healed without God's grace. In order to receive healing, we must first reconcile with God

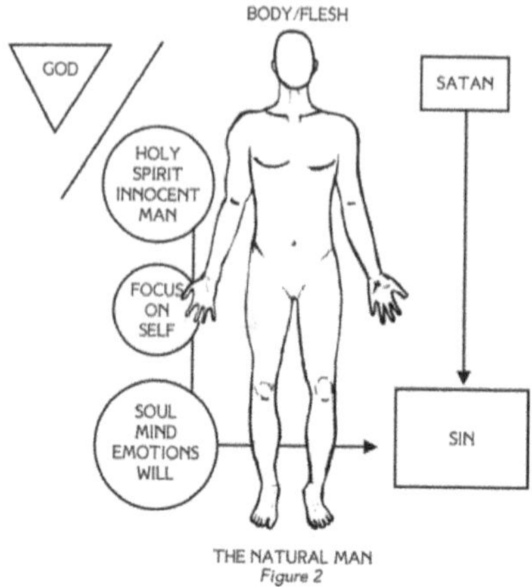

THE NATURAL MAN
Figure 2

Carnal Christians

A carnal or fleshy Christian has accepted Jesus Christ as their Lord and Savior. They are spiritually alive "in Christ" and have been justified by God. The carnal Christian follows the impulses of the flesh and enjoys living in the world. Flesh refers to our carnal desires and the world refers to how non-believers act.

First John 2:15-17 says, "Do not love the world or the things in the world. If anyone loves the world, the love of the Father is not in him. For all that is in the world—the desires of the flesh and the desires of the eyes and pride in possessions—is not from the Father but from the world. And the world is passing away along with its desires, but whoever does the will of God abides forever."

You cannot love God and the things of the world at the same time. When we focus on possessions, lust, power, greed, or drunkenness, we will not enter the kingdom of God. Even though the carnal Christian is spiritually alive, they continue to fall back on old habits. Pastors say the carnal

Christian has one foot in the spiritual world because they believe, but the other foot remains in the world where they feel comfortable. When you have one foot in each world, you cannot mature and move forward. God wants us to be spiritual Christians who make every attempt to stay out of the world.

Second Corinthians 5:14-17 says, "For the love of Christ controls us, because we have concluded this: that one has died for all, therefore all have died, and He [Christ] died for all, that those who live might no longer live for themselves, but for Him who for their sake died and was raised. From now on, therefore, we regard no one according to the flesh."

Our own sinful self is dead and gone. Our new spiritual self is alive with the power of Christ to resist sin. Too many Christians enjoy reliving their old lives that are dead and gone. They love to resurrect that sinful man, reliving their youth or the good-old-days.

Sin can be fun for a fleeting season, but soon afterwards the consequences of that sin results in negative emotions, resentment, and bitterness. These Christians believe that they can rise up the old self for one night a week or month, have some fun, then go back to the spiritual Christians life. This is not possible; this will break God's heart.

Satan is not our only enemy. We become our own enemy when we live in the world or in the flesh sabotaging our sanctification and spiritual well-being. This is the main reason why so many professed Christians live defeated lives.

When keeping one foot in the church and the other in the world, one cannot enjoy the abundant life that we inherited as God's children. I'm often told, "I can't do it," "I'm not strong enough to resist temptation." You have the power to do all things through Christ who strengthens you (Philippians 4:13). You are a child of the most powerful God in the universe; you are seated with Christ and God Himself in heaven (Ephesian 2:6).

As Christians we must make every attempt to walk in the spirit. It's not easy but with the power of Christ you can do anything, and without Him, you can do nothing.

When we look at figure 3, the Carnal Christian, we see that our spirit talks to God. But we still focus on ourselves. Our old man continues to influence our soul, mind, emotions, and our will. The old man's influence causes us to return to sin. We also must remember that when we sin and hold onto unrepented sin, we open the door to Satan's influence.

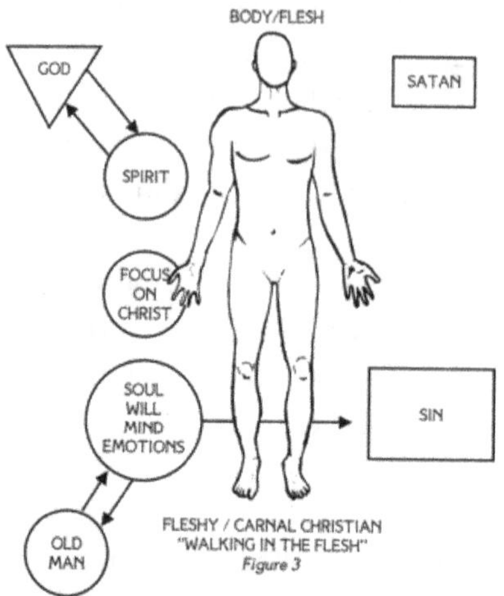

FLESHY / CARNAL CHRISTIAN
"WALKING IN THE FLESH"
Figure 3

Spiritual Christians

When we become Christians, our old self is dead, this is often called the "old man." During regeneration, our old self died. With Jesus' resurrection, we are also reborn. We are born again; we are a new man in Christ.

Second Corinthians 5:17 says, "Therefore, if anyone is in Christ, he is a new creation. The old has passed away, the old the new has come."

We can put away all the old habits that oppressed us, weighed us down, and separated us from God because the Holy Spirit now resides in our hearts.

We are now new Christians, just babies in Christ. I relate new Christians to a new high-horsepower race car engine. Well, I relate everything to car racing! The builder or creator has built it carefully making sure everything is just right and will be able to produce lots of horsepower.

However, to get every single horsepower's performance out of the motor requires an experienced tuner. Fine engine adjustments need to be made so that everything is just right. The motor needs to be broken in properly to ensure longevity and consistency. The engine needs to mature to make sure it operates in the way it was designed to. Jesus is the tuner of our lives; the Holy Spirit brings on maturity and continual sanctification.

Spiritual maturity and sanctification comes from walking in faith or walking in the Spirit. New Christians normally continue to walk in the flesh because they know no other way of life. What all Christians should strive for is to walk in the Spirit living a Spirit filled life.

Walking in the Spirit is simply developing a close loving relationship with our heavenly Father. During my career as a narcotic agent, I've been paired up with many partners. When I got a new partner, on our first shift together, we would talk to get to know one another. At first, we often misunderstand what each are saying, But as we work together more and more, we learn to communicate effectively.

In police work, new partners can be very dangerous and a miscommunication can be deadly. As time goes on, we develop trust for on another. Trust is extremely important. Without trust, we would live lives in fear and insecurity. After more time goes by, we can communicate without saying a word. Communication flows back-and-forth without mistake or misunderstanding. A new Christian can go through this same process as I did with my partners.

To become spiritually mature we partner up with Jesus. Communication at first may be uncomfortable. When I first became a Christian, I had a very difficult time calling God "Father." I did not want to disrespect my earthly father. But as I grew closer to God and trusted Him more and more the word "Father" flowed easily.

As we pray and talk to God we become more comfortable. As we praise and worship God we begin to see His blessings on our lives and we trust Him more. As we continue to walk in the Spirit making a sincere effort to break away from our sinful habits, praying and listening to His response, studying His word and in the Bible we mature in our walk with Him.

As we mature, we break free from those sinful activities. The more we become sanctified, the more we can resist the temptations of sin. We cannot do this without a relationship with Christ (John 15:5).

Galatians 5:16-17 says, "But I [Paul] say, walk by the Spirit, and you will not gratify the desires of the flesh. For the desires of the flesh are against the Spirit, and desires of the Spirit are against the flesh, for these are opposed to each other, to keep you from doing the things you want to do." This inner war keeps us in emotional pain.

Spiritual maturity is not easy to obtain, it requires work, faith and trust. But as you become Spirit-filled, you will be forever changed.

Galatians 5:22-26 says, "But the fruit of the Spirit is love, joy, peace, patience, kindness, goodness, faithfulness, gentleness, self-control, against such things there is no law. and those who belong to Christ Jesus have crucified the flesh with its passion and desires. If we live by the Spirit, let us also walk by the Spirit. Let us not become conceited, provoking one another, envying one another."

These are all character traits of a Spirit-filled Christian. Even Paul admits it is not easy road when he says; the desires of the flesh are against the Spirit. Never get discouraged, if you trip up and commit some sin. Confess and repent and move forward.

Paul, who was probably the most influential disciple had difficulty with sin. Paul writes in Roman 7:15-20 and 7:24-25, "For I do not understand my own actions. For I do not know what I want, but I do the very thing I hate . . . So now it is no longer I who do it, but sin that dwells in me, this is, my flesh. For I have the desire to do what is right, but not the ability to carry it out. For I do not do the good I want, but the evil I do not want is what I keep doing. Now if I do what I do not want, it is no longer I who do it, but the sin that dwells within me."

The Apostle Paul who met Jesus face-to-face still had trouble resisting sin. The flesh is very powerful.

We see from figure four that Spiritual Christians have their focus on Jesus. With the focus on Jesus we can possess that love that Jesus commands. We then have the strength to block out that "old man." A spiritual Christian walks in the Spirit following the prompting of the Holy Spirit. As we walk in the Spirit we produce good fruit and good works, not because we have to, but because we want to please the Lord.

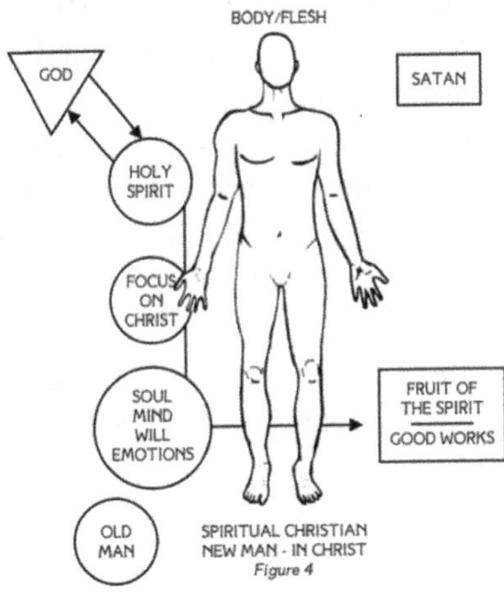

Figure 4

Walking in the Holy Spirit becomes easier as you mature in Christ. It is simple to see where you are currently by reading Galatians chapter five and then honestly evaluating the fruit you are exhibiting. If you are proud of the character traits you exhibit (the way you act) then you're on the right track. But if you are embarrassed or ashamed of the things you do, it's time to ask God for help. The battle is in the mind.

Satan attacks when you are on the correct path and you are maturing. This is when you have to be most vigilant and watchful. Keep your mind focused on Jesus Christ with worship, praise, prayer, and thanksgiving these will keep Satan at bay. This will eventually become a habit and soon you will be walking in the Spirit!

REMEMBERING WHO YOU ARE IN CHRIST

> *But we ought always to give thanks to God for you, brothers beloved by the Lord, because God chose you as the first fruits to be saved, through sanctification by the Spirit and belief in the truth. To this He called you through our gospel, so that you may obtain the glory of our Lord Jesus Christ" (2 Thessalonians 2:13-14).*

Most people, including Christians do not live the joyful life that they could and should be living. This is because most people see themselves in negative light. They think "If I were a little skinnier," "If I had a better job," "If I were better looking," or "If I just had a bit more money, I would feel better and have a happy life."

God created you, Psalm 139:13 says, "For you [God] formed my inward parts; You knitted me together in my mother's womb." God made you exactly as He planned. He did not make a mistake, your personality, disposition, skin color, your IQ, and looks was not an accident. God designed you with a purpose in mind, just the way you are. God has a plan and purpose for you, you must fulfill your destiny. Psalm 139:14 goes to say, "I praise You, for I am fearfully and wonderfully made."

Ephesians 2:10 says, "For we are His [God's] workmanship in Christ Jesus for good works, which God prepared beforehand, that we should walk in them."

You are God's workmanship! If He wanted you taller, smarter, or skinnier, He would have made you that way. You are one of a kind, original, and unique. You were put on this earth by God to fulfill His plan and purpose. You will never reach the potential that God has for you unless you see yourself as God's workmanship.

This is a fallen world ruled by Satan. It is his plan to make you feel you are not worthy of people's love and respect—that you are not smart enough, talented enough, or attractive enough to live a successful and joyful life. His plan is to keep you in pain and in defeat.

Stop accepting Satan's lies. Rebuke him. When these negative thoughts enter your mind, respond with positive affirmations: "I am wonderfully made," "I am a child of God," or "God gave me everything I need to succeed." It is so very important to understand and believe who God says you are.

In order to receive spiritual, emotional, and physical healing, we must understand who we are in Christ. We all hold certain beliefs about ourselves and others based upon our "worldview." Our beliefs and behaviors are first shaped by our parents. We were rewarded when we did something good and punished when we did something bad. Then we went to school and learned new beliefs, habits, and behaviors. Some confirmed and some differed from those of our parents. As we grow older, we are influenced by many other people throughout our lives.

We learn what is right and wrong through other people's opinions and actions. These life lessons determine who we are. Trauma also influences our beliefs and behavior depending on our response to the traumatic incident.

Our worldview impacts how we behave, what we believe, and what choices we make. If you believe you are a failure, unlovable, or a bad seed, you will behave in that manner. Trauma changes our worldview and our sense of who we are. You may begin to believe that you are what happened to you—a victim, a failure, an unattractive, or bad person. This may be how you view yourself, however, your identity and self-worth is not a product of what happened to you, what you did or did not do, or what you have or do not have.

Your identity—your position is "in Christ." Being in Christ gives you purpose and meaning. You are a child of God. Sadly, too many Christians are oppressed in this false sense of who they are. They see themselves as their failures, poor decisions, and mistakes. This false mindset keeps them in a cycle of depression, failure, and sin.

If we want to live the life God intended us to live, we must understand who God says we are. Each one of us is born spiritually dead. When we accept Jesus Christ as our Lord and Savior, we are born again and given a new spirit—the Holy Spirit of God. This is called regeneration.

Second Corinthians 5:17 says, " . . . if anyone is in Christ, he is a new creation. The old man has passed way, behold, the new has come." Ephesians 1:3-7 adds, "Blessed be the God and Father of our Lord Jesus Christ, who has blessed us in Christ with every spiritual blessing in the heavenly places, even as He chose us in Him before the foundation of the world, that we should be holy and blameless before Him. In love He predestined us for adoption as sons through Jesus Christ, according to the purpose of His will, to the praise of His glorious grace, with which He has blessed us in the beloved. In Him [Jesus] we have redemption through His blood, the forgiveness of our trespasses [sin], according to the riches of His grace . . . "

Paul is telling us that God chose you before He created the universe. God predetermined that you would believe and trust in His Son, as a result, you have been adopted into God's family and you have been blessed in Jesus Christ.

Ephesians 1:11-14 says, "In Him [Jesus] we have obtained and inheritance, having been predestined according to the purpose of Him [God] who works all things according to the counsel of His will, so that we who were the first to hope in Christ might be to the praise of His glory. In Him you also, when you heard the word of truth, the gospel of your salvation, and believed in Him [Jesus], were sealed with the promised Holy Spirit, who is the guarantee of our inheritance until we acquire possession of it, to the praise of His [God] glory."

As Christians we are in Christ and He is in us through His Holy Spirit. Being in Christ means that we have died with Him and have been resurrected with Him, thus, we are a new person. Our old sinful self has been crucified with Jesus on the cross, and our new self has been resurrected. This is also known as being "born again." We are a new person who never existed before.

Through this regeneration process God calls us saints. It is no longer what you do that determines who you are, but it is who you are that determines what you do. You are a child of God. Understanding this is essential to living a victorious life. If you see yourself as a child of God, you can no longer doubt your self-worth. We must be aware of Satan's schemes to try to return us to living an oppressed life. When Satan attacks with his negative thoughts, we must remind ourselves of who we are in Christ, the more your behavior will begin to reflect your identity.

When we believe who God says we are, we begin to experience success in our Christian walk. Just as it is important for us to believe who God says we are, it is equally important that we believe other people are also children of God. We are commanded to love one another and to treat others accordingly. When we meet someone for the first time, we judge them based on our worldview; we then treat them based on our judgments: good or bad. But if we suspend judgment and see them as children of God, we follow Christ's command to love one another.

The below statements are taken from Neil Anderson's book, "Victory Over the Darkness."

Who I Am in Christ? I Am Accepted

- I am God's child (John 1:12).
- I am Christ's friend (John 15:15).
- I have been justified (Romans 5:1).
- I am united with the Lord, and I am one spirit with Him (1 Corinthians 6:17).

- I have been bought with a price. I belong to God (1 Corinthians 6:20).
- I am a member of Christ's body (1 Corinthians 12:27).
- I am a saint (Ephesians 1:1).
- I have been adopted as God's child (Ephesians 1:5).
- I have direct access to God through the Holy Spirit (Ephesians 2:18).
- I have been redeemed and I have been forgiven of all my sins (Colossians 1:14).
- I am complete in Christ. I am significant (Colossians 2:10).
- I am free from condemnation (Romans 8:1-2).
- I am assured all things work together for good (Romans 8:28).
- I am free from any condemning charges against me (Romans 8:31-34).
- I cannot be separated from the love of God (Romans 8:35-39).
- I have been established, anointed and sealed by God (2 Corinthians 1:21-22).
- I am confident that the good work God has begun in we will be perfected (Philippians 1:6).
- I am a citizen of heaven (Philippians 3:20).
- I am hidden in Christ in God (Colossians 3:3).
- I have not been given a spirit of fear, but of power, love and a sound mind (2 Timothy 1:7).
- I can find Grace and mercy in time of need (Hebrews 4:16).
- I am born of God and the evil one cannot touch me (1 John chapter 3).
- I am the salt and light of the earth (Matthew 5:13-14).
- I am a branch of the true vine, a channel of His life (John 15:1, 5).
- I have been chosen and appointed to bear fruit (John 15:16).
- I am a personal witness of Christ (Acts 1:8).
- I am God's temple (1 Corinthians 3:16).
- I am a minister of reconciliation for God (2 Corinthians 5:17-21).
- I am God's coworker (2 Corinthians 6:1).
- I may approach God with freedom and confidence (Ephesians 2:6).
- I can do all things through Christ who strengthens me (Philippians 4:13).

Who Am I? I Am Restored

- I am the salt of the earth (Matthew 5:13).
- I am the light of the world (Matthew 5:14).
- I am a child of God (John 1:12).
- I am part of the true vine, a channel of Christ's life (John 15: 1, 2).
- I am Christ's friend (John 15:15).
- I am chosen and appointed by Christ to bear His fruit (John 15:15).
- I am a slave of righteousness (Roman 6:18).
- I am enslaved to God (Romans 6:22).
- I am a son of God; God is spiritually my Father (Romans 8:14-15; Galatians 3:26; 4:6).
- I am a joint heir with Christ, sharing His inheritance with Him (Romans 8:17).
- I am a temple—a dwelling place—of God. His Spirit and His life dwell in me (1 Corinthians 3:16; 6:19).
- I am a united to the Lord and I am one spirit with Him (1 Corinthians 6:17).
- I am a member of Christ's body (1 Corinthians 12:27; Ephesians 5:30).
- I am a new creation (2 Corinthians 5:17).
- I am reconciled to God and am a minister of reconciliation (2 Corinthians 5:18-19).
- I am a son of God and one in Christ (Galatians 5:17).
- I am an heir of God since I am a son of God (Galatians 4:6-7)
- I am a saint (1 Corinthians 1:2, Ephesians 1:1, Philippians 1:1, Colossians 1:2)
- I am God's workmanship—His handiwork—born a new in Christ to do His work (Ephesians 2:10).
- I am a prisoner of Christ (Ephesians 3:1; 4:1).
- I am righteous and holy (Ephesians 4:24).
- I am a citizen of heaven, seated in heave right now (Ephesians 2:6; Philippians 3:20).
- I am hidden with Christ in God (Colossians 3:3).
- I am an expression of the life of Christ because He is my life (Colossians 3:4).
- I am chosen of God, holy and dearly loved (Colossians 3:12; 1 Thessalonians 1:4).
- I am a son of light and not of darkness (1 Thessalonians 5:5).
- I am a holy partaker of a heavenly calling (Hebrews 3:1).

- I am a partaker of Christ; I share in His life (Hebrews 3:14).
- I am one of God's living stones, being built up in Christ as a spiritual house (1 Peter 2:5).
- I am a member of chosen race, a royal priesthood, a holy nation, a people for God's own possession (1 Peter 2:9-10).
- I am an alien and stranger to this world in which I temporarily live (1 Peter 2:11).
- I am an enemy of the devil (1 Peter 5:8).
- I am a child of God, and I will resemble Christ when He returns (1 John 3:1-2).
- I am born of God, and the evil one—the devil—cannot touch me (1 John 5:18).
- I am not the great "I am" (Exodus 3:14; John 8:24, 28, 58), but by the grace of God,
- I am what I am (1 Corinthians 15:10).

Since I Am in Christ, I Am Living in Restoration

- I have been justified—completely forgiven and made righteous (Romans 5:1).
- I died with Christ and died to the power of sin's rule over my life (Romans 6:1-6).
- I am free forever from condemnation (Romans 8:1).
- I have been placed into Christ by God's doing (1 Corinthians 1:30).
- I have received the Spirit of God into my life that I might know the things freely given to me by God (1 Corinthians 2:12).
- I have been given the mind of Christ (1 Corinthians 2:16).
- I have been bought with a price; I am not my own; I belong to God (1 Corinthians 6:19-20).
- I have been established, anointed and sealed by God in Christ, and I have been given the Holy Spirit as a pledge guaranteeing our inheritance to come (2 Corinthians 1:21-22; Ephesians 1:13-14).
- Since I have died, I no longer love for myself, but for Christ (2 Corinthians 5:14-15).
- I have been made righteous (2 Corinthians 5:21).
- I have been crucified with Christ and it is no longer I that live, but Christ lives in me. The life I am now living is Christ's life (Galatians 2:20).
- I have been blessed with every spiritual blessing (Ephesians 1:3).

- I was chosen in Christ before the foundation of the world to be holy and without blame before Him (Ephesians 1:4).
- I was predestined—determined by God—to be adopted as God's son (Ephesians 1:5).
- I have been redeemed and forgiven; I am a recipient of His lavish grace (Ephesians 1:7-8).
- I have been made alive together with Christ (Ephesians 2:5).
- I have been raised up and seated with Christ in heaven (Ephesians 2:6).
- I have direct access to God through the Spirit (Ephesians 2:18).
- I may approach God with boldness, freedom and confidence (Ephesians 3:12).
- I have been rescued from the domain of Satan's rule and transferred to the kingdom of Christ (Colossians 1:13).
- I have been redeemed and forgiven of all my sins. The debt against me has been canceled (Colossians 1:14; 2:14).
- Christ himself is in me (Colossians 1:27).
- I am firmly rooted in Christ and am now being built in Him (Colossians 2:7).
- I have been made complete in Christ (Colossians 2:10).
- I have been spiritually circumcised (Colossians 2:11).
- I have been buried, raised and made alive with Christ (Colossians 2:12-13).
- I died with Christ and I have been raised up with Christ. My life is now hidden with Christ in God. Christ is now my life (Colossians 3:1-4).
- I have been given a spirit of power, love and self-discipline (2 Timothy 1:7).
- I have been saved and set apart according to God's doing (2 Timothy 1:9; Titus 3:5).
- Because I am sanctified and am with the sanctifier, He is not ashamed to call me brother (Hebrews 2:11).
- I have the right to come boldly before the throne of God to find mercy and grace in time of need (Hebrews 4:16).
- I have been given exceedingly great and precious promises by God by which I am a partaker of God's divine nature (2 Peter 1:4).[15]

---

[15] Neil Anderson, *Victory Over the Darkness*, (Bethany Brothers Publishers, Michigan, 2013) 38-39; 51-53; 64-65.

All the above statements are true. There is nothing you can do to make them less or any more true. It is all based on God's grace. As we mature as Christians, our life becomes more meaningful.

Write these true statements on "3x5" cards and carry them with you or place them in a spot where you will see them every day. Anytime you feel under attack from Satan who is trying to deceive you into believing you are worthless, take out the cards and read the statement out loud. The more you reinforce who you are in Christ, the more you will change into the likeness of Christ.

As you move forward in your Christian walk, everyone will be able to see that your behavior has changed. The Holy Spirit changes us from the inside out. He changes our heart. We no longer enjoy the things we used to enjoy—like getting drunk, cursing, making fun of others, and other bad behavior. As we mature, we experience more and more fruit of the Spirit.

I cannot overly express the importance that all Christians understand who they are in Christ. The majority of Christians today struggle with habitual sin. They do not understand that they are children of God and are not required to worry about their performance on doing good deeds to earn their way into heaven. There is nothing we can do to earn our forgiveness, it is only given to us because of our trust in Jesus Christ and through God's grace. If we stress about doing enough good things to get into heaven, it drives us deeper into sin. Then it becomes a vicious cycle. But when we accept our position as a child of God we need not worry about anything. We can trust our Heavenly Father to provide our needs and that all things will work for good.

You are a child of the Most High God: You are a special. Our heavenly Father loves you not because what you have done or how good you are. He loves you because you are His son or daughter. Trust who God says you are. You are what you believe. As a child of God, there is nothing you cannot overcome.

FAITH IS THE KEY TO HEALING

> *"For by grace you have been saved through faith. And this is not your own doing; it is the gift of God, not a result of works, so that no one may boast. For we are His workmanship, created in Christ Jesus for good works, which God prepared beforehand, that we should walk in them" (Ephesian 2:8-10).*

Faith can be defined as having confidence, trust, or to hold something true. Faith is the most important aspect of Christianity.

Hebrews 11:6 says, "And without faith it is impossible to please Him [God], for whoever would draw near to God must believe that He exists and that He rewards those who seek Him."

And Galatians 2:16 adds, " . . . we know that a person is not justified by works of the law [good deeds] but through faith in Jesus Christ, so we also have believed in Christ Jesus, in order to be justified [not guilty] by faith in Christ and not by works of the law, because by works of the law no one will be justified."

Paul is telling us that it is only through our faith in Jesus that we are forgiven of our sins. We could never do enough good deeds to please God and earn His forgiveness. Faith is the one attitude of the heart that is the exact opposite of depending on yourself. It is our faith and trust in Jesus that makes us Christians.

Faith in Christ is essential in maturing as a Christian. Everyone has faith in something, it is the object of our faith that differentiates Christians and non-believers. We all live by faith every day.

When we go to sit down in a chair, we must have faith that it will not break when we sit in it. We have a great faith when we are driving on the road every day. You probably never thought about it, but even simply crossing a four-way intersection requires faith. If you're driving straight and the light is green, you probably drive straight through the intersection without thinking twice about the cross traffic.

Why? Because you have driven through intersections hundreds of times in the past with no problems. You have faith that the light for cross traffic will be red when your light is green. You have faith even though you cannot see the red light for cross traffic. We also have faith that the cross traffic will see their red light and stop for it. We have faith that they are not distracted or drunk-driving. Now that you have thought about this scenario, do you still have faith to drive forty-five mph through a green light? Or will you now slow down and think twice?

I worked traffic enforcement for five years and have investigated hundreds of vehicle collisions during my career. Most were at intersections. I have seen how people drive and I also have seen a number of vehicle malfunctions that caused collisions. When I am driving, I slow down when approaching an intersection to ensure the cross traffic slows for their red light. Why do I slow down? Because I have lost faith in other drivers.

Based on my experience, I know, most drivers are distracted by something. I know that there are also many drivers who are driving impaired due to lack of sleep, medications, drugs, or alcohol. How does my loss of faith affect me? It makes driving more stressful. I pay close attention to each cross street and intersection because I know that these are dangerous places where collisions often occur.

The fear of being involved in a collision causes stress and anxiety making our travels through life less enjoyable. Constant stress like this may even cause us to give up driving altogether and ride a bus. Once we lose faith, it is difficult to build it back up. The ultimate object of faith is in Jesus Christ.

We sense God is telling you to do something that may be uncomfortable. This is when your mind plays tricks on you, or is it Satan? You find ways to back out of what you believe God is asking you to do. If you back out you will miss the blessings that He has waiting for you upon completion of your task. You will miss out on God's plan and purpose for you. When you step out in faith that God has your back, I guarantee it will be one of the greatest experiences of your life. God's plan is always right.

The amount of faith we are able to have in someone or something is dependent on how much we know about and trust that person or object. I believe that lack of trust and faith in God is why many Christians live defeated lives. They profess their faith by going to church on Easter and Christmas and maybe a few times during the football off-season. They pray self-centered prayers, and sometimes say, "Praise God!" in front of friends and family and then expect God to respond to them favorably. The problem is that their lack of faith is corrupted by their lack of knowledge.

Hosea 4:6 says, "My [God's] people [you] are destroyed for lack of knowledge."

If you want to grow your faith and increase your knowledge, you must learn more about who God is and who He says you are. The more you learn, the more faith you will have.

Romans 10:17 says, "So faith comes from hearing, and hearing through the word of Christ." Paul is referring to the spoken word from the Bible. This is done by listening to preachers teaching the Bible and from testimonies of those who have experienced God's miracles and unconditional love. Faith also comes from reading the Bible, going to Bible studies, praying, and fellowship with other Christians. Faith is an action word. If we want our faith to grow, we must trust that what God says is true. For example,

Matthew 11:28-30 says, "Come to me [Jesus], all who labor and are heavy laden, and I will give you rest. Take My yoke upon you, and learn from Me, for I am gentle and lowly in heart, and you will find rest for your souls. For My yoke is easy, and My burden is light."

Jesus is telling you that if you are going through a difficult time that makes you feel as if a large weight is on your shoulders, you can go to Him in faith and find rest, peace, and joy. You can give Him all your troubles, cares, and worries. He will carry them for you. With Jesus in our lives, why do we need to worry? Who has ever added a single hour to their life by being anxious or worrying about problems? (Luke 12:25). In order for us to release our worries to Him, it requires that we have trust and faith that He will do what He promises to do.

Step out in faith and trust Jesus. In prayer, tell Jesus that you cannot live like this anymore. Tell Him that you trust and have faith in Him to take care of all of life's situations. I promise He will take care of it all for you and do a better job handling these things that you ever could have done, if you have faith. Remember that God promises that all things (even our trials) will work out for the good for those who love Him (Romans 8:28).

Throughout the years, as my faith grew, so did my trust, and so did my peace. I know that I can trust God to follow through on His promises. Stepping out in faith means to give Him all your worries and then forget about it. It is not easy but as your faith grows, giving it to God will become second nature. If you pray for Him to take all your worries but you continue to stress over your problem, you're not stepping out in Faith. Just try it and watch what God does in your life.

We can be assured of all of God's promises from the Bible. If we are assured, we can have the required faith. If God declares it, you can count on it! We cannot manipulate God's will through prayer or good works. This is why we must learn God's teachings, promises, and spiritual principles. As we become mature in our Christian faith, our trust and faith will grow.

I love racing cars. In order to drive fast around a closed racing course, you must drive on what is called "the racing line or groove." This is an imaginary line that if you can keep the car on or near, the car will not only handle its best, but will have consistently fast racing lap times. If you are off this groove by even a foot or two, you cannot smoothly drive the apex of each corner. Your lap times will increase and the car will not handle as well. You can't win a race like that.

Our walk with God is a direct result of our faith and trust in Jesus. If our faith is off just a little, our Christian walk will suffer. There is no better time to start than today. Begin by praying and telling God that you want to start your renewed relationship with Him today. Tell Him that you are starting with a small amount of faith, but you want it to grow.

As you begin you walk with God you will begin to see His blessings. Your trust begins to grow. Your faith begins to grow. The closer your relationship, the more trust and faith you will have. You have been saved by faith, you have been justified by faith, and you will be healed by faith.

CONFESSION & REPENTANCE ENSURE DAILY HEALING

> *"Repent therefore, and turn back, that your sins may be blotted out, that times of refreshing may come from the presence of the Lord . . ." (Acts 3:19-20).*

What do you do now? What happens when a Christian sins? When we first made Jesus Christ our Lord and Savior, our sins were forgiven, past, present, and future. God considers us not guilty; we are justified. God sees us as if we never sinned. This is not something we earned or achieved on our own, it is through the grace of God that He forgives us.

But what happens when we sin after becoming a Christian? When we commit a sin or do something that goes against God's principles, our relationship with God is disrupted. God still loves us, but our sin disappoints Him. For those of us who have children, we know that when they do something that is against our rules. We become disappointed in them. We do not stop loving them. We do not love them less because of their mistake, but our relationship is strained. Our relationship remains disrupted until our child has made amends for what they have done.

It is the same with God, our relationship with Him is strained until we have made restitution for our mistake. He does not love us less. When our relationship with God is disrupted, He does not listen to our prayers (Proverbs 15:29).

Jesus tells us that we cannot produce good fruit unless we abide in Him (John 15:4). Holding onto unrepented sin prevents us from abiding in Him, and Him in us. Peter tells us that sin wages war against our soul (1 Peter 2:11) that can affect our peace and can cause turmoil in our lives.

In order to restore our relationship with our Heavenly Father, we must acknowledge our sins. This is referred to as confession. When we confess our sin to God, He forgives us and cleanses us, we are forgiven (1 John 1:9) and our relationship is restored. This is a gift from God. Nothing can cleanse us from our sin on our own.

We can be more spiritual than all our friends. We can pray for hours a day, go to church, do volunteer work, pay tithes, or go to all the Bible studies but these things are just a waste of time. It is only through confession and repentance that we are cleansed. Some of us, like me, must confess and repent several times a day.

Since the fall, all humans are sinners. No one is less a sinner, no one is a worse sinner. Do not allow others to fool you; everyone falls short of the glory of God, everyone sins. God knows that we will not stop sinning until we go to our heavenly glory. This is why He sent His son to pay the price that was meant for us. Christ's work on the cross allows us to simply confess and repent instead of sufferings the death penalty that was meant for us. Jesus paid the prices for us.

Confession is so important that Jesus incorporated it into the Lord's prayer, " . . . forgive us our debts [sins], as we forgive our debtors [those who sin against us]" (Matthew 6:12). Confession should be done prior to or incorporated into all daily prayers as the Lord's prayer models. Some churches require public confession of sin, the Bible teaches both public and private confession.

It is important to acknowledge our sins to God in order to begin the healing process. A long time ago, when one of my daughters was young, she fell and scrapped her knee. She ran in the house crying. I got out the first aid kit antiseptic to clean the wound. She knew that the spray stung.

She cried out, "No!" She wanted me to put a band-aid on the wound without cleaning it. Most Christians do the same thing. We want Jesus to cover our sins, but we don't want the pain of cleansing our wounds so they will heal. We just want it covered up.

But if the wound is not cleaned, it gets infected and causes more pain. When we do not expose our sin to God's healing balm, we remain in our pain. If we deny or try to justify our sin, healing will not occur. Christ-Centered Healing was developed to bring these old wounds to the surface to be cleansed. It is not a pain-free process, but it will heal.

We must confess and repent to restore our relationship with God. Repentance means a genuine change of mind. We must change our mind from that of the world, to the mind of Christ. God hates sin, we should also. We are to confess our mistakes to God, then, turn away from that sin. Repentance is having a sincere regret for our sin.

2 Corinthians 7:10 says, "For godly grief produces a repentance that leads to salvation without regret, whereas worldly grief produces death."

You cannot fake true repentance. God knows the heart of each man. Never get discouraged, we are all sinners. If someone says they do not sin, they lie

(1 John 1:8). We were born in sin, even the Apostle Paul kept sinning and he wrote a large portion of the New Testament.

We know right from wrong. We know what we should and should not do. Even knowing these things, we do what we should not do. God knows this is universal to all humans. When we commit a sin, God does not say, "WOW! I didn't see that coming!" God knows we will sin. This is why He provided us with a way to pay restitution—confession and repentance.

It is so important for the mature Christian to understand and believe that we are forgiven, not by anything we do, but for what Jesus Christ has done for us on the cross. We can never earn our forgiveness or even purchase it. It is only God's grace that He forgives and heals us. When you sin (and you will) just acknowledge your sin to God and make a sincere effort to turn away from that sin and God will forgive you. The sin that caused the separation from God has been removed and your relationship with Him restored. Once our relationship has been restored, the healing will begin.

WALKING IN THE SPIRIT ENSURES CONTINUED HEALING

> *"But I say, walk by the Spirit, and you will not gratify the desires of the flesh. For the desires of the flesh are against the Spirit, and the desires of the Spirit are against the flesh, for these are opposed to each other, to keep you from doing the things you want to do. But if you are led by the Spirit, you are not under the law" (Galatians 5:16-18).*

It is so important for the mature Christian to understand Galatians 5:22-26 says, " . . . the fruit of the Spirit is love, joy, peace, patience, kindness, goodness, faithfulness, gentleness, self-control; against such things there is no law. And those who belong to Christ Jesus have crucified the flesh with its passions and desires. If we live by the Spirit, let us also keep in step with the Spirit.

The apostle Paul is telling us that a spiritually mature Christian "walks by the Holy Spirit" also referred to as "walking in the Holy Spirit." Walking by the Holy Spirit refers to living a Christian lifestyle. Why do we need to be spiritually mature? Because as we become spiritually mature, we align ourselves with God's will. As we live a life that is in God's will, He provides us the peace, joy, healing, and the abundant life that is promised in the Bible

(John 15:11, 1 John 1:4). As we rest in God's will, we experience the blessings and healing that God promises (Deuteronomy 28:1-14).

What do we have to do to become spiritually mature? We must put all our sinful responses to our traumas in our lives to death on the cross. We place the cross of Christ between us and our sin. We confess, repent, and renounce our sinful responses, and place them at the foot of the cross.

We also must acknowledge that we have a sovereign God who is in control of all things (Colossians 1:15-20). Equally important is understanding who we are in Christ; we are children of God, deeply loved and cherished. All humans are born in sin and self-centered. As we seek God and place our trust in Him, we are transformed by the renewing of our minds into a Christian lifestyle (Romans 12:2). As we mature in our faith, we become more in the image of Christ.

As we follow the leading of the Holy Spirit, we learn that sin does not have to enslave us because it is through God's grace that we are forgiven of our sin. We already have learned that when we become a Christian, God's Holy Spirit dwells within us. The Holy Spirit guides and directs God's elect.

The Bible gives us many examples of people being led by the Spirit of God. In Acts 8:26-40 describes an Ethiopian Court official that was reading scripture but was not able to understand the text. The Holy Spirit told Philip to go and talk with the official and help him understand God's word. Philip followed the leading of the Holy Spirit and explained the scriptures to the Ethiopian and then baptized the official bringing another person into the kingdom of God.

In Acts 16:6-10 we read that Paul and Timothy were preaching the gospel throughout the ancient world. They wanted to go and preach in Mysia, however, the Holy Spirit would not allow them to go into there. The Holy Spirit told them to go to Macedonia instead. They preached the gospel in Macedonia. We learn that the Holy Spirit can tell us to do or not to do or go somewhere to fulfill God's plan, either for our lives or the benefit of the church.

As we learn to hear God's voice, we can fulfill His plan and remain in His will. The Bible teaches that when you walk in the Holy Spirit you will be blessed. When you are in habitual sin, He may withdraw that blessing.

Remember, God hates sin. We see that when Samson, Saul, and David were in God's will, they were blessed. However, the Holy Spirit departed when they disobeyed God.

Living a spirit-filled life is walking in the Holy Spirit. It is called "walking" in the Holy Spirit because it is a journey, it is not just sitting around and waiting on God to do all the work. Walking in the Holy Spirit is a relationship with God where we listen for His directions and following His prompting in order to fulfill His will.

Consider it a partnership. God is a Spirit without a human body. We have a human body and as part of the *body of Christ* we carry out His plan and purpose on earth.

When we walk in the Spirit we will exhibit the fruit of the Spirit. One night when I was in prison, I was walking laps in the yard. I saw another man that I did not recognize also walking. He appeared to be new to this prison. I noticed that the man's body language showed that he was either deeply depressed or suffering with anxiety. I heard the Holy Spirit tell me to go talk to the man.

I was doing my own exercise program. I was on a mission. I did not want to talk to the guy. The Holy Spirit repeated the command. I hesitated. This was prison. You do not just go up to a stranger and start talking with him. Who knows what this guy was in for.

I stalled as long as I could and then approached the man. The guy had just arrived to this prison. He was in distress and was feeling depressed because he just left his family. We walked and talked. I gave him some "new guy" pointers and invited him to our nightly prayer group. A few days later he came up to me and thanked me for talking with him and calming him down. It was not me; I didn't even want to talk with him.

The Holy Spirit saw someone that needed comforting and I was the closest Christian to the man in need. God used me to comfort one of His children. This is what the body of Christ is meant to do. Without God's prompting, who knows what that guy would have done or who else could have taken advantage of him.

How will we know when we are walking in the Spirit? The proof of a proper relationship with God is the fruit we exhibit. We should be able to see changes in our lives that are positive. Good fruit or positive results of a spirit-filled walk with God are: love (not hate), joy (not depression), peace (not anxiety), patience (not anger), kindness (not arrogance), goodness (not selfishness), faithfulness (not disloyalty), and self-control (not rage) (Galatians 5:22-23).

Do these traits describe you? If not, your relationship with Jesus Christ might not be as it should. John 15:5 says, " . . . whoever abides in Me [Jesus] and I in him, he it is that bears much fruit, for apart from Me you can do nothing."

Because of what Jesus has done for us through His ultimate expression of love, we also show our love for Him by abiding in Him. He then abides in us. Abide means to dwell or live in. Abiding in Jesus is the same as walking in the Holy Spirit.

As we walk in the Holy Spirit, we mature in our faith and relationship with God, our character develops into the person God designed us to be. This results in sanctification. Our sanctification is God's will for our lives (1 Thessalonians 4:3). Sanctification is the process of conforming to the image of Christ. It is this process of sanctification that brings blessing and healing.

Renewing the Mind

A proper walk in the Holy Spirit includes taking every thought captive, 2 Corinthians 10:3-5 says, "For though we walk in the flesh, we are not waging war according to the flesh. For the weapons of our warfare are not of the flesh but have divine power to destroy strongholds. We destroy arguments and every lofty opinion raised against the knowledge of God, and take every thought captive to obey Christ, being ready to punish every disobedience, when your obedience is complete."

The daily battle is in the mind. We are attacked by Satan, his demons, and our flesh, every day. Our beliefs and attitudes are formed by our childhood experiences, life experiences, and traumatic experiences. Those beliefs and attitudes are assimilated into our minds over time. Our behavior then, is a result of our beliefs and attitudes. In Romans 12:2, Paul tells us that we are not to live by societal norms, but to allow the Holy Spirit to renew our minds from the inside out, and by this we learn God's will.

How do we renew our minds? The Bible says that when we make Jesus our Lord and Savior, we are a new creation. God places the Holy Spirit in our heart to lead and guide us throughout the day.

So, if we are a new person and our old self is dead, why do we continue to sin? As we learned previously, our behavior is based on our beliefs. Our beliefs are obtained from the events in our childhood. Unlike computers, we do not have a delete button. We cannot just forget our past bias and judgments. Our old self remembers our old beliefs because it has been ingrained since childhood.

The problem is now that our old self (flesh) is different than our new Spirit. The flesh and the Spirit oppose one another (Galatian 5:17). This opposition causes distress in our soul. This distress is the cause of our pain; it manifests in negative emotions. On top of this, Satan may still oppress us because of the unrepented sin. In computer terms, think of your brain as the computer hardware. Our thoughts are the software. Renewing your mind is similar to updating or upgrading the software. When you are born, the software is blank. As you grow up, data is being written on the software continually. The data comes from everywhere and every experience. This software then begins to influence your behavior—good and bad. By the time you become an adult, your belief system influences your behavior and has become habits. Habits are hard to change. The software has to be updated and overwritten.

When we become Christians, the Holy Spirit helps us overwrite the old data. Paul has told us that positionally we are dead to the old sins that held onto us. And we are now alive to Jesus Christ (Romans 6:11). With the help of the Holy Spirit, our thoughts slowly begin to change, one thought at a time. Every time you follow the Holy Spirits prompting, a piece of old self-centered behavior is overwritten and new godly belief is written, thus, renewing the mind. The more we follow the Holy Spirit, the more our old data is over-written.

This is called sanctification—the renewing of your mind. Because our old self-centered beliefs are habitual, this process is not easy. Our flesh is strong. It is a daily battle that many of us lose because we lack the knowledge to walk in the Spirit. Don't forget the influence of Satan.

This battle of the mind is depicted in cartoons and movies. It is often show by a person with a devil on one shoulder and an angel on the other. The devil whispers to do something wrong. Then we see the angel whispering to do what is moral and right.

Here is an example in everyday life: Let's say you're going to the store. There is someone following you several yards behind you. You open the door to the store, look back and see this person behind you. Do you wait and hold the door open for them? Does it matter if it is a woman or a man? If so, why?

The little devil whispers in your ear, "Go ahead and go inside. You're too busy to wait for this person." Or, "Don't wait. They need the exercise." But the Holy Spirit tells you, "Do the right thing, hold the door open. That's what Jesus would do."

Who would you listen too? The devil or the Holy Spirit? This is a simple example, but it is the one you listen to and follow that determines who you serve.

If you do not hold the door open, the devil becomes dominate in your beliefs and behavior. All decisions are then influenced by the devil. The same with the Holy Spirit, the more you listen to God, the more the old data will be overwritten, and the more you will be sanctified.

How do we discern who is speaking? How do we know who is talking to us? In the above scenario, the devil is influencing you to be self-centered. How does this compare to what the Bible teaches? Does the Bible teach us to be selfish? Or does it teach to love others and be kind to others? What lines up with God's word? If it is being kind, you hold the door open and wait for that person. This is selfless behavior.

This sounds like a long process, and it is, but once you begin, when a thought enters your mind, it will become a habit to compare it to God's moral standards. The ability to form this comparison is why it is important to understand what the Bible teaches.

Temptations are everywhere. Thoughts that appeal to our "old man" and tempt us into our old sins. When a temptation pops up, we consider whether or not to do it. As we contemplate this thought, our emotions get involved increasing the likelihood of giving into the temptation because it is familiar to us. We must learn to control our thought process.

When such thoughts surface, we take the thought captive and compare that thought to God's word. If the thought does not align with God's word, we are to reject that thought. This is difficult at first, but as it becomes a habit, the process will be automatically set into motion whenever a temptation arises. If we do not reject the thought and act on the temptation, we must then take responsibility for the sinful action.

Many times the strongholds that guide our behavior are difficult to overcome. How do we break strongholds? By renewing our minds through the word of God, going to church, volunteering to help those in need, going to Bible study, knowing who God is, and knowing who you are in Christ. We must also know how Satan works to keep us oppressed. By walking in the Holy Spirit, we learn to discern godly thoughts and those of Satan.

We must be aware of Satan's schemes (2 Corinthians 2:11). Satan's plan is to deceive us into doubting who God is and to tell us lies that try to make us believe we are unworthy of God's love and blessing. These schemes are why it is so very important to take every thought and evaluate it with God's word. If the thought is something like, "You're no good, look what you've done, God will never forgive you." Now, rationally compare that thought to God's word.

Does God say you're no good or cannot be forgiven? No! Does God forgive all that come to Him? Yes! What does the Bible say about God's love? Romans 8:38-39 says, "For I [Paul] am sure that neither death nor life, nor angels nor rulers, nor things present nor things to come, nor powers, or height nor depth, nor anything else in all creation, will be able to separate us from the love of God in Christ Jesus our Lord."

We must reject negative thoughts and move on. When we expose that thought as a lie, we win the battle. Satan has no authority over us unless we allow it by opening the door through our sin. We must shut the door by confession and repentance. As we practice this process it becomes a habit and a normal thought pattern.

In order to take every thought captive to compare it with the truth of God's word, we must be familiar with God's word. Attending regular Bible studies with other Christians is instrumental in learning God's word.

1 Timothy 3:16-17 says, "All scripture is breathed out by God and profitable for teaching, for reproof, for correction, and for training in righteousness, that the man of God may be competent, equipped for every good work."

And 1 John 2:14 adds, " . . . the word of God abides in you, and you have overcome the evil one."

Knowing the word of God helps you to discern the lies of Satan. Regular prayer helps us in our walk with the Holy Spirit. Regular conversation with God grows faith, trust, and brings healing.

2 Chronicles 7:14 says, " . . . if My [God] people who are called by My name humble themselves and pray and seek My face and turn from their wicked ways, then I will hear from heaven and will forgive their sin and heal their land [bodies]."

When you pray and give God your problems, you strengthen your relationship with Him.

1 Thessalonians 5:16-18 says, "Rejoice always, pray without ceasing, give thanks in all circumstances; for this is the will of God in Christ Jesus for you." Prayer is powerful tool in the Christian's toolbox.

James 5:16 adds, "Therefore, confess your sins to one another and pray for one another, that you may be healed. The prayer of a righteous person has great power as it is working."

It is God's will for you to call out to Him when in need or just to tell Him, "Thank you" for your blessings. After you pray remember to spend some quiet time alone with God—prayer is a *two-way* conversation.

As discussed earlier, we must listen for God's voice. When we start out it is difficult because of all the noise and static in our minds. As we focus on God, the static dissipates more and more. God does not speak to all of us in the same way. We must learn to discern His voice from all the others. Give it time and you will hear when He talks. Jesus told his disciples about the Holy Spirit.

John 16:13 says, "When the Spirit of truth comes, He will guide you into all the truth, for He will not speak on His own authority, but whatever He hears He will speak, and He will declare to you the things that are to come." The Holy Spirit will speak to you the truth of the gospel. Jesus tells us that the truth will set you free from the bondage of sin. As we mature in our faith in Christ and are being led by the Holy Spirit, we learn God's will.

1 John 2:15-17 says, "Do not love the world or the things in the world. If anyone loves the world, the love of the Father is not in him. For all that is in the world—the desires of the flesh and the desires of the eyes and pride of life—is not from the Father but is from the world. And the world is passing away along with its desires, but whoever does the will of God abides forever."

We all live in this world, but that does mean that we must be part of the world. God has set apart Christians from the world. As Christians living in this world controlled by Satan, we must focus on Jesus because He has overcome the world (John 16:33). When we abide in Jesus, we have His power to overcome the world.

When you do sin, and you will (we all do) do not stress and get down in the dumps. Simply confess and repent the sin and move forward.

THE IMPORTANCE OF BAPTISM

> *"Do you not know that all of us who have been baptized into Christ Jesus were baptized into His death? We were buried therefore with Him by baptism into death, in order that, just as Christ was raised from the dead by the glory of the Father, we too might walk in newness of life" (Romans 6:3-4).*

Baptism is extremely important. Every Christian should be baptized. Based on scripture there are three common types of baptisms. John the Baptist immersed people in the Jordan river after they repented their sins. The water is symbolic of cleansing. John's baptism was the forerunner to the current baptisms. Baptize means "immersion."

The first type of baptism is that of *salvation.* It is called the baptism of the Holy Spirit. At the time that a sinner makes Jesus Christ their Lord and Savior, God gives the new believer the Holy Spirit of God to reside in their heart, no water is required here.

Acts 2:38-39 says, " . . . repent and be baptized every one of you in the name of Jesus Christ for the forgiveness of your sins, and you will receive the gift of the Holy Spirit."

1 Corinthians 6:17 says, " . . . he who is joined to the Lord becomes one spirit with Him."

During salvation we are baptized into the same body; the *body of Christ* (1 Corinthians 12:13-26). The body of Christ is the church, every believer is a member of the body of Christ. We need not attend a church to be a member of Jesus' church. We are baptized by the Holy Spirit which brings redemption and salvation. With redemption comes adoption into the family of God, we become co-heirs with Jesus (Galatians 4:6-7).

A co-heir denotes equal share. When one dies they leave their estate to an heir, often there are a number of heirs to receive varying amounts of the estate. Being a co-heir means that we will receive an equal share with our older brother Jesus. This is an important principle to understand when believing what the Bible says about who we are in Christ. The baptism of the Holy Spirit is automatic. He begins the work of regeneration. We become a new creation, our sinful "old man" has died, and a new spiritual person is born, thus the term "born again" (2 Corinthians 5:17).

The second type of baptism is the *water baptism.* Water baptism is a public confession of the inward change produced by confession, repentance, and faith in Jesus. A proper water baptism is that the person is immersed in water. This is symbolic of dying on the cross and being buried. That death is represented by the immersion in the water. The resurrection of our body and rebirth is represented by coming out of the water.

Water baptism is primarily a public confession of faith. It is not required to receive salvation. Immersion is preferred, however, there are certain circumstances where a person may be required to be sprinkled with water.

For example, a person in the hospital who is not able to get out of bed cannot be immersed, so sprinkling is permitted. Many parents have their infants baptized by sprinkling with water. This is not Biblical. When we choose to be baptized, we make the decision to accept Jesus as our Lord and Savior. An infant cannot make that choice. It does no harm but, it would be better to have the church pastor dedicate the child to the Lord. Water baptism is commanded by Jesus. All believers should be baptized as soon as practical after their regeneration. Some scriptures teach the necessity to baptize include Acts 2:38, 22:16, and Matthew 28:17-20. However, water is not required to be saved.

The third type of baptism is the baptism *in the* Holy Spirit. It is often called the "filling of the Holy Spirit." This baptism is under the authority of Jesus. Through this baptism we are immersed into the Holy Spirit of God. There are some scholars who do not believe in this baptism. Scriptures that prove this baptism include:

- Acts 1:4-5: " . . . John baptized with water, but you will be baptized with the Holy Spirit not many days from now."
- Acts 1:8: "But you [disciples] will receive power when the Holy Spirit has come upon you, and you will be My witnesses in Jerusalem and in all Judea and Samaria, and to the end of the earth."

Some scriptures say, "baptized *in the* Holy Spirit" and Matthew 3:11, John 1:33, Acts 2:4, Mark 1:8, and Luke 11:11-13 use similar language.

In Luke 11:11-13 Jesus tells us that we have to ask for the baptism in the Holy Spirit, saying,

" . . . how much more will the Heavenly Father *give* the Holy Spirit to those who ask Him."

In Acts 8:14-17, Doctor Luke tells a story about new believers in Samaria. Philip preached the gospel in Samaria and everyone witnessed great miracles of healing. The Samarians were enemies of the Jews. They were considered lower class. It was a big deal that these people were accepting Jesus as their Lord. The apostles heard this great news and sent Peter and John to the area.

We are told that the Holy Spirit had not yet come upon these new believers because they were only baptized in the name of Jesus Christ. When the apostles arrived, they prayed and laid hands on the new believers and then they received the Holy Spirit. Through these scriptures we see that all believers have been baptized *by the* Holy Spirit, but not all believers have experienced the baptism *in the* Holy Spirit. The baptism *in the* Holy Spirit usually only occurs once in a believer's life.

Jesus told His disciples that after His death, resurrection, and ascension to heaven God the Father would send the Holy Spirit to them (John 14:16). Jesus was referring to the day of Pentecost. Pentecost occurred fifty days after Jesus' ascension into heaven.

On that day, Jesus' followers were all together in one house celebrating the Jewish Pentecost feast. While they were in the house, there was a great sound from the heaven like a great wind. All the believers in the room were filled with the Holy Spirit (Acts 1:1-4). The day of Pentecost marked the beginning of the Christian church. When the disciples were filled with the Holy Spirit, they received the supernatural ability to speak and preach in other languages from other nations. People were amazed and astonished that these common people were able to speak in languages they did not know (Acts 2:4-8). The baptism of and in the Holy Spirit sets us apart for God and empowers us to resist sin and praise God.

In order to be baptized *in the* Holy Spirit, we must ask God for that baptism. It is amazing what God will do if we just ask Him. James 3:2 says that we don't have what we want, because we do not ask. A simple and sincere prayer is all it takes. Some churches prefer to have a church elder lay hands and pray for another to receive the Holy Spirit.

Either way is fine because it is through faith that we are filled with the Holy Spirit. After prayer, you may feel something great happening inside you, or you may not feel anything, if you do not feel any different, no need to worry, God will answer your prayer. When this occurs, I guarantee that you will feel the peace that can only come with a personal relationship with our creator.

If you have not yet been baptized, please do not worry about your situation. You do not have to be baptized to receive salvation.

John 1:9 says, "If we confess our sins, He [God] is faithful and just to forgive us our sins and to cleanse us from all unrighteousness." Acts 16:31 says, " . . . believe in the Lord Jesus and you will be saved . . . "

Belief in Jesus is the only requirement to having eternal life in heaven.

FASTING KICK-STARTS THE HEALING PROCESS

> *"Then I turned my face to the Lord God, seeking Him by prayer and pleas for mercy with fasting and sackcloth and ashes" (Daniel 9:3).*

Fasting has become the new fad advocated by health experts for weight loss and the prevention of disease. Many believe that this is a new idea. Since ancient times people have abstained from food for therapeutic, spiritual, and healing reasons. Fasting or hunger strikes are even used by political and social activists to raise awareness for their cause.

Many religions including Christianity encourage followers to fast and pray in pursuit of their spiritual goals. The Bible refers to fasting no less than seventy-eight times in twenty-four books. Fasting is intended to bring about changes in the mind, body, and soul. The voluntary abstaining from food humbles oneself before God. During fasting we enter into God's presences seeking forgiveness and reconciliation through praise and prayer. Fasting often produces an internal transformation that leads to sanctification.

In the Old Testament, fasts were used by the Israelites to cleanse their sins, regain their loss of holiness, and receive blessing from God. In the New Testament, Jesus used fasting and prayer during spiritual warfare. Fasting is a powerful tool that should be part of every Christian's toolbox.

There are five fasts described in the Bible: a one-day fast, a three-day day fast. A seven-day fast, a fourteen-day fast, and forty-day fast.

God instituted fasting for the Day of Atonement which was one-day fast for the Jews to repent for sins and reconcile with God. Leviticus chapter sixteen explains the Day of Atonement; this is a once-a-year ceremony to atone for sin to be a statute forever. God said to Moses, "And it shall be a statute to you forever . . . " (Leviticus 16:29).

This became part of the Mosaic Law. For Christians, this law is no longer mandatory due to Christ's work on the cross and the advent of the New Covenant. We no longer follow the law of Moses. But this strong statement by God shows the importance of fasting in one's spiritual life.

Jesus used prayer and fasting in spiritual warfare. An example of this is in Matthew 17:14-21 which says, "And when they [Jesus and His disciples] came to the crowd, a man came up to Him [Jesus] and kneeling before Him, said, 'Lord, have mercy on my son, for he is an epileptic and he suffers terribly. For often he falls into the fire, and often into the water. And I brought him to Your disciples, and they could not heal him.' And Jesus answered, 'O faithless and twisted generation, how long am I to be with you? How long am I to bear with you? Bring him here to me.' And Jesus rebuked the demon, and it came out of him, and the boy was healed instantly. Then the disciples came to Jesus privately and said, 'Why could we not cast it out?' He said to them, 'But this kind [demon] never comes out except by prayer and fasting.'"

This passage is interesting because we read the man said his son was an epileptic. We would associate that with an illness. But Jesus removed the demon that was causing the epilepsy in the boy. This removal shows that many illnesses can have spiritual origins. Not all people with illness or disease are possessed by demons.

Christians cannot be possessed by Satan or demons. But Satan brought disease into this world and continues to use it as part of his plan to wage war against God's people. As Christians learn how to conduct spiritual warfare, they mature in Christ and often are healed spiritually, physically, and emotionally. Only Jesus can heal this fallen world. We also learn that faith goes a long way with prayer and fasting. Fasting seems to supercharge prayer. Prayer with fasting is a powerful weapon in our battle with Satan and his demons.

The prophet Isaiah in 58:6 says, "Is not this the fast that I choose: to loose the bonds of wickedness, to undo the straps of the yoke, to let the oppressed go free, and to break every yoke?"

God says that fasting with a repentant heart will break the bonds of sin and free you from sin's oppression. This chapter describes fasting from God's point of view. I recommend anyone considering fasting read Isaiah chapter fifty-eight.

Jesus tells us that when we fast properly, God blesses us. Matthew 6:16-18 says, "When you fast, do not look gloomy like the hypocrites, for they disfigure their faces that their fasting may be seen by others. Truly, I say to you. They have received their reward. But when you fast, anoint your head and wash your face, that your fasting may not be seen by others but by your Father who is in secret. And your Father who sees in secret will reward you."

Jesus was referring to the religious leaders, the Pharisees, who would put on a public display during their fasts. The Pharisees showed signs of mourning and sorrow to show how religious they were in order to gain the people's respect. The Pharisees were not fasting to please God, as they were seeking to obtain their reward from the people. Jesus called their respect as coming from the "world." But when we humbly fast to please God, not others, God will bless us.

We must fast with a repentant heart. If we fast with unrepented sin in our hearts, God will not hear our prayers, even when we fast. We see an example of this in the book of Jeremiah.

The Israelites practiced idolatry and were unrepentant. Although they continued to fast and pray, they had no desire to repent or reconcile with God. God is always watching. He is patient, He watched and waited for the Israelites to repent for seventy years. The law, prayer, and fasting were practiced as mere repetitive tradition.

The Israelites had hardened their hearts and were not sincere. God warned the people through His prophet Jeremiah, yet they still rebelled. When God finally had enough of the rebellion, God said to Jeremiah,

"Thus says the LORD concerning this people: They have loved to wander thus; they have not restrained their feet; therefore the LORD does not accept them; now He will remember their iniquity and punish their sins. The LORD said to me [Jeremiah], 'Do not pray for the welfare of these people. Though they fast, I will not hear their cry, and though they offer burnt offering and grain offering, I will not accept them. But I will consume them by the sword, by famine and by pestilence'" (Jeremiah 14:12).

We see that due to their rebellion, God punished them. Their hearts were not sincere. Even though they fasted, God would not hear them. This punishment shows that fasting is powerful, but not powerful enough to overcome unrepented sin. If you decide to fast, first spend some time confessing and repenting your sins. Just as prior to the Lord's supper, we need to examine ourselves prior to fasting and prayer. We must only come to God with a sincere heart, this pleases Him.

There are many reasons to fast—in a dangerous situation, an illness, or a trial. The Apostle Paul knew the power of fasting and praying. Acts chapter twenty-seven describes the time that Paul had been arrested and was to stand trial in Rome.

Paul and other prisoners had been put on a ship to Rome. During the journey, the Holy Spirit warned Paul of upcoming danger where great winds would cause a shipwreck and many would perish. Paul warned the people in charge, but they would not listen. Soon the winds of a northeaster tormented the ship. Huge clouds came and kept them in total darkness for several days.

Paul declared a fast. Every person aboard fasted, even non-believers. After fourteen days the Lord sent an angel to Paul who told him that the ship would run aground, however, there would be no loss of life. Paul told everyone to eat to regain their strength for what lie ahead. The ship struck a reef and broke apart but all 276 men survived. The reef was near the island of Malta. They were close enough that they all swam to the island safely.

This story shows the power of prayer and fasting. This is a powerful tool that should be used by every Christian. Fasting is an incredible way to get closer to God, when it's done with a sincere heart and proper motives.

CHAPTER 4

WHY GOD ALLOWS SUFFERING AND TRAUMA

"Blessed is the man who remains steadfast under trial, for when he has stood the test he will receive the crown of life which God has promised to those who love Him."

James 1:12

Some traumatized people blame God for their situation. God has a plan and purpose for each person on this earth. God is intimately involved in your life. Bad things happen in life, we can be assured that God will make your pain go away and make something positive out of it. It is important to know why God allows suffering in this world. This is just an overview of why God allows suffering.

The most frequently asked question by both non-believers and Christians is, "If God is so loving, merciful, and all-powerful, why does He allow people to suffer?" And, "Why doesn't He stop the suffering?" This is difficult question to answer. The Bible discusses suffering and provides a variety of reasons why every person on this Earth will go through a painful trial at some point in their lives.

As we learned in our Bible study, God created the heavens and Earth. He created them perfect. He created human beings in His image, also perfect. With the fall of man, sin entered into this perfect world. With sin came both spiritual death, physical death, pain, suffering, and sorrow. The fall turned control of the earth from Adam to Satan.

As Christians, we cannot be surprised when difficulties come into our life. About 2,000 years ago Jesus warned His followers that trials and pain will come into their lives (John 16:33). The Apostle Peter also warned the church about trials.

First Peter 4:12-13 tells us, "Beloved, do not be surprised at the fiery trial when it comes upon you to test you, as though something strange were happening to you. But rejoice in so far as you share Christ's sufferings, that you may also rejoice and be glad when His glory is revealed."

Every person living on this earth can expect to be put through painful trials. We can expect disappointment, pain, suffering, and loss resulting from an overwhelming life event or a traumatic incident.

PAIN AS TRIAL

The Bible teaches that God allows us to go through painful trials to test us, to humble us, and to know what is in our hearts. The story of the Israelites who were enslaved in Egypt for 400 hundred years teaches God's purpose of testing and humbling. Remember the movie of the Ten Commandments? The Israelites were slaves to the Egyptians. God chose Moses to deliver them from slavery. Under God's direction, Moses was sent to the Egyptian Pharaoh to ask the Pharaoh to release God's people. The Pharaoh refused. God then brought ten plagues upon Egypt. Each plague was horrific showing God's power to both the Egyptians and Israelites. After nine plagues the Pharaoh still refused to release the people. If the Pharaoh did not allow the people to go, all the first born in the land would die. The Pharaoh still refused.

Later an angel of the LORD killed all the first-born people and animals in Egypt; expect for Israelites. This was the Passover. Pharaoh's son died that night. The Pharaoh finally allowed Moses to take the people and leave.

As the Israelites fled Egypt, God led them on their journey by a cloud by day and a pillar of fire by night. When they were blocked by the Red Sea and the Egyptian army was closing in on them, God parted the sea so the Israelites could cross on dry ground. When the nation had crossed, God restored the sea causing the Egyptian army to drown in the sea. God demonstrated many miracles for the Israelites, but they never truly trusted Him. With every sign of trial, they complained and even suggested that their slavery was better than their freedom. The trip from Egypt to the Land of Canaan should have taken less than a month, but because of the people's disobedience to God, He led them around the wilderness traveling in circles for forty years.

Deuteronomy 8:2 says, "You shall remember the whole way that the LORD your God has led you [Israelites] these forty years in the wilderness, that He might humble you, testing you to know what was in your heart, whether you would keep His commandments or not."

The Israelites failed the test. God allowed them to wander around the wilderness until that entire disobedient generation had died off.

The Story of Job

The story of Job shows that God can use Satan to test us. The Book of Job is thought to be the oldest book of the Bible, we do not know who wrote it. In the first chapter we learn that God called Job, "A blameless and upright man, who fears God and turns away from evil" (Job 1:18). God was proud of Job.

One day Satan was talking with God, and God was bragging on Job. Satan, living up to his name as the "accuser" told God that Job was only praising God because God blessed Job (v. 1:9-11). God allowed Satan to test Job with a limitation that Satan was not allowed to injure him (v. 1:12). Satan had all of Job's children killed and had thieves steal all his wealth (v. 1:13-19). When Job heard the bad news, he tore his robe and shaved his head in mourning, he fell on the ground and worshipped God (v. 1:20).

Job said, "Naked I came from my mother's womb, and naked I shall return. The LORD gave, and the LORD has taken away; blessed be the name of the LORD."

Job did not sin or accuse God of the wrongdoing. When God and Satan met again, God still had reason to brag. Satan again accused Job again of flattering God due to His blessings. God allowed Satan to test Job again, this time with the limitation that Satan could do what he wanted but could not kill Job (v. 2:4-6). Satan inflicted a disease on Job, causing sores all over his body (v. 2:7).

Job's wife said, "Do you still hold fast your integrity? Curse God and die." Job responded, "Shall we receive good from God, and shall we not receive evil?"

Job did not sin against God (v. 2:6-7). Job mourned for a very long time. Some friends came because they heard what happened. They accused Job of sinning and because of his sin was being punished, Job maintained his innocence.

Job cried out to God asking why he was going through this trial in his life. In chapter thirty-eight, God asks Job who is he to ask why? God said that Job asks questions without knowledge. God asks Job where was he when God created the heaven and earth?

Basically, God tells Job He is sovereign over everything and everyone. God has a reason for everything He does.

Job finally responds, "I know that You can do all things, and that no purpose of Yours can be thwarted" (v. 42:1).

Job then repents for doubting God. God then restores Job's wealth and then doubles it. God then gave him ten more children. He already had ten children waiting for him in heaven.

The lesson is that God is sovereign. We must trust Him. He created all things and knows what is best for us. We do not need to know why God allows us to suffer, we just need to understand that God is in control of all things and loves us unconditionally.

Trial by Fire

As we saw in the Old Testament, God may test our faith. 1 Peter 1:6-7 says, "In this you rejoice, though now for a little while, if necessary, you have been grieved by various trials, so that the tested genuineness of your faith—more precious than gold that perishes though it is tested by fire—may be found to result in praise and glory and honor at the revelation of Jesus Christ."

Peter says we must be tested by fire. These tests are called "trial by fire." All valuable precious metals must be refined with incredible heat to be purified. Metal like silver and gold is placed in a container over fire. Soon the metal liquefies and impurities rise to the top. At the proper time the refiner skims off the impurities being careful not to skim off the precious metal.

This process is repeated several times, each time increasing the heat a bit more. Each time, more impurities are removed. The refiner may place a piece of charcoal into the liquid. The charcoal brings out the metal's sheen. Soon the refiner's reflection will appear in the liquid. This is what God does in our lives putting us through the heat of trials until His reflection is seen in us. God chose us to be molded into the likeness of His Son.

Romans 8:28-29 says, "And we know that for those who love God all things work together for good, for those who are called according to His purpose. For those who He foreknew He also predestined to be conformed to the image of His Son . . . "

Philippians 1:29 adds, "For it has been granted to you that for the sake of Christ you should not only believe in Him bit also suffer for His sake."

And Hebrews 2:10 adds, "For it is fitting that He [Jesus], for whom and by whom all things exist, in the bringing many sons to glory, should make the founder of their salvation perfect through suffering."

If Jesus was made perfect through His suffering, we may expect the same suffering to perfect us for the day we are glorified. God is the refiner. When He sees impurities in us, He turns up the heat. Maybe He sees that we have too much pride, He turns up the heat to humble us. If we become addicted to a sinful habit, He will turn on the heat so we seek out His help. Maybe He sees us running away from Him enjoying being our own god. He places a trial in our lives to bring us closer to Him. God may allow more than one trial in our life in order to bring us closer in the image of Jesus.

James the brother of Jesus gives us great advice while going through a trial. James 1:2-4 says, "Count it all joy, my brothers, when you meet trials of various kinds, for you know that the testing of your faith produces steadfastness. And let steadfastness have its full effect that you may be perfect and complete, lacking nothing."

PAIN AS PREPARATION TO FULFILL GOD'S PLAN

Another reason God allows pain in our lives is for training in preparation to fulfill His plan. His plan can be for your life or a much bigger plan as we see in the story of Joseph. Genesis chapter thirty-seven through fifty tells his story. It is a great story that everyone should read, but I have to summarize here.

Joseph was the youngest of eleven sons of Jacob. Jacob loved Joseph more than his other sons and did not hide his feelings. God was with Joseph at a young age. Joseph had dreams that his brothers would someday bow down to him. His brothers hated Joseph because of this dream and that he was father's favorite.

One day Jacob sent Joseph out to the pasture to see if his brothers were alright. When the brothers saw him approaching they conspired to kill him. One of the brothers stopped the plan. One brother said they should place Joseph in a dried up well and cover it up and leave him there. This brother intended to later go save him. When Joseph arrived, they ripped off his coat and threw him into the well. The brothers then ate lunch.

What a dysfunctional family! As they ate, a caravan of traders going to Egypt passed by. The brothers decided to sell Joseph to the slave traders for twenty shekels. The trader took Joseph to Egypt. The brothers killed a goat and dipped the coat into the blood. They went home and told Jacob that a wild animal attacked and ate Joseph. Jacob was so upset he mourned his son for a very long time.

The slave traders sold Joseph in Egypt to a man named Potiphar. Potiphar was the Commanding Officer of the Pharaoh's Body Guard. He was a very prominent court official. God was still with Joseph, in everything he did. He prospered. Potiphar placed Joseph in charge of his entire household.

Potiphar's wife liked Joseph and one day made a play for him. Joseph said, "How can I do this great wickedness and sin against God?" Potiphar's wife became angry and falsely claimed that Joseph had tried to rape her. Joseph was placed into prison without a trial. But God was still with Joseph in the prison. Everything Joseph did was prosperous. The jailer placed Joseph in charge of the entire prison.

One day, two of the inmates had troubling dreams. Joseph correctly interpreted their dreams. One was executed, the other set free. The one who was set free promised to tell the Pharaoh about Joseph. When the Pharaoh had a disturbing dream, he was told by the freed inmate about Joseph's ability to interpret dreams. Joseph was removed from prison to interpret the Pharaoh's dream.

Joseph told the Pharaoh that he was not a prophet but that God would tell him the meaning of the dream because God placed the dream into Pharaoh's mind. The dream was a warning that Egypt would have seven years of bountiful crops throughout the land. Afterword, Egypt would suffer seven years of famine. This worldwide famine would consume the land.

Pharaoh did not know what to do. Joseph suggested the Pharaoh choose a discerning and wise man to store up the crops during the first years of plenty to ration out the stored grain in the time of famine. The Pharaoh chose Joseph and placed him in charge of all the land of Egypt. Only the Pharaoh would be over Joseph. Joseph had been a slave and in prison for thirteen years before he took control of Egypt. Joseph was only thirty years old at this time.

In the first seven years Joseph stored up vast amounts of grain. When the famine came, Joseph oversaw the rationing of grain. Egypt sold grain to people from all over the world. The Pharaoh became very rich from the sales of grain during this time.

Jacob and his sons were also affected by the famine. Jacob sent his sons to go to Egypt to purchase grain. When the brothers arrived in Egypt, they did not recognize their brother Joseph, but Joseph recognized them. When the brothers met Joseph, they bowed down to him. Joseph's dream came true.

Joseph decided to play with his brothers; Joseph accused them of being spies. They told Joseph that they were twelve brothers, the youngest was at home with their father and the other had died. Joseph was surprised that they said there was another brother. He told his brothers to prove they were honest and go home return with the youngest brother. Egypt was to keep one brother in jail until they returned. They purchased their grain and went home.

When Jacob heard what happened he did not want to send Benjamin to Egypt, Benjamin was now his favorite. Jacob feared something bad would happen to him, like happened to Joseph. But the famine continued, requiring them to go purchase more grain. The brothers returned to Egypt.

When Joseph saw Benjamin, he was overjoyed. Joseph ordered a big feast for the brothers. After toying with them, Joseph revealed himself to his brothers.

Genesis 45:4-8 says, " . . . I am your brother, Joseph, whom you sold into Egypt. And now do not be distressed or angry with yourselves because you sold me here, for God sent me before you to preserve life. For the famine has been in the land these two years, and there are yet five years in which there will be neither plowing or harvest. And God sent me before you to preserve for you a remnant on earth, and to keep alive for you many survivors. So it was not you that sent me here, but God."

Joseph added, "As for you, you meant evil against me, but God meant it for good, to bring it about that many people should be kept alive, as they are today" (Genesis 50:20).

Joseph had his entire family move to a choice property in Egypt where they prospered.

God used Joseph to save his father, who became the father of the nation Israel, and his brothers, the leaders of the twelve tribes of Israel. Imagine the trauma and heartbreak Joseph went through when his brothers wanted to kill him. They sold him into slavery. He was falsely accused and imprisoned for years. I bet he felt hopeless, but the Bible says that God was with him throughout this entire time prospering all he did.

During this time, he did not know how God was using him. He kept in faith believing and worshipping God. God used Joseph to save the nation of Israel. Coming out of his pain, Joseph saw God's plan and purpose for his pain.

PAIN AS EXAMPLES OF GOD'S GLORY

Another reason God allows or ordains trials in our life is to show His glory. The Gospel of John gives us an example of this, Jesus and His disciples were in Jerusalem.

John 9:1-3 says, "As He [Jesus] passed by, He saw a man blind from birth. And His disciples asked Him, 'Rabbi, who sinned, this man or his parents, that he was born blind?' Jesus answered, 'It was not that this man sinned, or his parents, but that the works of God might be displayed in him.'"

The disciples believed that God was punishing the blind man for generational sin. The blind man could not have sinned because he was born blind. God allowed this man to be born blind so that later in life, Jesus would heal him to show God's power. This healing glorified God for all those who witnessed the healing. Many believed in Jesus after the man was healed.

Some people need to witness a miracle to believe. I know I did. I was on the fence with my belief, but when God healed my daughter, I believed!

Still another reason why God allows trial in our lives is to bring us closer to Him. A painful trial often drives us closer to our creator. We seek the comfort that only a loving God can provide. As we go through the pain, we learn to trust Him in the pain and to deliver us from the pain.

When we do not seek God in our trials we tend to respond in sinful ways, we become angry, bitter, depression sets in, we have a pity party, and we blame everyone but ourselves for our pain, including God. It is the sin that keeps us in our pain. As we draw closer to God, we recognize our blessings which builds trust. We can always trust in God's promises.

God promises us that even though we are in pain and things look like they will never be the same, even though we do not understand the reasons for our pain, and even though we feel that it is unfair, He will make our pain work for our good. He is doing a great work in you, you may not see it now, but you will come out of your trail better than you ever would have imagined. After we have been through the trial, we look back and see we become better because of it. Trials mold and shape us into the people we are today.

Whoever gets better by experiencing good times? King David agrees that trials make us better.

Psalm 71:20 says, "You [God] have made me see many troubles and calamities will revive me again; from the depths of the earth you will bring me up again. You will increase my greatness and comfort me again."

Knowing and understanding this doesn't make the pain any easier. But we know that God is with us every step of the trial to comfort us, and to promote us after we have persevered.

Psalm 23 comforts us, "The LORD is my shepherd; I shall not want. He makes me lie down in green pastures. He leads me by still waters. He restores my soul. He leads me in paths of righteousness for His name sake. Even though I walk through the valley of the shadow of death, I will fear no evil, for You are with me; Your rod and staff comfort me. You prepare a table before me in the presence of my enemies; You anoint my head with oil; my cup overflows. Surely goodness and mercy shall follow me all the days of my life, and I shall dwell in the house of the LORD forever."

PAIN AS CONSEQUENCE OF SIN

The last reason God allows or ordains trial in our lives is due to the consequence of sin.

Hebrews 12:5-11 explains, " . . . My son do not regard lightly the discipline of the Lord, nor be weary when reproved by Him. For the Lord disciplines the one He loves, and chastises every son [or daughter] who He receives. It is for discipline that you have to endure. God is treating you as sons. For what son is there whom his father does not discipline? If you are left without discipline, in which we all have participated, then you are illegitimate children and not sons. . . . He disciplines us for our good, that we may share his holiness. *For the moment all discipline seems painful rather than pleasant, but later it yields the peaceful fruit of righteousness to those who have been trained by it*" (Emphasis mine).

Those of us who are parents understand that we discipline our children because we love them. If we didn't care, we would let them run wild. All parents set rules and boundaries just like God has done with His commandments. We must understand that there are consequences for our behavior. When we break the rules, we must be corrected. If not, we would repeat the same offense again. One offense leads to another that leads to another.

God must discipline us because He knows the damage sin causes in our lives. Unrepented sin causes us emotional distress and the feeling of being disconnected from God.

When we sin, we must confess and repent. Confession and repentance restores our relationship with God, He forgives us our sin, however, there is still consequences for our sin. Let's face the truth, we are all sinners, we will always be sinners until we go home to heaven. The only way to mitigate the consequences is to quickly repent of the sin and make a sincere effort to stop.

One of God's most effective methods of discipline is through illness. God tells us in Exodus 15:26, " . . . If you will diligently listen to the voice of the LORD your God, and do that which is right in His eyes, and give ear to His commandments and keep all His statutes, I will put none of the diseases on you that I put on the Egyptians, for I am the LORD, your healer."

God repeats this several times in the Old Testament. In Deuteronomy chapter twenty-eight God tells us to choose right from wrong. If we follow God, we will receive blessing. But if we reject God, expect judgment. Illness will bring us to our knees and forces us to humble ourselves in front of our creator.

The Bible teaches us that we will all go through trials in our lives. We can lessen the pain by looking at our trial from a different perspective, a Christian perspective. When a non-believer goes through a trial, they see only pain, no purpose. The pain promotes anger and bitterness. But if we view it from a Christian perspective, we see that our pain has a purpose and once endured will fulfill God's plan for our lives.

A perfect example of pain causing a positive change is how a pearl is made. Pearls are made when a grain of sand somehow gets into the shell of an oyster. The grain of sand has jagged edges and irritates the inside of the oyster's shell. It causes a lot of discomfort and pain. The oyster will excrete a substance that will coat the grain of sand attempting to stop the pain. The oyster secretes more and more of this substance, again to try to stop the pain. This process continues in the oyster until the grain of sand has turned into a beautiful pearl.

The sand represents a trial in your life. We usually use poor coping mechanisms to minimize the pain of that trial. These coping mechanisms can be anything from alcohol, drugs, to cutting yourself. But the pain and discomfort are still present.

With us, it's only through a loving relationship with Jesus Christ can our pain be turned into a pearl. The substance we need to secrete is the love of God.

When a trial comes up in our lives, we try to fix it ourselves by manipulating the situation and worrying about it. We leave God out of our pain. We cannot fix our lives by ourselves, so the pain continues. We try to numb our feelings with alcohol or drugs to lessen the pain. Sometimes we involve ourselves in church or volunteer work to take our minds off the pain.

These may help in the short-term, but if we ignore the source of our pain hoping it will go away by ignoring it, the pain actually multiplies. Only God can heal a broken heart. When we come to Him in confession, repentance, forgiveness, renouncing sin, vows, judgment, and expectancies, we receive God's healing balm.

Maybe your childhood was difficult: your family failed you, your parents were not there for you, you had to go it alone from a young age, a parent was in jail, a parent was addicted to a substance, you suffered abuse, or something worse happened. This history is not your future. Your children do not have to suffer the same plight. You must say, "This stops with me right now!"

This generational trauma has to stop here and now. Why are you living your life angry? Why bitter? Why depressed? Why do you try to please everyone but yourself? Why do all your relationships fail? These are all results of a broken heart. Someone wounded you, something happened to you that you did not deserve. There is a hole in your heart from the abuse, divorce, illness, loss of promotion, betrayal, bankruptcy, or mistakes of the past.

That hole is God-shaped. Nothing will fill that hole except the one who created it—God. Only God can make your heart whole. There is no drug, amounts of alcohol, gambling, eating, starving, cutting, dangerous sexual behavior, that can fill that void. Hurt people, hurt people. The person who hurt you, was hurt by someone also—who are you hurting?

During my bout with the negative emotions of PTSD and depression, I was hurting my children and did not even know it. They were all adults during this time, their mid-twenties. I later heard that they did not want to come to my house to visit because my mood swings were so great that they did not know which dad to expect: the dad they grew up with or the mean dad that I had become. It broke their hearts to be treated the way I treated them. I did the same with my wife. I want to say I'm sorry to them.

God wants to heal us and restore our hearts with the hearts He originally designed us with, a heart of flesh! He can only do this if you trust Him and give Him your whole heart.

As Christians we must view our trials from a Christian perspective. The trials in our lives are opportunities for growth. It's all about perspective. How we talk and frame our situation sets the tone. If you complain, you magnify the problem. But when you magnify God in your pain, your entire attitude will change. Praise God through your pain.

Remember, God is sovereign. Your trial is not by accident or bad luck, there are no such things. God knew what was going to happen beforehand and either allowed it or ordained it. God would never have allowed you to be subjected to a painful trial if it was not for your own good. You may not understand it and it doesn't make sense, but God is on the throne, He knows what He is doing.

Change your perspective! Instead of asking, "Why?" Instead of trying to manipulate your circumstances, talk to God. Say, "God, I don't understand why I am going through this situation, but I know that you are in charge, and I trust you."

Through God's grace you will have a new hope, a new outlook, and a positive perspective that will make you stronger, builds your character, endurance, and perseverance.

Romans 5:3-5 says, " . . . we rejoice in our sufferings, knowing that suffering produces endurance, and endurance produces character, and character produces hope, and hope does not put us to shame, because God's love has been poured into our hearts through the Holy Spirit who has been given to us."

THE TWO BYPRODUCTS OF ENDURING TRIALS

There are two byproducts of enduring a trial. They are new growth and wisdom and testimony of what God has done in our lives. First, lets discuss new growth and wisdom.

New Growth and Wisdom

First is the new growth and wisdom we receive from going through a trial. Corinthians 1:3-8 says, "Blessed be the God and Father of our Lord Jesus

Christ, the Father of mercies and God of all comfort, who comforts us in all our affliction, so that we may be able to comfort those who are in any affliction, with the comfort, with which we ourselves are comforted by God. For as we share abundantly in Christ's sufferings, so through Christ we share abundantly in comfort too. If we are afflicted, it is for your comfort and salvation; and if we are comforted, it is for your comfort, which you experience when you patiently endure the same sufferings that we suffer. Our hope for you is unshaken in our suffering, you will also share in our comfort."

It is this growth in love and compassion we learned so that we can comfort others who are going through similar things that we went through. Many times we hear of a great tragedy in someone's life. Later we learn that they used that trial as a catalyst to help others.

In 1980, Candy Lightner, a divorced real estate agent lived with her twin girls and her son near Sacramento California. On May 3, 1980, her 13-year-old daughter Cari was hit by a drunk driver while walking to a church function with a friend. She was hit with such force that she was knocked out of her shoes and thrown 125 feet. Cari died a short time after the collision. The drunk driver never stopped to check on the girl.

The driver was later identified and arrested. This was not his first alcohol related arrest. A week or so after he hit Cari, he got into another collision while drunk. Law enforcement told Lightner that alcohol related deaths received minor punishments. The driver was convicted of vehicular man slaughter and was sentenced to twenty-one months in jail.

Lightner later told People Magazine, "Death caused by drunk drivers is the only socially acceptable form of homicide." Four days after Cari's death, Lightner channeled her grief and anger into fighting drunk drivers. She started an grassroots organization to advocate for stiffer penalties for drunk driving and to raise the drinking age to twenty-one years old. Lightner teamed up with Cindi Lamb whose daughter had been left paralyzed by a drunk driving collision. The pair began "Mothers Against Drunk Drivers" (MADD). MADD managed to change the laws and change the drinking age to twenty-one years old.

Lightner helped grow MADD into an international movement with almost 400 chapters, two million members, and 600,000 volunteers. Although there was controversy later in her career, it does not diminish her accomplishments. Cari Lightner's tragic death resulted in new legislation across the nation. MADD unarguably has saved thousands if not hundreds of thousands of lives since its inception. Candy Lightner used this horrific event to save lives and produce hope.

Testimony

The second byproduct is that our trials give us a testimony for what God has done in our lives. The best example of a testimony is that of Jesus Himself. After Jesus was crucified and resurrected, He appeared to His disciples.

John chapter twenty tells us, "On the evening of that day, the first day of the week, the doors being locked where the disciples were for fear of the Jews. Jesus came and stood among them and said to them, 'Peace be with you.' When He said this, He showed them His hands and side. Then the disciples were glad when they saw the Lord" (Verses 19-20).

"Now Thomas, one of the Twelve, called the Twin, was not with them when Jesus came. So the other disciples told him, 'We have seen the Lord.' But he said to them, 'unless I see in His hands the mark of the nails, and place my finger into the mark of the nails, and place my hand into His side, I will never believe. ' Eight days later, His disciples were inside again, and Thomas was with them. Although the doors were locked, Jesus came and stood among them and said, 'Peace be with you.' Then He said to Thomas, 'Put your finger here, and see my hands; and put your hand, and place it in My side. Do not disbelieve, but believe.' Thomas answered him, 'My Lord and my God!'

Jesus said to him, 'Have you believed because you have seen Me? Blessed are those who have not seen and yet have believed'" (Verse 24-29).

Jesus said, "You believe because you have seen."

Jesus wounds are His testimony to the trial that He endured. I believe that the wounds are still in His body. When we get to heaven, we will see them also. Without His wounds and scars no one would have believed.

We all make mistakes; we bring trouble upon ourselves and make poor decisions. God does not waste these experiences. He turns your mistakes and overwhelming life experiences into a powerful testimony that will glorify

God! It is only natural for you to have scars from your trial. But with God's help you will make it through this trial.

You will see the growth and maturity that will only come from the pain.

Now it is time to share your experiences with others, both believers and non-believers. Your testimony very powerful. Your story can comfort many going through the same trial. It can bring people to Jesus and reaffirm a Christian's faith. Proudly show your wounds: give your testimony to all who will listen.

The Bible says to rejoice in your pain and suffering because God allowed it and He will make everything work for your good.

CHAPTER 5

16 CRITICAL EMOTIONAL ISSUES TO HEALING

We have discussed what trauma is and how it affects our life and why God allows suffering. But we need to understand what God has to say about healing. I cannot express enough how important it is to understand who God is and who He sees you as. Some who experience over-whelming life events often feel resentment towards God. This is because most people do not understand who God truly is.

Let's begin with learning about our emotions. What we believe affects our emotions. As a result, our emotions dictate how we behave. If we are experiencing negative emotions, we know that it has an effect on our behavior. Negative emotions = negative behavior. Negative behavior tends to hurt others. When we understand our emotions and how we were designed to react, we can make necessary changes to begin the healing process.

"I am weary with my morning; every night I flood my bed with tears; I drench my couch with my weeping. My eye wastes away because of grief; it grows weak because of my foes. Depart from me, all you workers of evil, for the Lord has heard my plea; The Lord accepts my prayer" (Psalm 6:6-9).

God created man with an internal warning system that notifies us when someone hurts us or we move out of God's will. This warning system is our emotions. Our emotions are molded by our belief system or worldview. Our worldview effects what we believe and how we think.

Our worldview is based on many factors such as: age, education, gender, race, upbringing, prior trauma, education, religion, and much more. Our worldview influences our thoughts and our thoughts then influence our emotions. Our emotions finally influence our behavior, good or bad. If a person, group, or culture has a negative worldview, it has a great effect on their lives.

One can say there are as many worldviews as there are people. I believe there are only two worldviews. The first acknowledges that there is a God, that He is sovereign and the second believes that man himself is his own god.

When we act as if we are our own god, we are out of alignment with the true living God's will. When we are out of God's will, our internal warning system alerts us to the misalignment. When we are out of God's will for our lives, we often experience a wide variety of negative emotions.

Depending on the circumstances, emotions may include: depression, anger, anxiety, bitterness, guilt, or shame. These emotions if not properly managed steal our peace and joy.

Unresolved emotional wounds of the past prevent us from living the life of peace and joy that God intended us to live. Strong emotional behavioral responses to small events are a warning sign that there are unresolved wounds of the past. Some examples include:

1. A man becomes verbally or physically abusive when his wife complains about him not taking out the garbage.
    - **Possible reason:** the man may have been raised by an over-bearing mother who was always pushing him to do things.
2. A husband attempts to initiate sex by coming up behind his wife and hugging her in a loving way and kissing her neck. The wife recoils in fear and breaks down crying.
    - **Possible reason:** the wife may have been sexually abused and the touch brought back a negative memory.
3. A high school age girl eats excessively in an effort to become overweight believing that by being overweight will make her unattractive to boys.
    - **Possible reason:** her father may have been overly critical as she was developing into a young woman or over possessive/

protective as she developed causing her to fear attention from boys.

These negative emotions are symptoms. These symptoms were triggered by a present event that reflected a prior trauma that has not yet been brought to the cross. We all experience negative emotions at one time or another; some more than others. When we give into these emotions and dwell on them, we are in sin.

These emotions often come from spiritual battles in our minds: the battle of good vs. evil. Satan's goal is to keep us in emotional distress so that we remain out of God's will. Satan tries to get us to believe that God is not there for us, that only our own effort will solve our issues. There is no need for God, you are your own god.

When we believe that it is our own will that gets us through the day, we are in sin. This is called idolatry, we idolize ourselves. Satan tells us that we can overcome our trials by ourselves.

2 Peter 2:19 says, "For what overcomes a person, to that he is enslaved."

It is the sin that overcomes us, we are then slaves to the sin. This means that we remain in a cycle of sinful behavior. We believe we are our own god, then all our actions and behavior are dictated by sin. As human beings, we do not have the strength to win this battle with Satan alone. We need a deliverer who have His life to set us free from the oppression of Satan.

Roman 8:1-2 says, "There is no condemnation for those who are in Christ Jesus. For the law of the spirit of life has set you free in Christ Jesus from the law of sin and death."

The Holy Spirit gives the believer power over sin. As we remove the chains of sin and serve Jesus instead of Satan, our negative emotions begin to subside. Our depression, anger, and bitterness are removed through our trust in Christ.

Jesus reassures us in Matthew 11:28-30, "Come to Me [Jesus], all who labor and are heavy laden, and I will give you rest. Take My yoke upon you, and learn from Me, for I am gentle and lowly in heart, and you find rest for your souls. For My yoke is easy, and My burden is light."

A yoke is a farming term that is defined as a wooden frame work for harnessing two oxen together. Oxen were used to plow fields. One ox will only have so much strength. When two oxen are yoked together, their load is easier; they are stronger working together.

Jesus tells us that He will help us, so, give our cares to Him, He will take our burden and we can then rest our souls. The soul is linked to our thoughts and emotions. The Christ-Centered Healing method is intended to take our focus off ourselves and to focus on and trust in Jesus for our healing. Here is an overview of the common emotions that if not resolved keep us in a cycle of pain.

DEPRESSION

Depression is a mood disorder. Depression has been identified as a serious problem for thousands of years. All humans worldwide are affected by depression at some point in their lives. In the United States alone, it is estimated that seventeen million people suffer from clinical depression.[16] Depression disrupts lives and interferes with everyday activities and negatively impacts our relationships. Depression destroys families and opens the door to Satan. Depression has a major impact on job performance. It is estimated that the cost to the U.S. economy is billions of dollars per year due to slow work production, mistakes, and sick leave.

The term depression is not in the Bible. The terms turmoil, despair, downcast, and afflicted are used. Some examples include:

- "We are afflicted in every way, but not crushed; perplexed, but not driven to despair, persecuted, but not forsaken; struck down, but not destroyed; always carrying in the body the death of Jesus, so that the life of Jesus may also be manifested in our bodies" (2 Corinthians 4:8-10).
- "So do not lose heart. Though our outer self is wasting away, our inner self is being renewed day by day. For this light momentary affliction is preparing us for an eternal weight of glory beyond all comparison, as we look not to the things that are seen but to the things that are unseen. For the things that are seen are transient, but the things that are unseen are eternal" (2 Corinthians 4:16-18).

---

[16] "Depression," last modified July 22, 2021, accessed December 1, 2017, http://www.psychologyinfo.com/depression

- "Why are you cast down, O my soul, and why are you in turmoil within me? Hope in God; for I shall again praise Him, my salvation and my God" (Psalm 43:5).
- "My [Jesus] soul is sorrowful, even to death . . . " (Matthew 26:38).
- "Be careful, or your hearts will be weighed down with dissipation, drunkenness and the anxieties of life . . . " (Luke 21:34).

These scriptures reference pain or grieving. Even Jesus was in despair prior to His arrest in the garden of Gethsemane. The scriptures speaks of suffering with depression.[17]

There are four categories of depression. The first is "feelings." Based on a variety of circumstances, depression causes sadness. Sometimes we may not even know why we are sad. This often brings low self-esteem, feelings of guilt, shame, helplessness, hopelessness, or worthlessness. These feelings often turn into bitterness, irritability, and fits of anger.

The second is "behavior." Those who are depressed often lack motivation and find it difficult to make decisions. Depressed people complain constantly and often withdraw socially. They tend to neglect their responsibilities and isolate themselves from family and friends.

Third, "thinking." Negative thoughts are a byproduct of depression. Negative thoughts include: guilt, shame, and a lack of self-worth. Some who suffer from depression can be self-destructive or suicidal.

And fourth is "physical health." Depression brings a loss of energy, lack of interest in once enjoyed activities, body aches, headaches, and disruption of sleep patterns, too little or too much sleep.

I suffered with depression for over ten years. I would feel depressed for three to four months at a time. Then for unknown reasons I snapped out of it. Soon after, back to depression. I would just isolate myself on the couch not wanting any contact. I had difficulty controlling my temper. Any minor incident caused a rage in me. I saw that my self-worth was low. I could find nothing to make me feel better. I didn't know why I was depressed. Looking back now, it was the beginning of PTSD.

---

[17] John Cottone, "Four Types of Depression," *Psychology Today Magazine*, accessed May 5, 2020, Https://www.psychologytoday.com/us/blog/the-cube/202004/four-types-of-depression

I contemplated suicide several times. My wife saw that something was wrong, she asked me to seek help. I was too tough, I had it under control. I didn't. It was only through a close relationship with Jesus Christ that healing began.

Negative feelings or emotions like depression and anger cause stress. Stress can cause psychosomatic symptoms that the mind and body used to mask the emotional distress.

Many people going through distress suffer from body aches, pains, tremors, fatigue, seizures, numbness, speech impairment, and even paralysis. Sometimes sadness is so overwhelming that the subconscious cannot bear to deal with the emotions. Our conscious mind separates from the stressful situation. This cannot be faked. Physical manifestations of depression or stress is common and something we all experience to some degree. The Diagnostic Statistical Manual 5th Edition (DSM-5) refers to these physical manifestations as a somatic disorder. If you are going through any physical ailment mentioned above, please see a physician for a complete checkup to ensure there is no underlying illness.

Causes of Depression

Everyone will experience the emotion of depression at some point in their lives. There are many causes of depression. There does not have to be just one cause, there could be several causes that led to depression. I always suggest a medical checkup to ensure no medical cause for the depression exists. Some medical causes include: chemical imbalance in the brain, side effects of medication, or improper diet. These are also genetic reasons for depression, investigate your family history for depression, substance abuse, or medical issues.

Depression can be caused by a personal goal that seems impossible to obtain. We all set goals for our lives, some set a two-year goal, some a five-year goal, and still others a ten-year goal. We base our success and often our self-worth on achieving these goals. If the bar has been set too high, the goal is impossible to obtain. Things then appear hopeless.

No matter the type of goal set, financial, familial, or even a noble goal like giving a certain amount of money to charity, if it is not attainable, that goal will cause depression. Depression is rooted in hopelessness.

Another common cause of depression is negative thinking. Because of bitterness and anger we view ourselves in negative light. We often perceive ourselves as unworthy, inadequate, unattractive, or out of shape. This low self-esteem brings hopelessness, hopelessness breads depression.

Sin is the most common cause of depression. When we sin we feel guilty for that sin. We know we did something we should not have done, or did not do something we should have done. Guilt follows along with self-condemnation that leads into depression.

This series of emotions begins a vicious cycle. Sin causes guilt, guilt causes depression, depression causes more guilt and more sin: the cycle continues. It is during depression we try to protect ourselves from further pain by making inner vows or developing bitter root expectancies, these will be explained in detail later.

Some people try to hide their depression from others. Some do not understand why they are depressed. God may have shielded them from the pain of a traumatic incident. As with all negative emotions, depression will manifest through their behavior and build a stronghold in their character structure.

Our behavior will show bad fruit, not the good fruit of the Spirit. A spiritually healthy person cannot produce poor fruit. When we become spiritually healthy, we display good fruit or good character traits.

Depression can be displayed in the form of: outbursts, impulsive behavior, aggressiveness, and even destructive behavior like: gambling, addiction, and sexual promiscuity. There are too many to list here.

Journaling will help you find the root cause of depression, the initial wound—the seed that began this process. If you have difficulty determining the initial wound, ask God to reveal it to you. Use the starting prayer in the appendix asking God's Holy Spirit to reveal the original wound that caused you to end up where you are now. Once the root cause has been determined, you can then see your sinful reaction to that wound. Healing begins with the knowledge and understanding of who you are in Christ, who God sees you as, forgiving, renouncing the sinful response, and repentance.

ANXIETY

Uncontrolled anxiety is a disorder. Anxiety is an inner feeling of apprehension, uneasiness, or worry that is accompanied by a heightened physical arousal. When anxiety is heightened, the body readies itself to fight or run away, this is called the "fight, flight, or freeze" response.

Anxiety is not always bad. This response is proper if there is an existing danger or threat of danger. But if there is no perceived danger, the body is negatively impacted. God gave us the emotion of anxiety to protect us from threatening situations. But when anxiety is prolonged and uncontrolled it negatively affects our lives and steals our peace and joy.

Biblical writers use the word anxiety as well as terms like "down trodden," "worry," "concern," or "anguish" to describe anxiety. Jesus preached about worry and anxiety. He taught that we should not worry about anything.

Jesus said, "Therefore, I tell you, don't be anxious about your life, what you will eat or what you will drink, nor about your body, what you will put on. Is not life more than food, and the body more than clothing? Look at the birds of the air, the neither sow nor reap nor gather into barns and yet your heavenly Father feeds them. Are you not of more value than they? And which of you being anxious can add a single hour to his span of life? And why are you anxious about the clothing? Consider the lilies of the field, how they grow; they neither toil nor spin" (Matthew 6:25-28).

He later says, "Therefore, do not be anxious about tomorrow, for tomorrow will be anxious for itself" (Matthew 6:34).

God knows what we need even before we think we need it. God will provide our needs, maybe not all our wants, but He will fulfill our needs. God knows that we are weak and worry too much.

Proverbs 12:25 says, "Anxiety in a man's heart weighs him down, but a good word makes him glad."

Peter 5:6-7 adds, "Humble yourselves, therefore, under the mighty hand of God so that at the proper time He may exalt you, casting all your anxiety on Him, because He cares for you."

Matthew 11:28-30 says it best, "Come to Me [Jesus], all who labor and are heavy laden, and I give you rest. Take My yoke upon you, and learn from Me, for I am gentle and lowly in heart, and you will find rest for your souls. For my yoke is easy, and My burden is light."

Jesus is telling is to lay our burdens, cares, and anxiety on Him. He will carry them for us, we need not worry. Anxiety is felt as we turn away from God. Our spirit is burdened when we stray from Him. As we get further away from God, we act self-reliant—as if we are our own god. We then must absorb all the anxiety and stress upon ourselves.

To get rid of anxiety we must acknowledge God's sovereignty and set our sights on His heavenly kingdom instead of the worries of this world. God is in charge and in control. Our worry or anxiety cannot change one thing in our situation. Give it to God.

Feeling anxiety is not a sin. It becomes a sin when we become immobilized by excessive anxiety, fear or worry. It is only God who can release us from the paralyzing fear, anxiety, or worry through the process of Christ-Centered Healing. It is not easy to stop worrying, things happen. Living in this world is difficult. Jesus warned His disciples. "In the world you will have tribulation [trouble or distress]. But take heart; I have overcome the world" (John 16:33). We must give all our cares and worries to Jesus Christ.

Causes of Anxiety

We know that we get the feeling of anxiety from danger or a perceived danger. But since the fall it has blossomed from many other causes. Some life circumstances that cause anxiety include:

- **Traumatic Stress Disorder:** PTSD arises following a traumatic event or the perception of atraumatic event. Anyone suffering from PTSD will experience anxiety.
- **Unstable environment:** Living in or being in a high-crime area, financial stress, natural disasters, political instability, or even just contemplating large purchases such as a house or car, starting a new job, or living with a person who has been violent can cause anxiety. If you are living in a situation where there is the possibility of physical danger, please seek help from a friend, family member, clergy, or the police.

- **Low self-esteem:** Low self-esteem or low self-image of ourselves cause us to be self-conscious, especially in social situations. Self-conscious people develop anxiety because they believe they are not good looking, smart, think, young enough, or the correct race to fit in. This is solved by understanding who you are in Christ.
- **Conflict:** Whenever a person is subjected to two or more conflicting influences there will be a sense of uncertainty that leads to anxiety. An example is a person who has a job they are happy with. This person is then offered a different job at a higher pay and more responsibility. This offer may cause anxiety because this person may not be sure if they can handle the responsibility. The pay is better but they do not know if they will enjoy the new job. There is the conflict, uncertainty that brings on anxiety.
- **Uncertain Goal:** All goals should be attainable. As we move towards fulfilling the goal, there may be circumstances in our control or not that makes us uncertain if we will be able to attain that goal. When we are uncertain, anxiety develops.
  - For example, when I was a young officer I wanted to be promoted to sergeant. The first step was to be promoted to corporal. There was a position open and the testing process was to begin in a few weeks. I knew that there were candidates testing with more experience than me. I felt anxiety many weeks prior to the testing process. My anxiety prevented me from being able to study properly. I worried too much.
- **Fear:** Anxiety and fear although similar are different. When we fear someone or something, it causes anxiety. Everyone has a fear of something or many things. Each of us has our own list of fears. With me its spiders and snakes. Some other fears include: failure, death, rejection, intimacy, conflict, illness or disease, success, or loneliness.
- **Theology:** Who we believe God is can cause anxiety. If we see God as an angry vengeful Father, or, if one does not believe there is a God at all, they will develop anxiety. If we see God as a compassionate merciful Father who loves His children as the Bible teaches, there will be no need for anxiety.

Moses warned the Israelites that their disobedience would be punished. Moses told the people that God would give them an anxious mind and they would have no rest and their lives would hang in doubt, they would have no assurance in their lives. This does not mean that all fear is either a punishment from God or a curse on non-believers. However, if you know who you are in Christ, understand who God is, and walk in the Holy Spirit, anxiety and fear will be eliminated.

The Bible gives Christians clear directions for overcoming anxiety. Philippians 4: 4-7 says, "Rejoice in the Lord always, again I say, rejoice. Let your reasonableness be known to everyone. The Lord is at hand; do not be anxious about anything, but in everything by prayer and supplication with thanksgiving let your requests be made know to God. And the peace of God, which surpasses all understanding will guard your hearts and your minds in Christ Jesus."

Paul is telling us to give all our cares to God. I know it is not as easy as it sounds but through prayer and the worship of our Father, Jesus will provide the strength to release the cares of this world. When you do, God will bless you with a peace and joy that cannot be explained. God will guard your heart from further anxiety. You must trust God the He will fulfill all His promises.

ANGER

Anger is a universal experienced by every person. This emotional state is difficult to define or describe. Anger has many degrees of intensity. From just being annoyed to violent rage. Anger is expressed either openly for all to see or it is suppressed. Anger can be short lived or persist for years or even decades. Suppressed anger that is harbored turns into resentment or bitterness.

God created us in His image. This means that God also experiences anger. Anger in itself is not a sin and can even be healthy when expressed in proper situations. If we express anger for the good of another like pointing out a brother's sin, it can lead to repentance. Or anger at an unjust situation can bring change for the better. It is always sinful to deny, suppress anger or hold onto it.

Proverbs 10:18 says, "The one who conceals hatred has lying lips . . . "

Proverbs 26:24 adds, "Whoever hates disguises himself with his lips and harbors deceit into his heart."

Anger is the leading cause of depression.

The Bible has almost 600 references to anger and warns against human anger. Ephesians 4:26 says, "Be angry and do not sin; do not let the sun go down on your anger and give no opportunity to the devil."

We see it is permissible to be angry, but not to hold onto it. Holding on to anger is a sin, it opens the door for Satan's oppression.

Colossians 3:8 adds, "But now you must put them all away: anger, wrath, malice, slander, and obscene talk from your mouth."

Human anger is dangerous. If left unchecked can be harmful. This is why the Bible tells us to turn away from anger. Anger turns into bitterness, that turns into sinful judgments, hatred, then vengeance.

1 John 3:15 says, "Everyone who hates his brother [fellow Christian] is a murderer . . . "

1 John 2:10-11 adds, "Whoever loves his brother abides in the light [Jesus], and in Him there is no cause for stumbling [sinning]. But whoever hates his brother is in the darkness and walks in the darkness, and does not know where he is going because the darkness has blinded his eyes."

And 1 John 4:20-21 adds, "If anyone say, 'I love God,' and hates his brother, he is a liar; for he does not love his brother whom he has seen cannot love God. And this commandment we have from Him; whoever loves God must also love his brother."

Lastly, Paul brings it all together in Romans 12:14-21, "Bless those who persecute you; bless and do not curse them. Rejoice with those who rejoice, weep with those who weep. Live in harmony with one another. Do not be haughty [prideful], but associate with the lowly. Never be wise in your own sight. Repay no evil for evil, but give thought to do what is honorable in the sight of all. If possible, so far as it depends on you, live peaceably with all. Beloved, never avenge yourselves, but leave it to the wrath of God, for it is written, 'Vengeance is mine. I will repay says the Lord.' To the contrary, if your enemy is hungry, feed him; if he is thirsty, give him something to drink; for by doing so you will heap burning coals on his head. Do not be overcome by evil, but overcome evil with good."

God's command is to love each other. If we hold anger and bitterness, but how can we love? Out of control anger is a sin. We were created with emotion of anger, even God experiences anger, but it needs to be controlled and only use in matters of injustice. Uncontrolled anger opens the door to Satan. Satan will then push us into bitterness, resentment, hatred, and vengeance. Do not give Satan his opportunity.

Causes of Anger

Anger has many causes, some situational and others due to the actions or inaction of others. A few common causes of anger include frustration, injustice, genetics and wounding.

Frustration is a universal experience. Frustration morphs into anger. Frustration can come from a blocked goal. As we realize that a life goal is or has been hindered we can become frustrated and angry. We can become frustrated when others let us down because of what they have or have not done. We can become frustrated when negative or unwanted events or circumstances pop up in our lives.

Some unwanted events can include a dead car battery before a big meeting, a co-worker's promotion over you, or illness before a vacation. These are all circumstances that will cause frustration. The extent or duration of frustration depends on the importance of the goal, circumstances, or the size of obstacle.

Jesus felt frustration and anger. The Apostle Mark tells the story of when Jesus went to the temple and saw all the vendors selling animals for sacrifice and converting foreign money into Roman coins. Jesus knew that these people were taking advantage of the people who were poor and had little money to purchase an animal to sacrifice. Jesus became frustrated and angry. He overturned their tables and drove them out of the temple. Jesus said, "... my house shall be called a house of prayer for all nations. But you have made it a den of robbers" (Mark 11:15-19).

Jesus believed the vendors were using the temple of God in an offensive manner; thus, they were disrespecting God. An example of a good response that is common among siblings is when an older brother sees his younger sister being bullied by some boys. It is the emotion of frustration and anger that makes a brother protect his sister. Remember it is when frustration and anger are taken to the next lever is when it becomes a sin.

Genetics can create an overly aggressive response to frustration and anger. There may be a family history of anger outburst or a person's brain chemistry may be off. Rage and aggression can result from a negative reaction to medications, illegal drugs, or alcohol. I recommend a thorough medical examination if similar symptoms exist.

Wounding can arouse anger, especially if we have been betrayed, rejected, humiliated, or unjustly criticized. These all challenge our self-esteem and force us to consider the that we may not be who we think we are.

Anger is our sinful response to the wound that we suffer. We become angry to protect our heart. When we are wounded, we hurt, the response to hurt is anger. They often occur together.

Anger will take over our heart. This is the same response to shame-based anger, hurt and shame turn into anger. We become angry to hide the shame from those around us.

How Anger Affects Us

Anger affects people in various ways. The most common are:

Isolation: most of us withdraw or isolate ourselves when we hold onto anger. Isolation appears to be the default coping mechanism for almost every negative emotion because it is easy. But it is also the least effective way to deal with anger.

Aggression/Acting out: anger and aggression are similar but not the same emotion. They do in fact go together. Anger is an emotional arousal. Aggression primarily affects those close to us. We often hurt the ones we love.

Lashing out can be either verbal or physical, or both. This show of aggression will "blow off steam" and give us short-term relief, in exchange we hurt others. This lashing out often results in feelings of guilt or embarrassment. Some psychologist believe that it is good to release this pent-up anger, however, this often leads to more outbursts, often increasing in intensity.

Redirected Aggression: one of the most dangerous effects of anger is when we redirect our anger from those we are angry at to our loved ones. Often our anger is directed at those who we cannot lash out at. They maybe an employer, authority figure, or other person that are not allow to confront.

Since we do not want to suffer any consequences from authority figures, we then lash out at those we have authority over or at least are on an equal footing with. The people we lash out at are often innocent people like a spouse or children are living in fear every day that the angry parent will come home and redirect their anger at the family. These parents terrorize their family without knowing the damage they are causing.

The damage of taking anger out this way is two-fold. First, this behavior is modeled to the children who tend to repeat the same behavior with their families. Second, the children will end up hating their parents. They hate the offending parent for their aggression, and also the other parent who allowed it to occur and not stopping the abuse.

This hatred goes against God's commandment to honor your parents and keeps the child in habitual sin. Sin separates us from God and causes bitterness and depression. When this child grows up and has their own family, the cycle of sin continues as does the first example.

Positive Anger: uncontrolled anger is destructive. Controlled constructive anger can be positive. Constructive anger can help with marital problems, correcting disobedient children, or help in business situations. Anger gives us a sense of control where suppressive anger can make us feel out of control. We must make every effort to control our anger and view it as a problem-solving technique.

Dealing with Anger

Let's be honest, dealing with anger is not easy. Often our anger becomes so engrained in us and becomes part of our character. Everyone knows someone who they call an "angry person." No matter the reason for our anger, justified or not, it must be dealt with. If not, it infiltrates every aspect of our lives. Anger not only harms us, but everyone around us. Anger causes stress; stress can cause physical illness.

The first step is to acknowledge anger. Be honest and admit you are angry with someone who harmed you? You will never experience healing if your anger is denied. If you do not believe you have anger issues, ask those who you spend time with you. They will tell you. As Jesus said, "You will recognize them buy their fruits" (Matthew 7:16). You cannot hide flawed character traits. We often do not see our own actions, but other see all.

The worst thing we can do is to avoid the pain by distractions like gambling, over-eating, over-spending, or substance abuse. We tend to jump headfirst into these activities in an effort to cope (numb and forget) or subconsciously self-destruct. These things may work for a short time, but eventually the emotions will return. Denial will never promote healing.

I describe this suppression of emotions like being in a swimming pool trying to hold two inflated beach balls under water. It's hard to do! Due to the air in the plastic balls, they want to float on top of the water. You can hold each ball under the water only a short period of time before they pop out with great force. We When you suppress emotions for any period of time, they reveal themselves with even more power and often will overwhelm you. Denying or suppressing emotions goes against God's design, therefore it is sinful.

The next step is to determine the cause of your anger. It is very important to be honest with yourself. The cause is the seed; this is the initial wounding. It is possible that you will not be able to recognize the original wound. It may have been a long time ago, or you have denied or suppressed the incident to protect yourself. If this is the case, I recommend that you use the prayer in the appendix called the "Starting Prayer" and ask God to reveal the initial wounding to you. The Holy Spirit will reveal all things to you when you are ready to receive it.

Journaling is again an excellent way to get to the bottom of your wounding. It helps determine the initial event, your response, and how your life has changed since.

Most feelings of anger require forgiving our offender. Forgiving our offender is difficult. But it is necessary. Forgiving is a choice. It is not to benefit your offender. It is for you.

Forgiving takes the heavy burden of anger off your shoulders. There will be no healing without forgiveness, it is the most crucial step in dealing with uncontrolled anger. Once you have forgiven, the next step is to confess and repent the sin of uncontrolled anger and thoughts of vengeance that comes with it. Remember God created us with the emotion of anger. Even God gets angry sometimes, He understands. Tell Him about the incident and how it made you feel, confess it to God. God will forgive you of all your sins (1 John 1:9).

GUILT

Guilt can have a debilitating effect on one's life. Guilt comes when we believe we have violated some personal ethic, law, standard, or principle. Feelings of guilt arise from our moral failures.

There are basically two broad categories of guilt: objective guilt and subjective guilt. Objective guilt occurs when we intentionally break the laws determined by the county, state, or federal government. Subjective guilty refers to the emotion of remorse, regret, and self-condemnation, that we feel when we think we have done something wrong or failed to do something we should have done.

Objective guilt comes from violating the law. It is normal to feel guilt and remorse for violating society's norms. After punishment, restitution, confession, and repentance, the feelings of guilt subside. It is the subjective guilt that opens the door to Satan.

Some guilt is good, 2 Corinthians 7:10 says, "For godly grief, guilt produces a repentance that leads to salvation without regret, whereas worldly grief produces death."

The Holy Spirit will alert us to when we veer off the narrow path. This produces guilt so that we will repent for our sin. When we live in the world, our sense of right and wrong is much different than with Christians.

Our guilt can become sin when we dwell on our mistakes and do not accept God's forgiveness. Jesus Christ died for our sins. He took our place on that cross so that we could be forgiven and live an eternal life with Him in heaven. Through His death and resurrection we are forgiven; all sins, past, present, and future. John 3:16-17 assures us, "For God so loved the world, that He gave His only Son, that whoever believes in Him should not perish but have eternal life. For God did not send His Son into the world to condemn the world, but in order that the world might be saved through Him." And also, Romans 8:1-2 adds, "There is therefore now no condemnation for those who are in Christ Jesus. For the law of the Spirit of life has set you free in Christ Jesus from the law of sin and death."

We are forgiven, there is no need for self-condemnation, this is extremely important for Christians to understand. Once understood and accepted, we can live the abundant life God intended.

After my arrest I struggled with severe guilt. I had been a decorated police officer for over twenty-five years. I always tried to be honest and fair and taught all my agents to be as ethical as possible. Now I was a criminal, a person who I used to judge as bad.

I was remorseful for what I had done. I know that God had forgiven me, but I was having a difficult time forgiving myself. The man who brought me to the Lord Pastor Jeff Kenney visited me every week.

During one visit, Pastor Jeff asked me how I was doing. I told him that my guilt was paralyzing. He asked, "Has God forgiven you?" I said, "yes." He responded, "So, if God forgave you, why can't you forgive yourself?" I sat silently.

He looked at me angrily. He said, "Who do you think you are?" I just sat there dumbfounded not knowing what to say. Pastor Jeff said, "So your standards are higher than God's?"

I didn't know what to say. He explained, "You're telling me that you have higher standards than God. You believe your ethics are greater than His?" He added, "You're placing yourself above God."

That hit me like a ton of bricks. If the true living God, creator of the universe forgave me my sins, I can forgive myself. Sometimes we all need a swift kick in the tush to bring us back to the truth.

Causes of Guilt

Guilt can be caused by numerous circumstances such as past experiences, trauma, inferiority, lack of forgiveness, poor decisions, or other sinful actions. Let's discuss some of these:

Past experiences: We learn the difference between right and wrong from our parents when we are children. We also learn how to react when someone does wrong. We see how our parents respond to misbehavior and use that as a model of how to respond to adversity. Some parents model rigid standards that are so high no child could attain the standard. Others seem to have no standards or rules.

Some parents can be critical, blaming, and appear unjust in their punishment. Children grow up to accept the standards and morals of their parents. Children whose parents had high standards often grow up expecting perfection from themselves. This is called Performance Orientation. People with performance orientation punish themselves for not meeting their unattainable standards. The guilt from not being able to meet their self-imposed standards has a negative impact in their lives. In contrast, children who had no standards or rules often believe they are owed something from society and may feel guilt for being unproductive.

Lack of forgiveness: this is not the cause of guilt, but if not dealt with will continue a cycle of guilt. We *must* forgive others and ourselves for the mistakes that we have made. If you have hurt someone, you must seek forgiveness. If they do not forgive you, that's okay, you tried and the burden is lifted off of you. The burden now shifts on them. They will now be oppressed by their unforgiveness. You are now able to move forward without guilt.

Sin: God created man to be in harmony with Him. Perfect harmony means that there was no sin to be between them. In the Garden of Eden, Adam and Eve were naked and unashamed. But when they disobeyed God, they experienced guilt and shame.

They knew that God would be disappointed in them for their disobedience. When God came down into the garden, they hid from Him because of their guilt. Guilt or shame had never been felt prior to this event. Adam brought this through his disobedience.

Satan uses our guilt and shame to keep us oppressed and away from God. This is his best lie. Satan knows our weaknesses and uses them against us. When we fail, Satan is there to capitalize on our mistake. He tells us we are failures and that God will not accept us. These are all lies!

If we accept his lies, we are thrown into a downward spiral of guilt and shame. Shame is a deep feeling of inadequacy and personal failure based on one's inability to live up to a perceived standard of conduct. This standard is defined by man. A person experiencing shame will believe: "I am no good" "I'm not worth the space I take up" or "The world would be better off without me."

Remaining in guilt and shame keeps us in habitual sin and steals our peace and joy. Confession and repentance will restore our relationship with God. Failure to understand this concept will lead to more guilt and more shame, depression, fear, low self-esteem, loneliness, and the loss of inner peace.

SHAME

Prior to the fall there was no shame on the earth. Adam and Eve were naked and not ashamed of it. But then after they sinned, they realized they were naked, disobedience brought shame. Unchecked guilt turns into shame, shame is a dangerous feeling. Shame brings helplessness and hopelessness. Without hope we have nothing. Christians should never feel the emotion of shame.

Romans 10:8-11 says, " . . . the word is near you, in your mouth and in your heart (that is the word of faith that we proclaim); because if you confess with your mouth that Jesus is Lord and believe in your heart that God raised Him [Jesus] from the dead, you will be saved. For with the heart one believes and is justified, and with the mouth one confesses and is saved. For the scriptures says, 'Everyone who believes in Him will not be put to shame.'"

There is no self-condemnation for Christians. Jesus took away our guilt and shame by His work on the cross.

GUILT = FEELING BAD FOR WHAT YOU HAVE DONE.
SHAME = FEELING BAD FOR WHO YOU ARE.

Unrepented sin brings shame, as Proverbs 13:5b says, " . . . the wicked [sinners] brings shame and disgrace."

One benefit to trusting in Jesus and walking in the Holy Spirit is found in Isaiah 61:7, "Instead of your shame there will be a double portion [double portion of blessing] . . . "

Shame is a painful emotion. God allows this emotion for a reason. Guilt is a moral or legal state resulting from a violation of law or moral standard. Shame is the painful response to the perception of being guilty and judging oneself in a negative way.

Healthy shame is an emotional response to a violation of God's law. Shame results from the Holy Spirit's prompting pushing us to confess and repent. Healthy shame is a warning signal that we are out of sync with God.

Unhealthy shame is based on Satan's lies and distortions about God, your worth, and your sin. Shame distorts our own sense of self. We do not focus on our sin and on God's grace that forgives us, but we focus on our condemnation and the lie that God will not forgive us. Lewis Smedes describes unhealthy shame in his book, *"Shame and Grace: Healing the Shame We Don't Deserve,"*

" . . . [unhealthy] shame can be like a signal from a drunken signal man who warns of a train that is not coming. The pain of this shame is not a signal of something wrong in us that needs to be made right. Our shame is what is wrong with us. It is a false shame because the feeling has no basis in reality. It is unhealthy shame because it saps our creative powers and kills our joy. It is a shame we do not deserve because we are not, as bad as our feelings tell us we are. Undeserved shame is a good gift gone bad."[18]

Unhealthy shame separates us from God, isolates us from others, and ourselves. To restore our relationship with God we must acknowledge and renounce the shame and repent for the sinful response.

Effects of Shame

Some of the symptoms of shame include:

- **Depression:** if you believe yourself to be inferior or defective, the sense of hopelessness leads to depression.
- **Jealousy / Insecurity:** the feeling of worthlessness creates a sense of insecurity that leads to jealousy.
- **Low self-esteem:** a shame-filled person does not know or believe who God sees them to be.
- **Blame others:** insecurity and low self-esteem often fuels a "victim mentality" that leads to blaming others for their circumstances.
- **Unhealthy competition:** people suffering from shame always compare themselves to others.

[18] Lewis B. Smedes, *Shame and Grace: Healing the Shame We Don't Deserve*, (San Francisco: Harper, 1993), 37

- **Self-focused:** shame-filled people because of their insecurity focus on themselves. They assume that everything is about them, everyone is talking about them. The focus should be on God.
- **Substance abuse:** due to the pain chronic shame people often use alcohol or drugs to help them cope, to get through another day. This is done to desensitize the pain of their shame. Abuse leads to addiction. This applies to addictive behavior also: gambling, food, spending, video games, and even excessive volunteer work are poor coping mechanisms.
- **Lack of intimacy:** a person struggling with shame tend to sabotage their relationships prior to becoming intimate with another.
- **Lack of energy:** shame-filled people use all their energy coping with the pain of shame which leaves them exhausted.
- **Denying feelings:** shame-filled people experience different negative emotions, most are painful. They suppress their feelings so they will not experience the pain.

As we remain in shame, we begin a downward spiral of shame:

- I want to be loved and accepted
- I am flawed and ashamed
- I must try harder to be better (performance orientation)
- I want to give up
- My hard work failed
- I am a failure because I give up
- I try harder, but it's never enough
- I can't do it
- I escape through addictive behavior
- I feel more ashamed . . .

Dealing with Shame

We must acknowledge our shame. Journal the event that you believed caused the shame. And then answer these questions: Is my shame real or perceived? What do I need to take responsibility for? Who do I need to forgive? Myself, my offender, or God? What do I need to renounce or repent for? Is there restitution to be made? With the help from the Holy Spirit, we can break down the event and look at it from a different perspective.

When we have been hurt or abused by someone, we must place the shame on the offender. Through prayer we can ask God to remove our shame and place it on the offender. This is done with the intent to bring our offender to repentance and to seek forgiveness from those they harmed. As Christians we must not seek revenge, that's God's job. Through prayer we remove the weight and burden of shame from us to the offender. We must accept God's forgiveness and understand that we are God's children and are deeply loved. Our self-worth is not based on man's opinion, but who God says we are. We are not defined by what has happened to us or for what we have or have not done, we are defined by who God says we are.

You must renounce shame. Toxic shame is of Satan. Refuse to listen to Satan's lies about what happened to you or what you have done in the past. Choose to focus on Jesus whose work on the cross defeated Satan set you free from the bondage of guilt and shame. Jesus told us that the truth will set us free. So, stop listening to Satan. Renounce him and his lies. Focus on Jesus.

We should fellowship with other Christians. Shame isolates us from our family, friends, and God. The church will help overcome our shame. Find a Bible believing church in your community and go regularly.

God put the Christian community in place so that the wounded and oppressed would have a place to go and confess their sins (James 5:16), so we can meet each other's needs (Acts 2:45), give and receive love (Romans 16:16), and help each other when we sin (Galatians 6:1). As we develop friendships in the Christian community, we find the support to believe the truth of God and to renounce Satan's lies.

JOY VS. HAPPINESS

"Now there is great gain in godliness with contentment, for we brought nothing into this world and we cannot take anything out of the world. But if we have food and clothing, with these we well be content. But those who desire to be rich fall into temptation, into a snare, into many senseless and harmful desires that plunge people into ruin and destruction. For the love of money is a root of all kinds of evils. It is through this craving that some have wandered away from the faith and pierced themselves with many pangs" (1 Timothy 6:6-10).

We all search for happiness. Do we seek joy? Is there a difference between joy and happiness? These are all deep questions. The discussion on this topic could fill and entire book. Joy is a constant feeling of peace and contentment. Only God can provide this type of joy. God's joy is a strength that is very difficult to put into words or to describe. Nehemiah 8:10b says, " . . . do not be grieved, for the joy of the LORD is your strength." Happiness is dependent on something good happening to you. something good happens, like you find a twenty-dollar bill on the ground, your happy. But you can lose your happiness. After you spend the twenty dollars, your happiness is gone.

The only way you can lose your joy is to sin against God. It is better to have the joy of the Lord then temporary happiness.

Every once in a while, my wife and I visit Los Angeles California. We will go to the beach, Hollywood, Beverly Hills, and Rodeo Drive for window shopping. It seems like such a fun-filled glamorous place. Many of us equate happiness with fun. The people all appear to be rich and famous. Many of us equate happiness with fun. The truth is that happiness and fun have little in common. Fun happens when you are doing something like walking on the beach or going to an amusement park. Happiness comes after the fun.

Having fun takes your mind off our problems while we are participating in that activity. When the activity ends, so does the fun. I used to believe that people living in Los Angeles had it made. The cool cars, expensive homes, and parties made me jealous. Then came the "reality" television shows that depicted the rich and famous people living their everyday lives.

The reality of the shows told another story. Yes, there was expensive trips on private jets, but as shows went on, we saw a different truth. We saw constant conflict and drama. We saw divorce and petty fights. I realized that their happiness was a mask, a façade that showed the world how great their lives were, but when you watch, we see alcoholism, depression, dysfunctional families, loneliness, and promiscuity. We do not see any evidence of God in their lives.

Most people who watch these shows only see the "stuff." They do not see the pain. Their masks conceal it pretty well. The average TV audience sees the dysfunction, but they believe the money will take care of that. Most of us believe that money will make us happy. Another expensive car will make me happy. Fixing my nose will make me happy. If I only had that

20,000 square-foot mansion instead of this 10,000 square-foot, I will be truly happy.

These possessions actually diminish their chances of peace and joy. Riches do not profit in the day of wrath, but the righteousness delivers from death (Proverbs 11:4). I'm not saying that being wealthy is bad. But it is when you place money, possession, or status over God that it becomes sinful.

If it is fun that brings us happiness, then pain must be equated with unhappiness. But the Bible tells us the opposite is true; that through pain comes joy and happiness. We must endure pain to achieve joy. It is from the pain that we appreciate life and the blessings that we already have. We learn to appreciate the little things and should consider ourselves to be blessed to have them. Living is joy. There is an old saying, "The happiest people don't necessarily have the best of everything; they just make the best of everything."

I don't know who said that but it is true. People in prison know this. They have to make due with a small locker or just a drawer. Simple food and clothing. They learn to truly appreciate the blessings that they have. Often that is why they came to prison because they took what they had for granted and wanted more.

Wanting more is not bad, but if we place the more over God, we begin to lose our joy. The only thing that can steal our joy is unrepented sin. Once the joy of the Lord is gone, we seek other things to make us happy in an effort to achieve joy. Without God we cannot obtain joy. First Timothy 6:16 says,

"As for the rich in this present age, charge them not to be haughty [prideful], nor to set their hopes on the uncertainty of riches, but on God, who richly provides us with everything to enjoy."

1 John 2:15-17 adds, "Do not love the world or the things in the world. If anyone loves the world, the love of the Father is not in him. For all that is in the world—the desire of the flesh and the desires of the eyes and pride in possession—is not from the Father but is from the world. And the world is passing away along with its desires, but whoever does the will of God abides forever."

The world and the flesh are controlled by Satan. Satan wants to rob you of your joy. There is absolutely nothing in this world that will give you the joy that a loving, trusting relationship with Jesus Christ will bring.

Sin not only steals your joy, unrepented sin can make you physical ill.

Proverbs 17:22 says, "A joyful heart is good medicine, but a crushed spirit dries up the bones."

Our spirit is crushed when we carry unrepented sin. Studies show that the stress of guilt and shame can cause a variety of illnesses. The Bible teaches that unrepented sin opens the door to physical illness. Remember, sin has consequences.

In the Gospel of John, the Apostle John recalls the story of when Jesus and His disciples were in Jerusalem for a feast. Jesus saw a man lying at the pool of Bethesda. The man had been an invalid for thirty-eight years, he was paralyzed. Tradition holds this man-made pool had healing powers. It was said that an angel would stir up the water. Whoever got into the water first was healed of their disease.

This man was paralyzed, he could never get to the water first, others would pass him up. Who knows how many years he lay there trying to get into the water before everyone else. Jesus healed the man who then got up and walked away. Jesus saw the man later that day and said to the man, "See, you are well! Sin no more, that nothing worse may happen to you!" (John 5:1-17)

If you hold onto unrepented sin, a consequence may be an illness. Sin defiles the soul, sin overcomes and dominates our minds, it causes a broken heart, causes diseases in the body, defiles the spirit, and worst of all it saddens and disgraces God; it breaks His heart.

Where our heart is reflects in the person we are. The Holy Spirit works in us to bring peace, contentment, and joy. A joy that only a relationship with Jesus Christ can bring.

Would you like happiness or joy? In Jesus you can have both!

PERFORMANCE ORIENTATION

Self-worth = Performance + Other People's Opinion[19]

Most of us want people to like and respect us. Some people place so much value on other people's opinions that their joy depends on positive affirmation from others. This is called Performance Orientation. Frustration will occur when you believe this and it will keep you in a cycle of shame.

The above equation is how the world evaluates themselves, this is what non-believers base their self-worth on. Using this equation is the recipe for disaster. Unfortunately, most Christians use this same formula. This is a product of the fall. This worldly view that we are only as good as other people's opinions is false. It is a lie that Satan promotes.

If we accept this false belief, we will find ourselves stuck in a never-ending cycle of trying to please others by being perfect. No human can be perfect. There is nothing wrong with being a perfectionist at work or in the hobbies that you indulge in, however, it is when you try to do all the right things to seek the approval of others when it becomes sinful. You are making the people who you are trying to please an idol.

What is even stranger is that it is when we try our hardest to do good that we mess up the most. A great number of people withdraw and isolate themselves for fear of failing. The fear of making a mistake that may change someone's opinion of you will bring a cycle of frustration that will lead to shame.

If our sense of worth is based on other people's opinions, we are doomed for failure because very person has a different standard of what is right or good, that bar will always just be out of reach.

Performance Orientation is based on pride, low self-worth, and a need to control. Our pride is satisfied when others acknowledge our efforts. If we do not receive praise, we become frustrated and depressed. Then, we feel inadequate and believe we must work even harder to earn our acceptance Acceptance equals love. When we understand and accept who God is and how He views us, we free ourselves from this cycle of oppression that believing the lie of perfectionism keeps us in.

---

[19] Robert McGee, *The Search for Significance*, (Houston: Rapha, 1990), p 27

All Christians need to understand that we are deeply loved by God. When we are secure in who we are in Christ and know that we are God's children, we no longer seek our self-worth through trying to please others. If this sounds like you, renounce your perfectionism and repent for making others an idol over God. If you are not sure, pray asking God to reveal any performance orientation in you. If any performance orientation exists, use the sample prayer to renounce, confess, and repent those behaviors.

SECRETS

Everyone carries around secrets from their past. Some are significant and some now seem silly. Secrets can be as small as "I cheated on a college test" to "I was sexually abused by a family member." Deep secrets like the last example can be very traumatic. Keeping these deep secrets internalized breeds guilt and shame, that causes a bitter root to grow in your heart.

As children we learn to lie to keep our secrets hidden. We keep these traumatic events secret to protect ourselves from further pain; we often keep the secret to protect the offender. As we carry this secret, it becomes a heavier and heavier burden on us. Sometimes we bury the secret so deep that we no longer acknowledge its existence. But it is always there influencing our thoughts, feeding our shame. It becomes especially troublesome when the secret occupies the mind. The more we think about it the more negative emotions present themselves.

The keeping of secrets not only affects the heart but also takes a toll on our physical health. Secrets also reflect beliefs about ourselves. The secret of being victimized can manifest itself in feeling unworthy of a loving relationship. When we feel worthless, we may sabotage any new relationship that comes along. We do this to protect ourselves from experiencing more pain. Secrets can also lead to substance abuse or compulsive and addictive behavior.

Deep traumatic secrets must be taken from their dark recesses and exposed to light to bring healing. We should confess them to a trusted friend or a member of your pastoral staff. If you have no one to go to, journaling is a powerful tool. Journaling the experience will enable you to see your response to the wounding and make sense of the incident.

Your secrets do not have to define you. Do not allow your secrets to disrupt your life and steal your joy. Bring your darkest secrets and fears to the foot of the cross, between you and your past wounding and allow Jesus to begin the healing process.

INFERIORITY & LOW SELF-ESTEEM

Low self-esteem involves the belief that you are unworthy, incompetent, and inferior to others. This self-perception becomes engrained in your mind even though there may be evidence to the contrary. Low self-esteem affects and influences how you feel, think, act, and interact with others. The Bible talks about pride, not self-esteem. We should not confuse these terms. Pride is an arrogant, exaggerated, and unreasonably high opinion of oneself in relation to others. It comes with a sense of superiority over others. In a sense, it is placing oneself over God.

Pridefulness is a product of this fallen world. It is of the flesh. The scriptures condemn pridefulness. The Bible views humility in a religious context as a person who acknowledges that he/ she is a sinner, accepts their imperfections, sins and failures and maintains a healthy compassion and concern for the welfare of others. Humility is not self-loathing or a low sense of self-worth. Humility also relies on the dependence on God. Philippians 2:3-11 says,

"Do nothing from rivalry or conceit, but in humility count others more significant than yourselves. Let each of you look only to his own interests, but also the interests of others. Have this in mind among yourselves, which is yours in Christ Jesus, who, though He was in the form of God, did not count equality with God a thing to be grasped, but made Himself nothing taking the form of a servant, being born in the likeness of men. And being found in human form, He humbled Himself by becoming obedient to the point of death, even death on a cross.

Therefore, God has highly exalted Him and bestowed on Him the name that is above every name . . . " This is an excellent description of biblical humility. Colossians 3:12-17 adds, "Put on then, as God's chosen ones, holy and beloved, compassionate hearts, kindness, humility, meekness, and patience, bearing with one another and if one has a complaint against another, forgiving each other, as the Lord has forgiven you, so you also must forgive. Above all these put on love, which binds everything together in perfect harmony. And let the peace of Christ rule in your hearts, to which indeed you were called in one body. And be thankful . . . "

We begin to see a theme with the biblical definition of humility. The Bible tells us that we should be as humble as Jesus. 1 Peter 5:5b-7 says,

"Clothe yourselves, all of you, with humility toward one another, for God opposes the proud but gives grace to the humble. Humble yourselves, therefore, under the mighty hand of God so that at the proper time He may exalt you, casting all your anxieties on Him, because He cares for you."

Proverbs 15:33 adds, "The fear of the LORD is instruction in wisdom, and humility comes before honor." And Matthew 23:12 says, "Whoever exalts himself will be humbled, and whoever humbles himself will be exalted." God does not suggest that we have low self-esteem.

This may confuse some. We should love ourselves, but not to the point of being self-centered. We should not have an attitude of superiority over anyone. We should know that we are all sinners, but God loves us, we are His children, we should be confident but not self-absorbed, humility is not humiliation, and through God's grace we are worthy of God's love.

Causes of Low Self-Esteem

There are numerous causes for one to have low self-esteem. Some include:

- Having handicaps or deformities
- A belief of unattractiveness
- People with difficult childhoods
- Inability to reach goals
- Experiencing failures in life
- Divorce
- Rejection
- Unrealistic expectations
- Betrayal
- Sin

Sin is one of the most common causes of low self-esteem. When wounded, we often respond in a sinful manner. Sin separates us from God, this separation causes us to feel guilty. Guilt left unchecked results in shame. Shame triggers low self-esteem.

Effects of Low Self-Esteem

The effects of low self-esteem are very similar to those of shame. Some include:

- Jealousy / Possessiveness
- Isolation
- Withdrawal
- Feeling you're not worthy of love
- Anger at self, others, or God
- Blaming others
- Uncontrolled anger
- Hopelessness
- Difficulties in relationships
- Depression
- Loneliness

We must understand that our self-worth is not based on what a neighbor, co-worker, parent or supervisor says we are. Our worth depends on who God says we are. We are children of God and deeply loved. We also need to reevaluate our goals to make sure they are realistic and attainable.

I heard about one man that had a goal to earn a million dollars within five years. For most people this is not realistic, unless you begin with five million dollars. Then you sure to be a millionaire. Failure will result in disappointment.

Join a church and fellowship with like-minded Christians, join Bible studies and adult groups. Learn who God says you are. Volunteer at local charities and do nice things for others. Seek a loving relationship with Jesus. Experience the peace and joy only He can bring.

GRIEF

> *"For everything there is a season, and a time for every matter under heaven: a time to be born, and a time to die; a time to plant, and a time to pluck up what is planted; a time to kill, and a time to heal; a time to break down, and a time to build up; a time to weep, and a time to laugh; a time to mourn, and a time to dance ..." (Ecclesiastes 3:1-4).*

We know grief can put us through a rollercoaster of emotions such as denial, anger, and depression. Grief can also affect us physically through somatic issues. When we understand what grief is and how it relates in our lives, its emotional affects can be managed. The word grief is associated with a loss. The word loss can be used in a variety of contexts. For our purposes here, we will view it as a loss that negatively impacts our lives. Everyone will suffer loss during their lives. Suzane C. Thompson describes loss like this,

"Loss is a part of the human condition and an unavailable fixture of life. The inevitability of major loss, however, does not mean that many of us are well prepared to handle this type of stress. Significant losses in life are likely to engender overwhelming negative emotions, disruption in everyday life, and long-term problems is resolving loss."[20]

No one talks about loss. It is too uncomfortable. We all seem to have an unspoken agreement not to talk about our losses, especially death. Every loss we suffer presents an opportunity for growth, for change, and understanding.

Unfortunately, we do not see these positive changes for many seasons due to remaining in our grief. Years down the road we see God's fingerprints all over our loss. In our grief we seek the easy way out.

Kim Kluger-Bell points this out in her book, Unspeaking Losses, stating,

> *"As a culture, we seem to have an intolerance for suffering; we tend to want those who have experienced a loss of any kind to get on with their lives as quickly as possible. Often by minimizing the impact of significant losses, pathologizing those whose reactions are intense, and applauding those who seem relatively unaffected by tragic events, we encourage the inhabitation of our own grief."* [21]

Grief is a normal response to the loss of a person or something significant in a person's life. Significant things in our lives can include an object like a home, car, our health, our job, or a pet. A loss can even be a loss of an opportunity. Grief comes from a variety of causes but most often we associate

---

[20] Suzane C. Thompson, *Blockades to Finding Meaning and Control in Perspectives on Loss – a sourcebook*, (Philadelphia, Bruner-Mazel, 1998), 21.
[21] Kim Kluger-Bell, Unspeakable Losses, (New York: Quill, 1998), p. 22.

it with the loss of a loved one or someone special in our lives. The loss of a loved one is never easy.

We do not want to admit that they died, we say, "They passed on to a better place," they "departed," or "God called them home." Christians should take comfort because "God so loved the world, that He gave His only Son, that whoever believes in Him should not perish but have eternal life" (John 3:16).

Even though we know this truth, it does not take away the pain and emptiness of losing a loved one. Loss can be devastating and our sorrow overwhelming.

For Christians, death is not the end of existence. It is just the beginning of our eternal life in heaven with God. Physical death is a result of the fall of man orchestrated by Satan. But Jesus defeated death by His work on the cross and all those who put their trust in Him will have eternal life. The Bible tells us that at the rapture Christians who died will be resurrected first, then the living Christians will meet them in heaven.

We should be comforted that at the rapture the Christians who have died will be resurrected first and then all the living Christians will be brought up to be reunited with our loved ones who were in Christ. When in heaven, we will all be given our resurrection bodies. Our bodies will never age, never be subjected to illness, and never cause us any pain.

This comforting but it still does not reduce the pain and grief we experience when we suffer a loss. The grieving process is necessary. God Himself experienced grief.

Genesis 6:5-6 says, "The LORD saw the wickedness of man was great on the earth, and that every intention of the thoughts of his heart was only evil continually. And the LORD was sorry that He had made man on earth, and it grieved Him to His heart."

And John 11:32-33 says, that Jesus also grieved, "Now when Mary came to where Jesus was and saw Him, she fell at His feet, saying to Him, 'Lord, if you had been here, my brother would not have died.' When Jesus saw her weeping, and the Jews who had come with her also weeping, He was deeply moved in His spirit and greatly troubled."

Jesus understood grief and spoke about it during His Sermon on the Mount, "Blessed are those who mourn, for they shall be comforted" (Matthew 5:4). Jesus knew the importance of the grieving process. This shows that grieving is healthy, but under certain circumstances it can be unhealthy if taken to the extreme.

Causes of Grief

Some of the causes of grief include:

- Loss of the significant person in your life
- Miscarriage
- Abortion
- Divorce
- Loss of property
- Loss of health
- Illness or disease
- Loss of credibility
- Loss of promotion or job
- Loss of innocence
- Financial loss
- Loss of social status
- Loss of goals or dreams
- Loss of identity
- Loss of attractiveness

Everyone will experience grief in different ways and lasting various time frames. Grief is emotion-filled. During normal grief, we experience intense sorrow, anger, frustration, guilt, loneliness, and bitterness. Some people who experience loss my deny the loss which brings on much stronger negative emotions. Normal grief includes denial intensified or prolonged. Some emotions when suffering grief include:

- Sorrow
- Depression
- Loneliness
- Fear
- Self-pity
- Anger
- Bitterness
- Irritability

- Guilt
- Helplessness
- Hopelessness
- Emptiness
- Absence of grief
- Denial
- Isolation
- Numbing of emotions
- Hyperactivity
- Lowered self-esteem and self-worth
- Moodiness
- Suicidal ideation
- Substance abuse or addiction

Grief is a normal response to a loss. Grief has been defined as intense emotional suffering. Those who grieve feel as though they are carrying a heavy weight on their shoulders. A grieving person may even feel physical symptoms like shortness of breath, heart issues, upset stomach, disrupted sleep and eating patterns.

Effects of Grief

Grief begins with shock, denial, uncontrolled crying, and disbelief. As time goes on, we can feel restless, lonely, and feel deep sorrow. As mentioned earlier grief can cause physical pain on the body. Grief causes stress. Stress can lead to headaches, body aches, high blood pressure, stroke, cancer and more. This is because grief interferes with the body's immune system, thus stress makes us more susceptible to illness or disease.

Depression is very common during grief. Feelings of anger, guilt, loneliness, and helplessness cause us to withdraw from friends and family. Those who grieve often withdraw or isolate themselves, so they do not have to face their grief.

Grief can affect our relationship with God and members of the church. Feelings of anger towards God for taking a loved one too soon are in the forefront of our thoughts.

Others turn to God in their grief and mourning seeking to find comfort and peace. Turning away from God will keep us in our pain and grief. Turning to God will bring healing.

Unhealthy grief occurs when grief is denied, delayed, ignored, or continual, with no end in sight. Unhealthy grief occurs most often when death is sudden, traumatic, violent, or unexpected. Unhealthy grief can cause:

- Isolation or withdrawal
- Self-destructive behavior
- Unwillingness to talk about the deceased loved one
- Intense sadness
- Alcohol or substance abuse
- Persistent illness
- The grieving person keeps themselves busy to avoid or deny the death
- The grieving person to show no emotion

Dealing with Grief

It is very important to understand that the process of grief is different for every person. Depending on the severity of the incident, the grief process can last a short time (weeks or months), whereas some may grieve years or more, especially where there is a death of a child or spouse. Some mourn for the rest of their lives.

What we don't want to do is to delay or deny the pain of the loss or minimize the loss. This will only intensify the pain and make the process last longer.

When I was sixteen years old, I worked at my father's auto repair shop on weekends and after school. I became friends with one of the mechanics whose name was Gary. He began to teach me everything about cars. He gave me my first tool to start my toolbox.

One day after school, I arrived at the shop. Everyone was sad. Dad told me that Gary was involved in a solo motorcycle collision on his way to work, and died from his injuries. I fell apart with grief I did not understand how my dad could have kept the shop open after learning the news. I went home and cried.

This was my first experience with death. My dad came home a couple hours later. I was in my room still crying. My dad came into my room and instead of consoling me, he yelled at me for crying, shouting, "STOP IT, MEN DON'T CRY!"

I was so upset I could not stop crying. This made him angrier and he slapped me across the face and ordered me to stop crying. This taught me to suppress or deny my emotions to show that I was a man.

When we both got much older, I learned that this was the way he grew up: he was taught to show no emotions. This worked well for him during the depression in Germany in the 1930's, then in World War II. I believe he suffered from PTSD because of his war experience. He never spoke about it. He got through life by suppressing his emotions.

I followed in my father's footsteps and suppressed all my negative emotions also. I believe if I would have been able to share my negative emotions with someone that I trusted, maybe I would not have gone to prison.

It is very important to go through the grieving process, no matter how difficult it may feel. The process must be completed.

For those who are grieving, it is beneficial to evaluate their feelings. Many struggle with trying to identify and express their feelings. The best method to evaluate our feelings is by journaling. There are various journaling techniques. I suggest keeping it simple.

Document the date and time of entry and just describe what's in your heart. For example: "I miss my wife" or "I'm scared to be alone." You can write about memories that trigger positive and negative emotions. You can journal positive memories like a vacation or you can document the milestone of your grief

You can begin a scrapbook, or you can just write a letter to your loved one, yourself, or to God. Explain how you feel, explain your anger, detail your emotions. You never have to show this to anyone if you do not want to, or if you prefer, show it friends and family. Any of these examples are positive ways to get your emotions out in the open and begin the healing process. Journaling will help you express your emotions. Anger is a common emotion during the grieving process.

Some reasons we become angry include:

- God for taking our loved one
- The deceased for leaving you behind

- Not doing enough
- Being forced into a different lifestyle
- Those who appear to be coping well

Anger is a warning sign. It's normally the first emotion we become aware of. It is not normally the first emotion we feel. Emotions that precede anger are hurt, fear, and frustration.

Anger camouflages the pain. It is easier to be angry than to endure the pain. Once we determine the reason for our anger we can work on the specific issue. Holding onto anger keeps us in our pain, the pain then infiltrates into every aspect of our lives.

It is extremely important that we do not grieve alone. This is the time we need comfort and support from family and friends. Talking about our loved ones helps us bring out the emotions and bring closure. If you know someone grieving, it is important to simply be supportive. Do not feel that you must provide words of wisdom to make them feel better. Silent support with a hug or two is the best medicine.

When I was a police officer, I hated to work the overnight shift. During the early morning hours, it is common to get a call for a death notification. If someone dies in another jurisdiction, that department will call the police who work the area where their next closest relatives live to notify them of the death. This is a very difficult call. It's normally from 2:00 to 4:00 A.M. One morning at about 2:00 A.M I received a call to notify a mother that her son had died in a vehicle collision.

I went to the house and rang the bell. I'm sure the couple inside already knew something was wrong when the cops come to the house at such an early hour. As I told her what the originating department told me to tell her, she broke down. This made me begin to cry. This was the first time I cried during a notification. I don't know why I cried. I reached out and hugged her. I sat on the couch with her and her husband for about an hour. When other relatives began to arrive, I left to respond to other calls for service. She later sent me a note that thanked me for staying as long as I did and sharing in her grief. It is always best to be quiet and supportive.

FORGIVENESS

> *"Put on then, as God's chosen ones, Holy and beloved, compassionate hearts, kindness, humility, meekness, and patience, bearing with one another and if one has a complaint against another, forgiving each other, as the Lord has forgiven you, so you also must forgive" (Colossians 3:12-13).*

Without forgiveness there is NO healing. If you do not forgive others, God will not forgive you. Without being forgiven, the promises of God are no longer valid. Most of us do not realize how important forgiving others is to our wellbeing. Forgiving others is probably the most important spiritual law in the Bible as the above scripture indicates. Let's see why.

Have you ever watched the television show called "Hoarders?" Our lives are a lot like the people depicted in the show. From a very young age we accumulate emotional garbage. Emotional garbage is from heartbreaks, wounding, and traumas that we have all been through.

This emotional garbage keeps piling up with each betrayal by friend, a loss of a job, divorce, or angry words by a family member. Like the people on the show, we do not want to let go of our garbage. This garbage keeps building up and building up, for some unknown reason we hold onto the hurt feelings. Hurt feelings turn into anger, bitterness, and hate.

Being human, we often revisit the negative memories of our wounding. Throughout our lives we all experience victories. I love to go back when I won a car race; it brings back great memories. But for some reason we just love to remember that negative event that caused us to be wounded. We like to recall every word, every emotion, and every action in minute detail as if it were a victory.

Why do we do this? I'm not sure. But I do know that we all love to feel sorry for ourselves. We do not realize it at the time, but we bring back these negative thoughts and emotions that draw us deeper into bitterness, self-pity, and resentment.

We also love to share these memories with others. Like a badge of honor, we bring up our wounding's to show people how much we hurt to garner pity from others. This sharing of our woundings engrains our memories into our story; we become defined by our pain. These negative thoughts and feelings will slowly eat away at our joy until it overflows causing us to live that defeated life I talk about so much.

There are times when we fake our joy. We put on our "happy" mask that shows others how composed and strong we are. But on the inside, our hearts hold anger, bitterness, and hatred. Not only are these sins but they will seep into every aspect of our lives and will negatively affect every relationship in our life. Bitterness and anger become our worldview.

We know that the unrepented sin of unforgiveness opens the door to Satan's oppression. Unforgiveness and its consequences will become a stronghold. Strongholds prevent healing and draws us deeper into sin.

Not only can unrepentant sins become a stronghold, but they render our prayers ineffective. God does not hear the prayers of those in unrepented sin. The sin of unforgiveness causes a restless soul. It produces stress and anxiety. Research by the American Psychological Association shows that anger, bitterness, and stress poisons our spiritual health, mental and emotional health, and even affects our physical health.[22]

You may ask: What can I do to get healthy and heal? The answer is simple—FORGIVE! Forgiving the person who offended us cancels out the stress and anxiety and removes Satan's oppression. The definition of forgiveness is "the act of setting someone free from an obligation to you that is a result of a wrong done to you."

What does the Bible say about forgiveness? Forgiveness is an important spiritual law, a very necessary step towards our freedom and healing. Forgiveness is so important that Jesus incorporated it into the Lord's Prayer.

Matthew 6:9-13 says, "Pray like this: Our Father in heaven, hallowed be Your name. Your kingdom come, Your will be done, on earth as it is in heaven. Give us this day our daily bread and forgive us our debts [sin], as we forgive our debtors [those who sin against us]. And lead us not into temptation, but deliver us from evil."

---

[20] How Stress Affects Your Health," last modified October 31, 2022, accessed July 7, 2023, https://www.apa.org/topics/stress/health#:⊠:text=This%20can%20put%20you%20at%20increased%20risk%20for,problems%2C%20weight%20gain%2C%20and%20memory%20and%20concentration%20impairment.

Jesus went one step further in verses fourteen and fifteen, "For if you will forgive others their trespasses [sin against you], your heavenly Father will also forgive you, but if you do not forgive others their trespasses, neither will your Father forgive your trespasses [sins]."

If you forgive those who hurt you, God will also forgive your sins. But if you refuse to forgive your offender, God will not forgive your sins. This is a powerful statement by Jesus. This alone should prompt you to forgive anyone who is perceived to harm you.

Paul warns us that unresolved anger from unforgiveness allows Satan to reign in your heart. We all know the damage Satan can cause if allowed, forgiveness is not optional. God commands us to forgive and ask for forgiveness when necessary. We do not want to forgive. It's hard to forgive. We must because we have been forgiven.

Forgiveness is a choice. It is an act that begins the process of spiritual and emotional healing. Forgiving others restores our relationship with God. If we are to experience healing, we must forgive our offender from the heart. Forgiving restores fellowship with God.

Mark 11:25 says, "And whenever you stand and praying, forgive, if you have anything against anyone, so that your Father also who is in heaven may forgive you your trespasses."

It's as plain as day. If you want God to hear your prayers, confess and repent all sin. Forgiveness is such an important concept that Jesus tells us to forgive multiple times.

Matthew 18:21-22 says, "Then Peter came up and said to Him [Jesus], 'Lord, how often will my brother sin against me, and I forgive him? As many as seven times?' Jesus said to him. 'I do not say to you seven times, but seventy times seven.'"

The message here is that we must forgive others, even if they sin against us multiple times.

You may say, "I'm doing good. Sure, people hurt me, but I don't care. I don't need to forgive." Well, let's find out if your right. Answer these simple questions:

- Has life not worked out for you as planned?
- Have you:
- Lost a job or promotion?
- Had a friend or family member betrayed you or let you down?
- Had your parents abandoned or abuse you? Abuse you?
- Made a vow to not be like your parent(s)?
- Been a victim of divorce or infidelity?
- Been a victim of a violent crime?
- Had to give up a life goal for family or financial reasons?
- Wanted to exact revenge upon someone?
- Had outbursts of anger?
- Often felt down or depressed?
- Lost hope in achieving joy in your life?

If you answered "yes" to any of these questions you may need to forgive someone for a wrong done to you. Forgiveness will set you free from the spirit of unforgiveness. When we hold onto an unforgiving spirit, we retain all the pain of what was done to us. It is in our nature make every effort to avoid pain.

We always search for a simple solution to our pain. It is easy to isolate ourselves by avoiding triggers that remind us of our pain. We sometimes avoid people, places, and thoughts of the incident. We use substances like drugs and/or alcohol to forget. Or, we could simply forgive our offender and heal the negative emotions, but instead we do everything possible under the sun so we will not have to forgive. Our pride and ego will not allow it. The truth is that we will remain in bondage to those who we don't forgive. Time does not heal wounds.

No matter what happened to you in the past, remember it is not the event that wounds the heart and keeps you in a cycle of pain. It is your response to that event that brings the anger and bitterness. Withholding forgiveness will cause you to suffer under the weight of Satan's oppression. Your offender will not suffer, they probably have long forgotten the incident while you hold on to it forever.

BITTERNESS

Bitterness is the primary byproduct of unforgiveness. Bitterness builds a wall between us and God. God's will for us is to forgive. When bitterness fills our heart, others can easily see the bitterness because it comes out in the way we act and talk. It becomes part of our character. It will dominate our lives no matter the mask we use to cover it up.

"You will recognize them [people] by their fruits [the way they act]. Are grapes gathered from thorn bushes, or figs from thistles? So, every healthy tree [person] bears good fruit [character traits], but the diseased tree [emotionally / spiritually unhealthy] bears bad fruit. A healthy tree [Christian] cannot bear bad fruit, nor can a diseased tree bear good fruit. Every tree that does not bear good fruit is cut down and thrown into the fire. Thus, you will recognize them by their fruits" (Matthew 7:16-20).

In the proper context, Jesus is referring to false teachers of religion who act as if they are holy, but they are actually just out for themselves. But this statement applies to us because if we are true Christians, Christ is in us and we are in Him. We cannot be spiritually unhealthy and produce good fruit. A healthy person is rooted in Jesus Christ who promotes forgiveness. A spiritually or emotionally unhealthy person is rooted in Jesus and fertilized with unforgiveness, bitterness, and anger that results in negative character traits.

Bitterness is always destructive. Nothing good will ever come from harboring bitterness and anger towards your offender. I remember being passed up for a promotion as a young officer. I complained. I blamed others. I was angry that another officer got the promotion I felt should have been mine. I had more seniority and a higher college degree. I was angry and complained for months to whoever would listen. My bitterness was on display for all to see. After several months other officers got tired of listening to my complaining. They told me they did not want to be around me due to my complaining spirit.

I never realized that my pain was out there for all to see. I was ashamed on how I acted. Looking back now I realize that I was a very unhappy person during that time. I would not have wanted to be around myself the way I was acting.

Most of us know it is better to release the anger and move on, but too often we believe that our current circumstance warrants an exception. Please do not let this bitter root take hold in your life. Don't feed a wound with unforgiveness, anger, slander, gossip, or hate. Prevent that bitter root from growing and taking hold by forgiving others, having empathy for their situation and above all else, love one another as Jesus loves you.

Forgiveness is a command of God. If we believe that God has forgiven us our sins, cannot justify not forgiving others.

Paul explained this spiritual law in Romans 12:14-21, "Bless those who persecute you; bless and do not curse them. Rejoice with those who rejoice; weep with those who weep. Live in harmony with one another. Do not be haughty [arrogant / proud] but associate with the lowly. Never be wise in your own sight. Repay no one evil for evil, but give thought to do what is honorable in the sight of all. If possible, so far as it depends on you, live peaceably with all. Beloved, never avenge yourselves, but leave it to the wrath of God, for it is written, 'Vengeance is mine, I will repay, says the Lord.' To the contrary, if your enemy is hungry, feed him; if he is thirsty, give him something to drink; for by so doing you will heap burning coals on his head. Do not be overcome by evil, but overcome evil with good."

The Apostle Paul is telling us to pray for good to come to those who are mean to us. Don't return evil with evil. Don't seek revenge, God will avenge His sons and daughters. And most of all, overcome evil with good. Love overcomes a multitude of sins (1 Peter 4:8).

LETTING GOD AND LETTING GO

Forgiving your offender is letting go of the pain you are experiencing after being hurt. Letting go of the pain through forgiveness does not mean what happened was okay; what happened to you was wrong. You didn't deserve it. When you choose to forgive, you choose to release the pain, anger, and bitterness you harbor against you offender.

Letting go is not letting them off the hook, but it is a conscious decision to give your pain to God. Christians should never seek their own revenge. Vengeance is God's job. When you follow these principles, you will feel as if a weight has been lifted off you. Forgiveness is not for the offender; it is to set the victim free from the oppression of the negative emotions unforgiveness causes.

God's commands are not arbitrary. He has a specific reason for each commandment. God tells us not to sin. He knows that sin defiles us. He knows that when we sin, we lose fellowship with Him; He knows that sin allows Satan to begin oppression of the sinner. The command to forgive is based on the proven fact that holding unforgiveness is toxic and poisonous to the heart. Forgiving others purifies our heart before God.

Refusing to forgive is a sin. Again, if we withhold forgiveness, our relationship with God is damaged. If we remain in unforgiveness we are telling God that our anger at an individual is more important that our relationship with Him.

Proverbs 15:29 says, "The Lord is far from the wicked [sinner], but He hears the prayer of the righteous."

This may sound harsh but God hates sin. He knows the damage it causes. Forgiving is not easy, matter of fact it is very difficult. I know, that I have a difficult time with forgiving, but we all have to forgive. Many say, "I don't have the strength in me to forgive." I tell them, through Christ you can do ALL things because He strengthens you (Philippians 4:13). Pray for the strength to forgive, God will answer that prayer!

Forgiving your offender does not require reconciliation. You are not required to restore your relationship with your offender, you are letting go of the power they have over you. You do not have to forgive them face-to-face. If you choose to forgive them personally, reconciliation may follow. It's your choice.

If you are still hesitant to forgive, think about what Jesus endured so you could be forgiven. Jesus was arrested, beaten, whipped, scourged, and nailed to a cross. Why did this happen to the creator of the heavens and earth? So that He could take upon Him all the sins and illnesses of all the people on earth. He did this voluntarily because of His love for us. As He hung on the cross bleeding and barely breathing due the position that the crucifix placed Him in, Jesus said,

"Father, forgive them, for they do not know what they do" (Luke 23:34).

If Jesus was able to forgive the those who murdered Him, you can surely forgive the person who hurt you. Forgiveness brings closure and healing into your life. It has unbelievable liberating power.

Seeking Forgiveness

Most of us have hurt someone in our life. God commands us to make amends to them. You may feel regret for what you have said or done to cause a friend pain. Regret can manifest itself into guilt and then shame.

In order to be set free from the feelings of regret, you must seek out those you hurt and ask their forgiveness. Seeking forgiveness can be a risky task. You may not be welcomed into a person's life that you wronged. They may reject you, but the reward of receiving forgiveness is priceless.

The emotional and spiritual reward is growth. God will provide you with the strength needed to seek forgiveness. They may not forgive you, but you have done as God has asked.

The anger and bitterness will eventually destroy their life. You are not required to reconcile if you choose not to. Forgiveness works both ways, without forgiveness there is no healing.

Forgiving Ourselves

We have all done things we regret. We made stupid decisions that affected not only our life, but our loved ones as well. We all experience guilt for the things that we have done, maybe even shame for those mistakes. Even though we know that God has forgiven us our sins, we still have a difficult time forgiving ourselves. We often believe that we are beyond forgiveness. Many believe, "God will never forgive me, look at what I did" or "Look what I did to my family, I destroyed it."

The true emotion we are experience is the emotion of disappointment. We are disappointed in ourselves for making mistakes and the poor decisions that led us to sin. Satan influences us to believe that the greater the sin is, the less we can forgive ourselves. This is dumb! In God's view, sin is sin. We are all capable of doing bad things if put in certain situations.

Paul tells us in no uncertain terms in Romans 3:10-18, " . . . as it is written: none is righteous, no, not one; no one understands; no one seeks for God. All have turned aside; together they have become worthless; no one does good, not even one. Their throat is an open grave; they use their tongues to deceive. The venom of asps [poisonous snake] is under their lips. Their mouth is full of curses and bitterness. Their feet are swift to shed blood; in their paths are ruin and misery, and the way of peace they have not known. There is no fear of God before their eyes."

We are all sinners. I am a sinner and you are a sinner. You may not want to hear that, but you are. No matter what the sin, no matter what you have done, Jesus' work on the cross cleanses you of all your sin, every sin, past, present, and future. If you do not accept Jesus' sacrifice, you can expect to receive the consequences of an unforgiving spirit.

If we refuse to forgive ourselves for our mistakes, we may develop a sense of worthlessness. Based on the mistakes of our past we feel not worthy for love—all based from guilt. This is Satan's greatest play in his playbook.

Satan will whisper in your ear, "Look what you did," "Everyone knows what you did. You're stupid," "No one can love you now, not even God." We punish ourselves for our mistakes. Our mistakes play on a never-ending loop in our minds.

This punishment begins the cycle of guilt and shame. Guilt and shame keep us in a self-imposed prison. Behind these spiritual bars we live in fear and uncertainty of our future. Just what Satan wants! You must understand, God has already forgiven you the minute you became a Christian. Through the perfect sacrifice of His Son, He forgave you and promises never to bring it up to you again.

God did not say, "All your sins are forgiven except for ___________." Feeling worthless is a sin. As you drift further away from God, you become less effective as a Christian because people will see your pain. How can you have a testimony about God's love when you don't feel it yourself? Making Christians ineffective is the goal of Satan. If he can keep us from peace and joy, he knows the poor fruit will show.

RESULTS OF UNFORGIVENESS

By not forgiving ourselves we cause havoc with our emotions. One result of not forgiving ourselves is Performance Orientation. Because we do not feel worthy of our forgiveness, we tend to feel that we must work harder so that others will accept and love us. We believe that if we do better, or work harder, people will like us. We believe in our current emotional state we are unlovable.

Another result of unforgiveness that is common is exhibiting some type of compulsive behavior. This comes from our attempts to cope with the negative emotions. We never seem to use positive coping mechanisms to combat negative emotions. We make every effort to bury or totally suppress our emotions that cause discomfort. We do this by participating in some sort of activity that may take our minds off our emotions for a short time.

Some compulsive behaviors include: drinking excessive amounts of alcohol, using mind altering substances, gambling, over-eating, not eating, compulsive sexual behavior, excessive use of video games, working 24/7, excessive shopping, and even excessive volunteer work at the church. This compulsive behavior is an attempt to escape our guilt and shame. We expend huge amounts of energy and time diverting our attention from the real problem, our inability to forgive.

This is sinful behavior because we are placing ourselves above God, our unforgiveness is an idol. This habitual sin has consequences. The downward spiral of addiction, financial debt, neglecting our families, or continual isolation are just a few of the negative consequences of compulsive behavior. The most hazardous is that we divert our attention away from God. We idolize things that distract us like money, power, possession, praise, sex, or the rush that some obtain from drugs, gambling or alcohol.

When you focus on these behaviors instead of God, you are basically telling God that His Son's sacrifice was not good enough for you. Christ's painful death on the cross was good enough for others but not for you. The only solution for your freedom is to accept God's forgiveness and forgive yourself.

Jesus' purpose on earth was to proclaim freedom for the oppressed and those in a spiritual prison that Satan has customized for them. The spirit of unforgiveness will reign in your life if you allow it. You will be in a prison without bars, held captive to unforgiveness. I wish someone would have told me about this years ago. It took me going to a real prison with metal bars and doors to be set free. Jesus Christ set me free.

Forgiving Parents

It is during our infancy and childhood that we develop our conception of authority figures according to the nature of our parents. They set the model for us. For example: if we need to be comforted, we may seek out our mother. If she is not available for our distress, we make a judgment that she is not available when we need her. Or, if we make a childhood mistake, our father may turn discipline into abuse. We judge and believe that when we fail, our father will love us less. These feelings are called "bitter root" judgments.

As we grow up, we do not intellectually understand that we have sinfully judged our parents. We do know that our heart is broken, we know that something is missing. A broken heart often results in resentment. Resentment turns into anger and bitterness. These judgments are in violation of God's spiritual law to honor our parents.

Deuteronomy 5:16 warns us, "Honor your father and your mother as the Lord your God commanded you, that your days may be long and that it may go well with you . . . "

And Proverbs 20:20 adds, "If one curses his father or his mother, his lamp will be put out in utter darkness."

God cannot be any clearer than that. God commands us to honor our parents. Honor is defined as: esteem or respect. The wounds of abuse, sexual, physical, or emotional, are difficult to overcome; especially when the perpetrator is a parent.

God gave us His Holy Spirit to help provide the power and strength to overcome our wounds. We must not allow our judgment against a parent continue. It is only through forgiving our parents and renouncing our judgments that we will obtain a newfound freedom and peace. God understands that our parents may not deserve to be honored, but it is God's command to honor them all the same. As with forgiveness this does not require that your relationship with the offender parent be reconciled. But it is necessary to begin the healing process.

Renouncing the sinful judgment and confessing and repenting for your resentment and anger removes the weight of this pain from your shoulders. Through this we release the power that sin has over you. As you heal, you often see that the offending parent has been a victim. You will see your circumstances from a different perspective—God's perspective.

Forgiving God

When we think of forgiveness, we associate this with forgiving someone who harmed us. We never reveal the angry feelings we have towards God. We ask ourselves, "How could God allow this to happen to me?" or "I'm a good person, why is God punishing me?" This leads to turning our backs on God and moving away from Him.

I grew up in a family that believed in God, however, we only went to church on Christmas and Easter. I knew nothing about who God is or what He represents.

When I went into Law Enforcement, I saw so much evil. I witnessed children victimized and more death than I care to remember. First Responders witness this evil every day. I could never understand how people could victimize each other with such cruelty. Witnessing this evil, I came to the conclusion that there could not be a loving God that would allow this all to happen. I knew nothing of Jesus or the gospel. It was not until I began to study the Bible and learn about who God is that I began to understand the purpose of evil.

Did I forgive God? God does no evil; He requires no forgiveness—He did nothing wrong. God is perfect and He makes no mistakes. He has done nothing wrong for man to forgive Him. I did renounce my feelings and accusations I made against God and repented for my thoughts. I became a Christian and was baptized. God is good, you can question Him, but do not accuse Him. Praise Him!

Steps to Forgiveness

1. Recognize and acknowledge that you are holding unforgiveness in your heart. Is it unforgiveness of others, yourself, or God? You must accept responsibility for your unforgiveness.
2. Repent from the sin of unforgiveness.
3. Renounce any bitter root judgments, expectancies and inner vows.
4. Believe and trust that God has forgiven you and He will never again bring it up to you.

5. Accept your release from your self-imposed prison and walk, in freedom, peace and joy.

Forgiveness Conclusion

Forgiveness is powerful. Forgiveness breaks the bonds of sins, sets you free from Satan's oppression. If mankind could humble themselves to this truth it would change the world. We hold the key in our hand, we hold the power, but we tend to get in our own way.

Pride, arrogance, anger, resentment, and bitterness prevents us from experiencing the healing power of forgiveness. We close ourselves off to God's blessings and healing. We readily accept God's mercy and forgiveness but are too self-centered to extend it to others. You hold the power of healing. You can choose to forgive and accept God's healing or continue to remain in sin harboring anger and bitterness, living a joyless life. It's your choice!

It should be understood that if you are in an abusive relationship, God does not expect you to forgive and forget. NEVER remain in an abusive relationship. Get out and go to safe lace and call the police. It is only when you feel safe that you can begin to work on healing. Without forgiveness, there is no healing.

SEXUAL ABUSE

The issue of sexual abuse has been a serious problem for thousands of years. It is only within the last few years that we are beginning to understand the its widespread prevalence.

New focus on abuse from the media and the #MeToo movement has shed light on the exploitation of children, sexual violence, sexual harassment, and clergy abuse. Historically, society has denied the presence of sexual abuse. Even the times when it was acknowledged the results were indifferent minimization. Research shows that forty to sixty percent of teenagers experience either sexual, physical, or psychological abuse. Thirteen percent of the girls in the study report that they had been raped by a boyfriend.[22] One abusive incident can result in a lifetime of pain. Incest, sexual abuse, molestation, unwanted sexual advances, and harassment have

---

[22] Linda Charmaraman et al, "Is it bullying or Sexual Harassment? Knowledge, Attitudes, and Professional Development Experiences of Middle School Staff," *Journal of School Health* 83, no. 6 (2013); p. 438-444. https://pubmed.ncbi.nlm.nih.gov/23586889/

been commonplace in our society. One incident of abuse can infect generations within a family—both victim and abuser.

A vast majority of those who abuse children were abused themselves as children. This cycle can continue for generations. Sexual abuse sinks into the abused person's heart, breaking it into pieces. The pain is great, permeating into every facet of their lives.

The abuse is often kept secret, which deepens the pain. There is nothing more damaging than sexual abuse by a parent or trusted family member. These sexual sins not only destroy a child's trust for authority figures, but also fractures their self-esteem and self-worth. It instills guilt and shame, while opening the door to Satan's influence through bitter root judgments, expectancies, inner vows, and unforgiveness.

Biblical stories describe many accounts of sexual assaults by invading armies and biblical characters. The Bible never approves of any form of abuse sexual nor physical.

The Bible teaches us to love our wives, our children and not to aggravate them. Employers are to treat employees, and customers fairly, to remove from them sexual immorality, and to be kind and loving to one another. Abuse affects its victims in a variety of ways. Victims of incest are more inclined to distrust others, have feelings of guilt and shame, have low self-esteem, conflicts over sexual identity, and experience helplessness.

Most victims of incest or molestation do not report the incident. If and when they do have the strength to tell someone, family abuse can often gets worse. Sexual abuse can lead to anxiety, anger, sexual dysfunction, sleep disturbances, addictions, hyper-sexuality, relationship problems, self-esteem issues, and depression.

Many victims become angry at God. They ask, "Why did God allow this to happen?" "Why didn't God stop it?" They may lose their faith and their trust that God loves them and will protect them. These feelings can be projected onto family and friends, straining relationships.

As with other types of trauma, sexual abuse manifests itself long term into our physiology.

Those who experienced sexual abuse can expect physical ailments to manifest as well as emotional distress. If you believe this maybe you, advise your medical provider of the prior abuse. Your doctor needs to be fully informed prior to a diagnosis.

Victims of sexual abuse often try to anesthetize themselves by making inner vows that try to protect them from further pain. They may feel what happened to them was their fault: "If I wasn't bad, daddy would not have hurt me" or "If I wasn't wearing a dress, that man would not have raped me." Satan uses these types of statements to condemn victims. They make a vow to themselves to never wear makeup or a dress again, or they may even gain weight to make themselves less attractive. They tend to judge themselves as "bad" or "evil."

Judgments often turn onto the offender, "My parents are bad" or "I hate my dad." Inner vows change to "I'll never trust a man again" or "I'll never allow anyone to get close to me again." These vows are based on lies and sinful judgments.

These vows and judgments open the door to and gives Satan the authority to commit other acts of harm in the victim's life with impunity and secrecy. This keeps them in a cycle where guilt and shame grow like weeds. They remain in their pain until the judgments and vows are renounced and forgiveness given.

We must forgive those who harmed us. The forgiveness must be sincere, false or fake forgiveness only reinforces the harm. Forgiveness and the renouncing of judgments and vows evict Satan, destroys strongholds, and shuts the door to oppression. Inner vows must be renounced and broken individually. Blanket renouncements do not last. With each vow being broken, hearts will open to receive the love of Jesus.

Trauma rewires the brain. Some people who suffered childhood sexual abuse may become aroused by dangerous situations, this includes sexual arousal during re-experiencing the initial trauma, via flashbacks or nightmares. This is common. It is this arousal that keeps them in destructive patterns. Destructive patterns include involvement in relationships with others who are similar to their abuser.

These relationships never work out. It is not until the abused begins that they realize they are in a destructive pattern. Sexual abuse, like all trauma, must be exposed to the light to begin healing.

Journaling will help process what happened. During the journaling process, not only must we evaluate the traumatic incident, but we must examine the familial relationships at the time the abuse occurred. We must place each family member into context and hierarchy of the family. Submissive relationships must also be understood in the context of the abuse; these wounds must be opened to the air and cleansed with the blood of Jesus.

Sexual abuse is the most difficult trauma to heal and will require time, effort, patience, love, and additional pain. You must own up to the fact that the abuse occurred. It was not your fault and it was wrong. You must also recognize that the abuse has harmed you and it is the result of this abuse that negatively affect your present life.

Journaling allows you to process what happened to you and produces positive results in all forms of trauma. However, due to the array of issues that need to be dealt with, I recommend having a trusted friend or family member with you as you go through this process. Tell your story in a safe place. As you come to a natural stopping point make notes in your journal. At this point your helper may have some questions.

They should gently ask clarifying questions or things that need to be expanded upon. Trauma awakens trauma. This means that more details may be remembered. Every detail should be brought to light. The understanding and growth will come from remembering the truth in detail. Do not neglect explicit, shameful and heartbreaking details.

Avoiding the painful details prohibits healing. Work together with your helper to find the sinful responses like unforgiveness, vows, expectancies, and judgments that keep you in pain. It is important to go slow and take the time to go through ALL the details. Questions like:

- “What happened first?”
- “What happened next?
- “How did that make you feel?”
- “What were you thinking during what happened?”
- “Did you do anything to protect yourself after the incident?”

These and similar questions are helpful to explore the issues that will arise. Make lots of notes during this process. Sexual abuse stories can be very complex. Moving forward requires baby steps. Pushing through this process will not promote healing; there are no quick fixes.

An important aspect in this process is for the abused to think about how they managed the trauma, stress, and emotions after the incident:

- Did they withdraw and isolate?
- Did they lash out at others?
- Did they become suicidal?
- Did they make judgments about the offender or themselves?
- Did they make vows to protect themselves?
- Do they need to forgive someone?
- And did they bottle up or express their emotions?

The helper should never offer advice. Their role is to help in the exploration of the incident and its aftermath. The goal is to gain insight, grieve, and determine the sinful responses so that these sins can be put to death on the cross we go through the process, God heals our heart, a new awareness is realized, insight is learned, faith and trust in God is reinforced, and healing is obtained. The scars and memories do not disappear, but now provide deeper meaning and understanding.

Forgiveness evicts Satan and closes the door to future oppression. Forgiveness must be sincere, and this takes time. Fake or insincere forgiveness does not heal. Forgiving too quickly prevents us from experiencing the pain of our story. Our story is so very important to bring to light in order to heal the broken child within.

As with forgiveness, shame is not easily overcome. Satan uses shame and guilt to keep us in habitual sin. He does not want us to be free from our shame.

Satan will fight tooth and nail to keep us in our shame. The warfare over our shame can be great. But in Christ we have the power to persevere and overcome. Overcoming shame can be a slow process and filled with pain. This is where depth and detail must be told. It will be painful, but when relinquishing and renouncing, healing begins. Shame is greatest when we experience sexual arousal from the memory of the abuse. Not every abused person experiences this arousal but it is very common and natural.

God made our bodies to experience sexual pleasure. It is because of this pleasure we have condemned and despised our bodies and now live in guilt and shame. We must put the shame onto the cross to be put to death so that we can bless our childhood bodies, not condemn them. The abuse was not your fault. It was cruel and a violation of trust. As an adult we grieve and honor the abused inner child. The power of shame cannot overcome God's love. Love always prevails!

As you make progress during the healing process, you can expect ramped up attacks by Satan. He does not want you to heal. He will mock you, lie to you in an attempt to have you slip back into shame. He tries to get you to sabotage your healing. He may use the lie: "This won't work, God doesn't love you" or "Why is this so painful and time consuming? Just quit."

God loves you. You are His child. No matter what you have or have not done, God will never leave you. It is God's will to have a close personal relationship with you.

As we go through the steps of forgiveness, renouncing vows, expectancies, and judgments, we often come to the realization that live is precious. We understand that life is meant to be engaged in all its sorrow and joy. This is a volatile time; we make some progress but then we may take a step backwards. This is common, do not be disappointed. Keep working and moving forward.

We may find a sense of purpose and realize God's calling. We usually see our emotions leveling out at this point and laughter and joy returns. Triggers that used to set us into a tailspin are slowly eroding and sexual pleasure may slowly return.

As you continue to work on your healing and growing deeper in your relationship with God, you see some of the damage that was left in your wake. Through honest and open discussions with family and friends, you will often see relationships that require our asking for forgiveness. Asking for forgiveness releases your guilt and restores relationships.

If a friend or family member does not accept your apology, the burden will be on them. You have followed God's command of asking for forgiveness. You release that person to God. Pray for them and move on.

The goal from all this is to understand that what happened to you is part of your story. It can be a story of sorrow and grief, but it is also a story of redemption and healing. A declaration of blessing. Our emotional and physical scars of abuse is your testimony to God's goodness. Just as Jesus proudly showed His scars on His hands and side to His doubting disciple Thomas as a testimony of His love; we can do the same.

God wants us to use our trials to help others. God allows us to go through trials for various reasons, one is to bring us closer to Him. As we draw closer to Him, He comforts us and helps us through these tough times.

He then wants us to comfort others who are going through similar trials so that we can show them the love God. It is your scars and your testimony of how God brought you out of your pain that will be a comfort to others. You are blessed to be given the opportunity to comfort others, you may even see purpose in our pain.

PRAYERS AND THEIR IMPORTANCE TO YOUR HEALING

To reveal any sinful use of your body:

Father,
I ask You to please reveal to my mind now every sexual sin where I used my body that was displeasing to You.
In Jesus' name I pray, Amen.

Note: As certain incidents come to mind, write them down so you won't forget them. Once you feel that God has revealed all there is to reveal, it is time to renounce these incidents.

To renounce sinful use of your body:

Father,
I renounce the sin of________ with ________. I repent for this sin and I ask You to please break any bond that occurred during this sin. I also ask You to remove any ground that Satan or his demons have taken due to my sin. I affirm that Jesus is my Lord and Savior.
In Jesus' name, Amen.

Note: When someone has experienced a sexual assault, they often feel as though they are now "dirty." This can carry over into all relationships and marriages, especially during times of intimacy. It is normal to feel as though you did something wrong. These feelings are promoted by Satan and must be renounced.

To renounce lies of sexual abuse:

Father,

As a result of my childhood trauma, Satan has lied to me, convincing me that as a result of my victimization convinced me that what happened was my fault and that I should be ashamed. This shame has infiltrated into my relationships with others. I renounce this lie and I expose Satan for who he is—a liar. I choose to believe the truth that I am Your child and that I am deeply loved. I know that I am forgiven for this false belief and for role I played at the time that I was molested. Thank You for being my Lord and Savior.

In Jesus' name, Amen.

CHAPTER 6

WHY JOURNALING IS KEY TO YOUR HEALING PROCESS

If you are reading this, you are most likely tired of living a life of pain and despair. You're probably also tired of hurting the loved ones in your life. Maybe your life is not heading in the direction that you intended since you went through an overwhelming life experience or a traumatic event. Maybe you see your emotions and your life spiraling out of control and you don't know why.

Exposing the trauma will begin the healing process. Talking to a trusted friend will help, but journaling is the single most effective way to begin your healing journey. Journaling will help you see God's purpose in your pain.

A traumatic event is like a seed that gets planted in our heart. If we fertilize the seed with forgiveness and understanding the seed will sprout roots that will grow into a tree that produces positive fruit. The term "fruit" in the Bible refers to character traits and deeds of the heart, good or bad.

But if the seed is fertilized with unforgiveness, anger, and resentment, the seed will sprout roots that will grow into a tree that will produce bad fruit or poor character traits.

Remember: how we behave is based on what we believe. This includes our out-of-control emotions and symptoms of PTSD. The Bible refers to this as the root of bitterness.

Hebrews 12:15 says, "See to it that no one fails to obtain the grace of God; and no root of bitterness springs up and causes trouble, and by it many become defiled."

The writer of Hebrews is warning us that anger turns into bitterness and will infiltrate our hearts and causes a root of bitterness to take control the heart. This root will take over our heart and our lives and that bitterness will hurt other people; most likely those we are close to like family and friends. Bitterness causes our emotions to play havoc in our lives.

BEGINNING THE HEALING PROCESS

In order to begin the healing process, it is important for you to know the original incident that wounded you. Our wounds are sometimes hidden from us. Like an iceberg, our wounds and heart breaks are hidden below the surface. Healing occurs when our wounds are exposed and resolved.

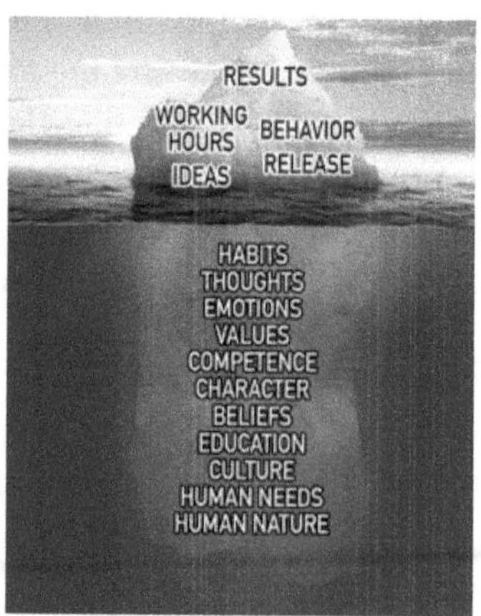

Most people know the incident and remember it well. But some do not remember the original incident. Your spirit may have blocked the memory to protect you from further wounding or at some point you just denied the incident to the point that your mind refuses to acknowledge it.

Exposing your trauma is crucial to healing. This can be done by opening up to a close friend or family member. Or, by writing your story down on paper detailing the event. Most people prefer journaling because it allows privacy.

You must reveal what happened, who did it, how you responded, and how did you dealt with the pain. Talking or writing about it allows you to let go of the trauma and helps the brain process the event. The more you write or speak about it, the less its hold is over you. You may see patterns in your life that require change and you may also see positive traits that you never thought you had. Journaling will also help you see how present Jesus was in the midst of your pain.

The goal is to pinpoint the original wound. You must realize there may be more than one event that is causing issues in your life. Once the original wound has been determined, you look for your response to the wound.

- How did you cope with the pain?
- How did you protect yourself from more pain?
- Was your response learned from your parents?
- Did it work?
- Are you withholding forgiveness?
- Are you judging your offender?
- Have you made inner vows or expectancies?

Think about how your life has changed since the incident, good or bad. It is very important to be honest. No one has to read the journal. If you want healing, be detailed and honest. People in pain have a tendency to blame others. Blaming others is a universal human trait that makes wounded people feel better. Blame is associated with anger and resentment.

Avoid blaming others. Acknowledge your role in your pain. Try to include as much detail as possible. If the pain gets to be too much, go slowly and just write an overview. Go into detail later when you are ready.

When you return to the overview, write out the emotions you felt and how you responded to them. Why do you believe you responded the way you did? Did thinking about it bring up another incident?

Detail every aspect of the event:

- What was the trigger?
- What happened next?
- Did you tell someone about the event?
- Who?
- Why or why not?
- How did your life change?
    - Better or worse?
    - How?
- Why do you believe it affected you as it did?
- Has your pain affected any relationships?
    - How?

Resist the urge to justify your actions, this is between just you and God. Spend about twenty to thirty minutes a day at first. If the writing brings uncomfortable memories, write less. If you seem to be feeling better, spend more time on the journal. Don't worry about spelling, grammar, or sentence structure.

If you seem to have writers block, just doodle as your spirit leads. Use this time to explore your thoughts and inner secrets. Get them out. Write them down. Keeping a secret is bad for your emotions. They will haunt your thoughts. Confess them to God through the journal. No has to ever read your thoughts.

Write about anything that comes to mind. If you're having a conflict with someone, write it out. Write down any frustrations with family, friends, co-workers, or with God. Keep track of negative feelings like grief, anger, bitterness, or depressive episodes. As the negative emotions comes on to you, write the date, time and details of the episode. Think if there was a triggering event, what emotion was felt, and using a one to ten scale, one being the least emotional intensity and ten being the most severe, document the level of emotional response. After the emotions subside, write what you did to lower that number and how you feel now.

At the end of the week look back and see if a pattern appears. Is there a common trigger? Was there a similar time of day? Location the same? People were present the same? If a pattern emerges, analyze the reason for the trigger and pray on it. Remember to write down all the positive things you did to overcome your problems at that time and coping skills that worked well and what did not.

EXAMINING YOUR RESPONSE TO THE WOUND

When you are all done writing the incident in detail, it's time to determine your response to the wound. Examine what you wrote and evaluate what it was you did after the wounding. Responses that keep us in a cycle of trauma include: unforgiveness, judging others, harboring anger and bitterness, making expectancies, and inner vows. You will notice at least one of these, but most likely you will notice all of them from the same incident.

After you identify the specific responses, write out what they are and the reason you made that particular response. Why can't you forgive? How did you judge the person? Was it an honest judgment or one made out of anger? Did you promise to do or not to do something to prevent more pain? Through this you may learn something about yourself and see where the pain is coming from.

If there is more than one traumatic event, take your time and begin with the one you believe was the most severe first. Then go the next incident. Do one at a time. Each incident is its own event. Writing them all together will bring no healing.

Make a "to do" list of the things you found you have to do begin the healing process. It may look like this:

- I need to forgive for ________.
- I need to renounce the inner vow of ________.
- I judged ________ for being judgment
- I need to renounce the sin of ________.
- I need to confess and repent for blaming God in my pain.
- I need to forgive myself for ________.
- I need to ask forgiveness from ________ for ________.

TRAUMA TIMELINE

There is a technique that is helpful for some people, that is to make a trauma timeline. A trauma time line is made by drawing a horizontal line on a blank paper. At the beginning or the far left, write the year you were born. As you move to the right of your birthdate, write down any and all traumatic incidents that you remember. If you remember the date or year of the event, write the date down. At the bottom of the line write down exactly what happened. For example, if you were bitten by a dog at the age of five, write it down just right of your birthdate. Continue from there to the present date. Place a notation for both negative and positive life events as you move to the present date. Take this exercise slow.

Pray that God will bring incidents to your memory, good and bad. If you feel anxiety or stress, take some time off.

When your done with the timeline, examine it to determine if there are any patterns that appear. I suggest that you then take each life event and journal them out as described herein. See if you made any sinful responses that need attention.

A trauma timeline is not required. It will help you to see each event in a different light. Because journaling gets all your emotions out on paper, it helps you process the incident much better.

Here is a list of question that will help you get started on the journal:

- How are you wounded? What happened?
- Who wounded you? Were they close to you?
- How did it make you feel?
- What did you do immediately after the incident?
- Have you confronted the person who hurt you?
- How has your life changed since this incident?
- Are you holding onto anger, resentment, or unforgiveness?
- Did you forgive them? If not, why?
- Do you need to seek someone's forgiveness?
- How have you dealt with the pain of the incident?
- Are you doing something to make yourself feel better? Activities? Alcohol? Workaholic?
- Did you judge the person who harmed you? In what way?

- Have you made a judgment about yourself? About life? About God? In what way?
- What are you doing to cope with your anger and pain?
- Have you made yourself some type of promise to protect yourself from further pain? What is your promise?
- Do you isolate yourself from others, friends or family?
- Do you drink in excess? Use drugs?
- Do you have problems in your relationships with others? If so, what do you believe is the issue? Do you seem to sabotage your relationships?
- Do you hurt others before they can hurt you? If so, why do you believe you do this?
- Have you had thoughts of revenge against the person who harmed you? In what way?
- Have you had thoughts of suicide? Are they realistic? If so, please seek help immediately.
- Have you thought about physically hurting other people?
- Does it seem like you and your family have a lot of bad luck?
- Have you become like the person who harmed you?
- Do you believe your emotions seem out of control?
- Do you cry more than you used to? If so, why?
- Do you get angry easily? Does your anger turn into rage?
- Have you found yourself to be impatient?
- Do you have more fear after the incident than you did before? What are you afraid of?
- Does it feel like people are out to get you?
- Since this incident do you think about sex more or less often? Good context or bad?
- Do you try to prevent yourself from thinking about sex?
- Does it bother you to be touched? By everyone?
- Do you avoid sexual situations?
- Do you practice safe sex?
- Do you seek out excitement? Danger? Driving fast? Gambling? Drugs, etc.?
- Do you often believe that you are going crazy? Why?
- Do you feel guilt over something that you have done? Why?
- Do you feel ashamed? Why? Of what?
- Are you keeping a secret or secrets? What are they? Why are they secret?

- Are you angry at God?
- Have you respected your parents? If not, why?
- Can you trust others?
- Do you trust God?
- Do you feel joyful? If not, why? Do you feel depressed? If so, why?
- Do like your job? If not, why?
- Do you feel disrespected by your co-workers? Do you know why?
- Do you feel like your life has purpose?
- Has someone you love betrayed you? If so, explain.
- Do you get enough sleep?
- Are you afraid to go outdoors?
- Do you feel safe? If not, why?
- Do you have support from family or friends? If not, why?
- Have you been abandoned? If so, by who? Do you know why?
- Has anyone not allowed you to express an opinion or be heard? If so, who?

These questions will help you get started. If one of them applies to you, expand on it in your journal.

If you are experiencing extreme emotions and are considering injuring yourself, please call this 24/7 phone number for help 1-800-273 -TALK (8255).

Below is a list of symptoms that persons diagnosed with PTSD suffer from. If you are experiencing any of the symptoms, write your feelings and the symptoms down in your journal. Go into as much detail as you are comfortable with.

- Intrusive memories: flashbacks, nightmares, etc.
- Inability to remember parts of the event
- Irritability
- Sleep disturbances, both too much and not enough
- Using alcohol or drugs to excess
- Isolating yourself from others
- Feelings of depression
- Feelings of anger, bitterness and thoughts of revenge
- Feeling jumpy or agitated
- Difficulty concentrating
- Feeling that your life will be shortened
- Participating in dangerous behavior

- Coping with life by addictive behavior such as:
    - Gambling
    - Dangerous sex
    - Pornography
    - Over/under eating
    - Spending money that you do not have, etc.
- Becoming hypervigilant in public
- Fear of going out in public
- Suicidal Ideation
- Cutting yourself to relieve the pain

One of my issues that I needed to evaluate and determine the seed of was my own isolation. I didn't like being around anyone. I had felt this way for several years. At a social event, I would experience anxiety. I tried to figure out why, but never came up with an answer. I prayed asking God to reveal the root cause to me. God brought many different incidents to memory, not one lead to an answer.

I began to journal my feelings. As I thought about what God revealed and related my anxiety to work, I thought about people at a social event. I felt uncomfortable in public, even at family events. Why? I felt that even though it was a family event, friends of friends were often present. I would often watch these unknown people closely.

I then thought about people who I had arrested that saw me off-duty in public and approached me. This was always a hypervigilant moment. You never know their intentions. They often recognized me before I did them. Once in Reno, Nevada a guy I arrested approached me and my dad near a casino. He only wanted to let me know that he changed his life and was doing good now. Some of the people called me names and threatened me, others just wanted me to know they recognized me.

When I had this all down on paper, I saw that this was my concern. No matter where I went, even other states, I could not get away from people I arrested. This made me uneasy. This was the cause of my isolation. It was easier for me to isolate than to deal with life's situations.

I saw that I was judging these people before I knew their intentions. So, I made an inner vow to stay at home and feel safe. I stayed away from friends and family for my own selfish purposes.

I renounced my inner vow and judgment of these individuals. I feel a lot better about the public now and feel more at peace. Journaling will help you sort out your feelings.

GETTING STARTED

It is best to find a quiet place without the distraction from phones, knocks on the door, or television to begin your journal. If necessary, send the kids off on a play date. Privacy is important but not as important as journaling in a place you feel safe. If you feel safe and secure, your thoughts will flow easier. If you have secrets that you never want to get out, bring separate pieces of paper to write the secrets on so that you can shred them when you have followed the instructions here.

Do not destroy them too soon, remember you need to see if you had any sinful responses to whatever your secrets contain. Purchase a notebook or a book specifically for journaling. Make sure you have extra pens or pencils and are comfortably dressed and fed. You want no distractions. An empty stomach is a huge distraction for me. Sit down and just let your thoughts flow into your mind. Begin in prayer, asking the Holy Spirit to help bring things to your memory that need to be dealt with. Here is an example of a prayer.

Prayer to Reveal Trauma

Heavenly Father,

I have been wounded and this wound is causing poor fruit in my life. I need to reconcile myself to you. Please reveal to me the details of the incident(s) that caused this wounding. Show me the seed of trauma that was planted in my heart causing this bitter root to grow. I have been bound by my pain and sinful responses for so long, I want to be set free. I know the truth of what happened will set me free. I want the peace, joy, and abundant life You promised. Give me the courage to identify this wound and expose the bitter root to the light. Reveal my sinful responses so that I can confess and repent for them so that the process of healing may begin. Please keep me safe during this process as I write down what your Holy Spirit reveals to me. In Jesus' name I pray.

Once this process is completed, journaling can be used as stressful life events come up. This will keep you from going back into your old sinful responses that failed you in the past. I also suggest journaling your daily prayers.

A prayer journal can increase your trust in God. Write down all the things you prayed for with the date and time of prayer. As these prayers are answered, go back and make a note of how each prayer was answered and when. You will begin to see a pattern of God answering your prayers. This will provide you with awesome testimony. Keep journaling for healing!

CHAPTER 7

OBSTACLES TO YOUR HEALING

The key to emotional, spiritual, and physical healing is to be in complete fellowship with God and be aligned with His will. In order to align with His will, we must clear out all the obstacles that prevent our relationship from growing. Obstacles can be habitual sin, violation of spiritual laws and principles, and engrained strongholds. These obstacles separate us from God, and puts us out of His will. They prevent us from fulfilling His will for our lives, and blocks our healing. Being able to recognize these obstacles is key to healing.

I have explained this earlier, but it is so important that I want to repeat it here also. Being involved in a traumatic event or an overwhelming life situation is a seed that gets planted in our heart. We can respond in different ways.

Our response is based on our beliefs and attitudes from previous life experiences and how our parents modeled coping behaviors for us. If we respond to the wound with forgiveness, understanding, and love, the seed grows into a healthy tree that produces good fruit. Good fruit is positive character traits that promote growth, wisdom, and healing. But if we fertilize that same seed with anger, hate, bitterness, and unforgiveness, that seed grows to produce an unhealthy tree that produces poor fruit. An unhealthy tree cannot produce good fruit.

This unhealthy tree has bitter roots. As the bitter roots take over our hearts, it causes us to exhibit behavioral structures such as anger at the world, bitterness of the things that have happened to us, victim mentality, envy of what others have, thoughts of revenge, and more.

All these responses to a wound are considered sinful. Sin opens the door to Satan's oppression. Most of us respond in a sinful manner because this is how our parents modeled how to deal with adversity. They did not know how to properly cope with their own overwhelming life events. Do not go out and blame them because the sinful responses have been engrained into our minds over generations based on society's belief system. Society normally does not recognize God. Society promotes us to be self-centered. Society tells us that only winners succeed. We must seek money and power if we want to be the best and be happy.

The Apostle Paul warns us of this thought pattern, "Do not be conformed to this world, but be transformed by the renewal of your mind, that by testing you may discern what is the will of God, what is good and acceptable and perfect" (Romans 12:2).

The "world" is the society we live in. Do not allow what society says you should be to be your truth. As you place your trust in Jesus, your mind will be transformed daily to be in fellowship with God.

When we go against God's will by sinning, we give authority to Satan to harass us. When we hold unrepented sin we begin to be ruled by what Satan's will is, not God's will. We are ruled by our sin. It controls us. The longer this goes on, the stronger Satan's hold gets in our lives. This hold will influence our thought patterns and behaviors leading us to more sin and deeper oppression. Sin controls our life.

When we are born again, we are saved. Our new position is "in Christ." When we are in Christ, we have already been healed. God gave Abraham the land of Canaan and the promise land. Even though Abraham and his descendants did not live there and were even held as slaves in Egypt, positionally, they owned the land promised to them.

The Israelites were required to overcome many obstacles that prevented them from living in the land they already owned. Those obstacles were their own sinful behaviors. Those of us who are in pain due to traumatic events of overwhelming life events are positional already healed. We must conquer our own obstacles in order to heal our broken heart that through Jesus' work on the cross has already been healed. These obstacles are identified by the character structures we exhibit. Once identified, we need to bring them to death on the cross.

We have a choice to make: we can either live as a slave to our sin and remain in our self-imposed prison, or we can decide to regain control of our lives by renouncing our sinful activities and evicting Satan from his stronghold in our lives. We go from living in the darkness to stepping into the light; walking in the light brings healing.

There are spiritual laws and principles that if violated, prevent our healing. These are absolute. We must follow them and to remain in God's will. Below are the spiritual laws and principles that must be understood.

LACK OF KNOWLEDGE

> *"My [God] people are destroyed for a lack of knowledge;*
> *because you [Israelites] have rejected knowledge"*
> *(Hosea 4:6).*

Without the knowledge of God, you are destined to remain in your pain until you die and doomed to an eternity in hell. God is the only one who can save and deliver you from emotional, spiritual, and physical pain.

It is only through the knowledge and faith in God that we obtain knowledge. Proverbs 1:7 says, "The fear of the LORD is the beginning of knowledge; fools despise wisdom and instruction." The word "fear" here not only means to be scared of, but to have reverence for God. Proverbs 2:6-7 adds, "For the LORD gives wisdom; from His mouth come knowledge and understanding; He stores up sound wisdom for the upright; He is a shield to those who walk in integrity."

God teaches wisdom. The world teaches knowledge. Merriam Webster defines knowledge as: the fact or condition of knowing something with familiarity gained through experience; or to be familiar with or acquire comprehension. Dictionary.com defines wisdom as the quality or state of being wise. Proverbs 1:7 and 2:7 say that you cannot have wisdom without the knowledge of God.

God is our creator. It is only through Him that we are forgiven of our sins and healed of our emotional wounds. If you do not have a personal knowledge and relationship with God, please do it now and begin the healing process.

DEMONIC INFLUENCE

> *"There are two equal and opposite errors into which our race can fall about devils. One is to disbelieve their existence. The other is to believe and to feel an unhealthy interest in them, they themselves are equally pleased by both errors and hail a materialist or a magician with the same delight."—C.S. Lewis*[24]

The Bible clearly teaches that there is a spiritual world made up of good and evil. Satan and his demons are on one side while God and His angels are on the other. Satan's goal is to deceive people to keep them from trusting in God. He wants us to believe that we can be our own god. Often, we fail to see that these lies are from Satan and not our own. But the self-defeating thoughts are from the king of all lies. Satan cannot control our thoughts or behaviors. He can try to influence our thoughts making us think that they are our own.

The Bible tells us to resist the devil (James 4:7). But before we can resist Satan, we must submit ourselves to God. If we don't submit to God, we do not have the authority and strength to resist the devil—we remain in bondage. When we make Jesus Christ our Lord and Savior, He gives us the authority to defeat Satan. The Bible teaches that Jesus gives His disciples the authority over Satan. Disciple means student or follower. All Christians are followers of Jesus. We have the same authority that Jesus possessed.

The Bible makes a distinction between the Devil's *oppression* and the demon *possession* of a person. Matthew 9:32-33 and 12:22 describes a demon *oppressed* man. Matthew 8:28-34 describes the demon *possession* of two men. Christian doctrine holds that a Christian who is possessed by the Holy Spirit cannot be possessed by demonic forces. But Satan can try to *influence* us without permission.

---

[24] C.S. Lewis, *The Screwtape Letter*, (Old Tappan: Flemming H. Revell, 1978), 43

We have already learned that unrepented sin opens the door and gives Satan authority to *oppress* us. When we are in unrepented sin, demons attach themselves to our lives and try to keep us in constant torment. The Bible clearly teaches that the devil can place thoughts into your mind in and an effort to influence you to move away from God (see 1 Chronicles 21:1, John 13:2, and Acts 5:3). The question now becomes: How we as Christians stop Satan's oppression?

Jesus' work on the cross defeated Satan (1 John3:8) and reclaimed authority once and for all times (Matthew 28:18). As Christians we have the same authority over evil as Jesus did. We must understand and believe this to reclaim our authority. Our position *in Christ* is victorious! Satan has been defeated (Colossians 2:15). So many Christians live defeated lives because they either do not know or do not believe that Jesus gave all believers His authority.

How do we use this authority? Mark gave us an excellent example of how Jesus removed a demon from a man. Jesus rebuked the demon in the possessed man, Jesus said, "... come out of him!" (Mark 1:25). The name of Jesus is all powerful. Satan and the demons know who Jesus is and they must obey Him. When we feel there may be a demonic attack in our lives, take these steps:

1. Confess out loud that Jesus is your Lord and Savior. No need to shout, just speak normally
2. Confess all sins
3. Renounce all obstacles to healing presented in this book
4. Renounce out loud Satan and his demons, again, no need to shout or speak angerly or use profanity.

Completing these steps reclaims your authority over Satan. But remember that if you return to unrepented sin, Satan and his demons will return with a vengeance. This is taught by Jesus in Matthew 12:33-45, we will go into more detail later.

Prayer To Renounce Demonic Activity
Pray out loud:

Father,
In the name and authority of Jesus Christ, I command Satan, his demons,

and any evil spirits to release their hold on me. I am a child of the Most High God and I choose to do my Father's will. I bind every evil spirit and trust that my Father will send them to hell forever and ever. I will no longer listen to the lies of the evil ones. The truth of the gospel has set me free.
In Jesus' name I pray, Amen.

PRIDE

> *"Everyone who is arrogant in heart is an abomination to the LORD; be assured, he will not go unpunished" (Proverbs 16:5).*

The teaching regarding the spirit of pride in proverbs is very powerful. What we believe in our heart is how we behave. A prideful heart promotes and arrogant spirit.

Proverbs 16:18 says, "Pride goes before destruction, and a haughty spirit before a fall."

Haughty means arrogant or superior. This proverb could not be more true. If I were to point at one of the listed obstacles that contributed to my downfall, it would be excessive pride.

During the eight years when I went through all my foot surgeries, I was humbled. But I still had to be humbled more. Recovering from my surgery, I would be in a leg cast and had to remain stationary.

During this time, I would not allow anyone to help me. I was too prideful. I would even crawl on the ground to the kitchen to get a drink. My wife wanted to help, but I would not allow her. My thoughts would be that if I accepted help, I was less of a man. Asking for help is a sign of weakness. I know this is a stupid philosophy, but it was engrained into me. This attitude made my wife feel like less than a woman. I broke her heart. Again, hurt people hurt people.

Pride will negatively affect all of our relationships. Pride goes against God's will and desire for our lives. I renounced my prideful spirit. I prayed for God to help me overcome my excessive pride. And he did! I also asked forgiveness from my wife for being an idiot. She forgave me.

The Proverbs say, "There are six things that the LORD hates, seven that are an abomination to Him: haughty eyes [pride], a lying tongue, and hands that shed innocent blood, a heart that devises wicked plans, feet that make haste to run to evil, a false witness who breathes out lies, and one who sows discord among the brothers" (Verses 6:16-19).

The first trait listed is pride! Pride, selfishness, and independence cause us to judge others, causes us to focus on material things, causes us to gossip, and causes us to criticize others, and destroys lives and prevents healing. "Pride goes before destruction, and haughty spirit before a fall" (V. 16:18).

"Before destruction a man's heart is haughty, but humility comes before honor" (V. 18:12).

We must do whatever possible to rid ourselves of our prideful spirit. Since pride is a sin, we must renounce our pride, confess, and repent of it.

OCCULT ACTIVITY

> *"There should not be found among you anyone who burns his son or his daughter as an offering, anyone who practices divination or tells fortunes or interprets omens, or is a sorcerer, or a charmer or a medium or a necromancer or one who inquires of the dead, for whoever does these things is an abomination to the LORD" (Deuteronomy 18:10-13).*

If you watch television these days you will see shows featuring mediums, psychics, witches, vampires, and the living dead. These are new age ideals. Many people enjoy going to psychics or palm readers to predict their future fortunes. Even some law enforcement agencies have used psychics in cold cases. God strictly forbids His followers from participating in any occult activity. Merriam Webster defines occult as: matters regarded as involving the action or influence of supernatural or supernormal powers or some secret knowledge of them.

Leviticus 19:31 says, "Do not turn to mediums or necromancers; do not seek them out, and so make yourselves unclean [sinful] by them; I am the LORD your God."

Verses 20:6 adds, "If a person turns to mediums and necromancers, whoring after them, I will set My face against that person and will cut him off from among his people."

Necromancy refers to a form of witchcraft that attempts to talk to the dead. Divination is a practice of fortune telling or foretelling the future. The majority of mediums and psychics are con artists. They prey on the weak, the grieving and the lonely. But there are some who practice the occult that have this gift from Satan, sometimes called the spirit of divination.

Acts 16:16-18 tells the story of when Paul was in Philippi spreading the gospel: "As we [Paul, Silas, and Luke] were going to the place of prayer, we were met by a slave girl who had a spirit of divination and brought her owners much gain by fortunetelling. She followed Paul and us, crying out, 'These men are servants of the Most High God, who proclaim to you the way of salvation.' And this she kept doing for many days. Paul having become greatly annoyed turned and said to the spirit, 'I command you in the name of Jesus Christ to come out of her.' And it came out that very hour" (Luke 16:19-40).

Some other types of occult activity include:

1. Ouija Boards, Levitation, Spirit Guides
2. Magic Eight Balls, Mental Telepathy
3. Fortunetelling, Tarot Cards, Trances, Satanism
4. Spells or Curses, Talking to the Dead, Witchcraft
5. Mind Reading, Hypnosis, Seances
6. Palm Readers, New Age Movement which includes: a broad range of philosophies and practices traditionally viewed as occult, metaphysical, or paranormal.

All these listed activities are perpetrated by Satan and his demons. Any person involved in these activities is giving Satan authority to oppress them. Satan uses these activities to gain a foothold in your life that will certainly become a stronghold.

The only way to cleanse yourself is to renounce each involvement in these activities, confess and repent for your part in them and you will be forgiven.

A CRITICAL SPIRIT

> *"I [Jesus] tell you, on the day of judgment people will give account for every careless word they speak, for by your words you will be justified, and by your words you will be condemned" (Matthew 12:37).*

Our words have tremendous power—power to build up and power to tear down. Jesus tells us that on the day of judgment, each one of us will have to explain the words we spoke. Jesus' half-brother James explains it this way:

"And the tongue is a fire, a world of unrighteousness. The tongue is set among our members, staining the whole body, setting on fire the entire course of life, and set on fire by hell. For every kind of beast and bird, of reptile and sea creature, can be tamed and has been tamed by mankind, but no human being can tame the tongue. It is a restless evil, full of deadly poison. With it we bless our Lord and Father, and with it we curse people who are made in the likeness of God. From the same mouth come blessing and cursing. My brothers, these things ought not be so. Does a spring pour forth from the same opening both fresh and salt water? (James 3:6-11)

We use the same mouth to bless and praise God, and then use it to put down others. It is very easy to have a critical spirit. When we talk about being critical, I not only referring to being mean with our words, but also gossiping about others.

Gossiping about others is usualy in a negative context. Criticism and gossip have their roots in pride and the judgment of others. Every single person on this earth is a child of God and deserves to be treated as such. God's will is that we love others and not criticize them to their face or behind their backs.

The Bible says: "Do not grumble against one another, brothers, so that you may not be judged" (James 5:9).

There are many people who spend vast amounts of energy and money being careful with what they eat and drink. But Jesus tells us to watch what comes out our mouths,

"Do you not see that whatever goes into the mouth passes into the stomach and is expelled? But what comes out of the mouth proceeds from the heart, and these defiles a person. For out of the heart come evil thoughts, murder, adultery, sexual immorality, theft, false witness, slander. These are what defile a person" (Matthew 15:17-20).

Jesus was talking to His disciples who were telling Him that religious leaders were speaking against Him. The religious leaders were speaking against Jesus and His disciples because they did not follow the Jewish law of washing their hands prior to eating. Jesus here explains to them that it is not the dirt that goes into our mouths from unwashed hands, but it is the evil that comes out of our hearts that makes us unclean (Matthew 15:17-20).

A critical spirit comes from a bitter heart. We must heal our heart to remove the bitter roots that cause a critical spirit. Pride and judgment are sins. These habitual sins will steal our joy and keep us in pain. We must realign ourselves with God's will by renouncing the pride and judgment, confess and repent to initiate healing.

Proverbs 10:11 says, "The mouth of the righteous is a fountain of life." and 12:18 adds, " . . . the tongue of the wise brings healing."

In Matthew 22:36-39, Jesus tells us that the greatest commandment is to love the Lord with all your heart and with all your soul and with all your mind. And the second greatest commandment is to love your neighbor as yourself.

When we love one another as Jesus commands, we cannot tear them down with our words or deeds.

A SPIRIT OF ENVY

> *" . . . if you have bitter jealousy and selfish ambition in your hearts, do not boast and be false to the truth. This is not the wisdom, that comes down from above, but is earthly, unspiritual, demonic. For where jealousy and selfish ambition exist there will be disorder and every vile practice" (James 3:14-16).*

To envy or covet is to have the desire to possess something that does not belong to you. Envying anything is a waste of time due to the law of diminishing returns (more on this later). If and when we obtain the object of our envy, we become bored with that object and want more or something else. This law is absolute. Envy brings anger and judgment that will weigh us down and opens the door to Satan's oppression.

When we envy, we place that object of our envy above God. Objects of envy include: a big house, expensive car, powerful job, fame, fortune, clothing, and even religion. The object of our envy becomes our idol. This violates God's first commandment. We must place God first in our lives. Anything or anyone we place above Him is an idol and is sinful.

Paul talks about those who worship idols in Romans 1:28-32, "And since they [non-believers] did not see fit to acknowledge God, God gave them up to a debased mind to do what ought not to be done. They were filled with all manner of unrighteousness, evil, covetousness [envy], malice, deceit, maliciousness. They are gossips, slanderers, haters of God, insolent, haughty [prideful], boastful, inventors of evil, disobedient to parents, foolish, faithless, heartless, ruthless. Though they know God's decree that those who practice such things deserve to die, they not only do them but give approval to those who practice them."

Look at the order of the sins Paul lists, he places envy before murder. Think about that. This placement shows the importance of the commandment of not to envy. What is interesting in this text is that Paul talks about approving of those who practice sin. Non-believers who are slaves to their sin encourage others to sin and vicariously enjoy when others sin.

Envy is a difficult emotion to resist. But when we place God above all things, people we will experience the feeling of contentment that only God can provide.

1 Timothy 6: 6-10 says, "Now there is great gain in godliness with contentment for we brought nothing into the world, and we can take nothing out of the world. But if we have food and clothing, with these we will be content. But those who desire to be rich fall into temptation, into a snare, into many senseless and harmful desires that plunge people into ruin and destruction. For the love of money is a root of all kinds of evils. It is through this craving that some have wandered away from the faith and pierced themselves with many pangs."

Money itself is not evil. It is the love of money that makes it an idol. Paul tells us that the love of money has caused many people to leave Christianity. When we have a spirit of envy, we are blocked from doing God's will in our lives and prevents healing.

"A tranquil heart gives life to the flesh [body], but envy
makes the bones rot" (Proverbs 14:30).

Application

We must renounce our envious nature, then confess and repent for placing something or someone above God. Spiritual laws are absolute. We cannot deny them, ignore them, or not believe in them. This is an absolute immutable fact. These laws and principles are not complex. They are constructed for the operation of human nature. When we understand these laws that encompass all human relationships, we will have insight into every difficult trial.

All things are governed by the same basic laws. When expressed in physics: "For every action there must be an equal and opposite reaction." If your action is good, good is returned to you. However, if your action is bad, bad is returned to you.

We must clear all these obstacles from our lives by placing them to death on the cross. By doing this we place the cross between us and the things that prevent our healing. When we complete this process, healing will begin.

This will not be an easy process, but it will be well worth the effort to be free from the sin that keeps you in a prison without bars. I learned this firsthand, even though I was in a real prison with bars and locks on the doors. Afterword, I felt better than I had in years. I was set free from my emotional bondage. I had been in a self-imposed prison for so long that the experience of freedom from my bonds was the best experience I ever felt (yes, even better that winning a race).

As you go through this process, deal with each obstacle by itself. Resist the urge to speed through this process. Yes, there will be pain and it will not be easy, but trying to go the easy route will not work. Use the prayers in the appendix to help guide you through the healing process. Listen to the Holy Spirit who will help you through each step. Make sure you document your journey in your journal. God bless you as your healing begins.

CHAPTER 8

SPIRITUAL LAWS THAT AFFECT HEALING

"The law of the LORD is perfect, reviving the soul; the testimony of the LORD is sure. Making wise the simple; the precepts of the LORD are right, rejoicing the heart; the commandment of the LORD is pure, enlightening the eyes; the fear of the LORD is clean, enduring forever; the rules of the LORD are true, and righteous altogether. More to be desired are they than gold, even much fine gold; sweeter also than honey, the drippings of the honeycomb. Moreover, by them is Your servant warned; in keeping there is great reward"

Psalm 19:7-11

As with the obstacles to healing, we must understand the biblical laws and principles that lead to; or prevent our healing. These laws and principles are in the scriptures. All are equally important to follow.

UNREPENTED SIN

> *"Behold, the LORD's hand is not shortened, that it cannot save, or His ear dull, that He cannot hear; but your iniquities [sins] have*

> *made a separation between you and your God, and your sins have hidden His face from you so that He does not hear [your prayers]" (Isaiah 59:1-2).*

Sin separates us from God. He doesn't love us any less, but our relationship is disrupted. This is a consequence of sin. If you have been saved, you are forgiven.

1 John 1:9 says, "If we confess our sins, He is faithful and just to forgive us our sins and to cleanse us from all unrighteousness."

If you have not been saved, please make Jesus your Lord and Savior right now. Have Him cleanse you from the sin that is causing you so much pain. In the appendix there is a prayer called the "sinner's prayer," pray this to receive forgiveness and eternal life in heaven.

FORGIVENESS

Forgiveness is a spiritual law. Without forgiveness there is no healing. Unforgiveness is the number one method that Satan uses to oppress Christians and keep them in habitual sin.

2 Corinthians 2:10-11 says, "Anyone whom you forgive, I [Paul] also forgive. Indeed, what I have forgiven, if I have forgiven anything, has been for your sake in the presence of Christ, so that we would not be outwitted by Satan; for we are not ignorant of his designs."

Jesus paid a huge price so that we could be forgiven. For Jesus' sake we must also forgive. We must base our relationship with others on the same criteria on which God bases His relationship with us: love, acceptance, and forgiveness.[25]

Forgiveness is an issue in almost every traumatic or overwhelming life event. Forgiveness is a command from God. In Matthew 6:14-15, Jesus tells His disciples, "For if you forgive others their trespasses, your heavenly Father will also forgive you, but if you do not forgive others their trespasses, neither will your Father forgive your trespasses."

---

[25] Neil Anderson, *Victory Over the Darkness*, (New York, Bethany House Publishers, 2013), 190.

Forgiveness Means:

- We give up the right to judge others and to seek our own revenge
- We release the debt owed to us by the person who wounded us
- We release the person who wounded us to God
- Knowing God will dispense judgment.

Forgiveness Does Not Mean:

- What happened to you is alright
- That the offender is no longer accountable
- That we must forget the wounding ever happened
- That we must reconcile with our offender and trust them again

Forgiveness does mean, however, that we must do our best to ask forgiveness from those that we harmed, because God commands us to seek forgiveness from those we harmed (Matthew 5:23-24). If the offender does not forgive you, the sin is then on them.

You did the right thing. Forgiveness is not about our feelings; it is about our obedience to the word of God. God has forgiven you; you must also forgive yourself and others.

We must choose to forgive. Faking forgiveness will not result in healing. Blanket forgiveness does not work. We must forgive each of our offenders individually.

An example of blanket forgiveness: "I forgive all those who harmed me." An Example of proper forgiveness: "I forgive my father for beating me." The difference matters.

It may take several attempts to feel the forgiveness. Keep forgiving until you feel peace in your heart. When you no longer experience negative emotions when speaking about the incident or offender, you have truly forgiven. Take it slow and do it properly for long-lasting healing.

BITTER ROOT JUDGMENTS

Judging others is another important spiritual law that impedes healing. Jesus commands us not to judge one another.

Matthew 7:1-2 says, "Judge not, that you be not judged. For with the judgment you pronounce you will be judged, and with the measure you use it will be measured to you."

The word judge should be changed to "condemn." We can judge others for their behavior, but we should never condemn that person for who they are. It is when we condemn others for who they are that we sin. Christians should love the sinner but hate their sin.

Jesus goes to say in verses 3-5, "Why do you see the speck [sin] in your brother's eye [life], but do not notice the log [lots of sin] that is in your own eye? . . . You hypocrite, first take the log out of your own eye and then you will see clearly to take the speck out of your brother's eye."

Humans love to fix other people. We are quick to judge them for something they did, but we rarely acknowledge our own sins or shortcomings. Jesus tells us to look at ourselves before we condemn others. Paul knows this principle and understands human behavior.

Paul writes in Romans 2:1-3, "Therefore, you have no excuse O man, every one of you who judges. For in passing judgment on another you condemn yourself, because you, the judge, practice the very same things. We know that the judgment of God rightly falls on those who practice such things."

Paul warns us that when we judge and condemn others, we are condemned to do the very same thing. The law is absolute. God will judge us for this hypocrisy.

We can judge a person's behavior but never judge the person for who they are. When we judge others, we automatically place ourselves above that person. We are telling everyone that we are better than them. We become judge and jury, like God we determine guilt.

Our relationship with that person is broken. Everything they now do is filtered through our glasses of judgment.

We must never make judgments against our parents. This is a violation of one of God's commandments. We often bury these bitter root judgments we have against our parents until they pop up at a triggering event.

Judging our parents is always a sin, because it goes against God's will. Judgments against our parents will affect every aspect of our lives, as well as our physical well-being. It is not our will that we must follow, but God's. When we condemn others, it is impossible to forgive. Even if we are able to forgive and we do not renounce the judgment; we remain in sin. We must renounce the judgment and forgive our offender.

Because of my judgment and hatred of drug dealers, I would later become just like them. Because of my sinful judgments, I doomed myself and became addicted to opioids and gave drugs to someone else. I became the same as the people I hated and condemned for who they were. I didn't just hate their sin, I hated them. I now have a better understanding on how and why people do the things they do and can empathize with wounded people.

Violation of this law has serious consequences. Judgments must be renounced, confessed and then repented of in order for healing to begin.

Bitter Root Expectancies

Although this is not a law, expectancies are obstacles to healing. A bitter root expectancy is a stronghold that occurs when we fertilize the seed of trauma with unforgiveness and anger. The bitter root forms in our heart. The roots from the seed overtake our hearts and infiltrates our belief system, our emotions, and thus effects our behavior.

When we are wounded from a traumatic incident(s) or overwhelming life event(s) we experience pain from the wound. In order to alleviate the pain and cope with what happened, we often make a false assumption based on what happened to us. For example, we might think that our lives will never be the same. We then expect our life to move forward in a negative direction. We seldom expect our life to move forward in a positive direction.

Thus, when we hold onto these negative expectancies in our life, it is like a self-fulfilling prophecy. When we believe our life will move forward in a certain way, it almost always does. In the Book of Job, Job is lamenting on what is happening to him. He says,

"What I have feared has come upon me; what I dreaded has happened to me" (Job 3:25). What Job believed would happen to him did. An example of an expectancy is:

A female child who had been sexually abused by her father. Her mother never interceded and stopped the abuse. The young female victim of sexual assault often makes the expectancy that all men are abusers, she cannot trust authority, and that she is not worthy of being loved. Her mother did not love her enough to stop the abuse. The expectancy is that she is not lovable and that all men are abusers.

Having this thought pattern engrained in the mind of the victim, we can see how she might respond to a new love interest. She will most likely sabotage each relationship. She will always be drawn to a man who will abuse her because this is what she has been modeled, and this is what she believes she deserves.

Another example is in a marriage where a spouse commits adultery, the victim spouse is wounded because of the betrayal. The victim spouse will most likely never trust the offending spouse again. They will often create the expectancy that "every man/woman cheats." If they stay together, their expectancy will cause a lack of trust and jealousy that will eventually tear apart their marriage. If they divorce, he/she may never trust their new spouse and they will almost always sabotage the relationship because of their belief system.

A final example is being raised a child of a critical parent(s) with constant verbal abuse. This situation may make the child create an expectancy that says, "I'm no good," or "I'm not good enough," or "I must work very hard to deserve people's love." It may also cause that child to make the expectancy that they will always have to perform and work harder to gain other's approval—even God's approval. They may never be at peace with their inner self.

Expectancies cause us to fear the future and prevents us from taking risks in life. 2 Timothy 1:7 says, "God gave us a spirit not of fear but of power and love and self-control."

The expectancies we form in our hearts are influenced by Satan. They are meant to keep us in our pain so that we remain defeated. Expectancies are in opposition to God's will.

All relationships will be negatively affected by bitter root expectancies. Wounded people who create expectancies will often sabotage every relationship they are involved in so that the expectation will come true and confirm their belief system. Expectancies must be renounced to kill this stronghold.

INNER VOWS

As with bitter root expectancies, inner vows are not a spiritual law or principle, but is an obstacle to our healing. Inner Vows are a result of a traumatic event(s), or overwhelming life events(s) where we experience a broken heart. We make inner vows to protect us from further wounding. We try to protect our heart in any way we can. We make ourselves a promise to do or not to do something that will prevent us from being wounded again. Inner vows tend to make us push people away and prevent us from having healthy relationships. Inner vows are sinful because they are about our will, not God's will.

Examples of inner vows include:

- When a close friend betrays your trust, you may make inner vow that says, "I will never trust anyone again." If a person becomes the victim of a robbery or a physical assault, the person may make an inner vow that says, "The world is not safe, I will never go out in public again."

When we try to protect ourselves, it prevents us from taking risks. Life is about risk. We will never enter into new friendships or relationships unless we take a risk on getting to know new people. We will never try a new job because we fear what the new co-workers will say about us.

We need to be open to new things and new people. There is never a guarantee that we will be disappointed in other people, but we are always richer for having known that person, we will always learn something from every single person we meet. Inner vows prevent us from moving forward our lives. Inner vows must be renounced.

Things we must understand about inner vows: Inner vows are a determination of our will, not God's.

Inner vows are motivated by bitterness and fear. Inner vows are defense mechanisms that opens the door to Satan's oppression. Inner vows lead to destructive patterns in our lives that are based upon fear, disbelief, or lack of faith and trust in God. Inner vows tend to multiply, one vow leads to another, then another. Inner vows often result in isolation. God created us to be in fellowship with others, not to live in fear alone away from other Christians. When God created Adam, He said it was not good for man to be alone.

SOWING AND REAPING

> *"Do not be deceived; God is not mocked, for whatever one sows, that will he also reap. For the one who sows to his own flesh will from the flesh reap corruption, but the one who sows to the Spirit will from the Spirit reap eternal life" (Galatians 6:7-8).*

Sowing and Reaping is a very important spiritual law to understand. If you do not care about the other laws and principles discussed herein, please make sure you follow this one. Paul is telling us that no one can fool God. Nothing can be hidden from Him. Everything we do has consequences, good consequences for good behavior and bad for negative behavior.

Sowing and reaping are agricultural terms that the people during biblical times would understand. Remember, the only way people could survive back then was through farming. Farmers would sow (plant) seeds and when the crops or plants matured, they were harvested. At harvest time the farmer would harvest their crops by cutting them with a sickle. This harvesting is called reaping. When we read and study the Bible, we need to understand the traditions and customs of that time to place scripture in its correct context.

If you practice biblical principles like loving one another, forgiving one another, helping those in need, and remaining humble, you will be in God's will. Also, if you practice these things, you will reap blessing and healing.

Proverbs 11:24-25 says, "One gives freely, yet grows all the richer; another withholds what he should give, and always suffers want. Whoever brings blessing will be enriched, and one who waters will himself be watered."

We see that when we do good, good will return to us, and when we do not do what is right, bad things will return to us. A lot of people live a lie. They tell others that they give to charities and volunteer at soup kitchens to appear godly. They may be able to fool some of the people, but they cannot fool God. God sees and knows all.

This principle can be summed up by saying. "Always do the right thing." The law of sowing and reaping is very simple: so simple that it is deceiving. We do not think about it, but when we realize how it works in our lives, we will be prepared for the difficult trials and we can then prevent condemning ourselves to failure.

THE LAW OF INCREASE

This spiritual law goes hand-in-hand with sowing and reaping. Whatsoever you sow will be returned to you with increase. If you sow for the good, all blessings returned to you will be with increase. When you sow bad or evil things, the bad that you will reap will be return with increase.

2 Corinthians 9:6 says, "The point is this: whoever sows sparingly will also real sparingly, and whoever sows bountifully will also reap bountifully." And Mark 4:24 says, "And He [Jesus] said to them [His disciples], 'Pay attention to what you hear': with the measure you use, it will be measured to you, and still more will be added to you."

Mark is describing when Jesus was telling the parable about the sowing the seed of God's word. It is in a different context but is still the same principle of increase.

And finally, in Hosea 8:7 we read, "They sow to the wind, and reap a whirlwind." In other words:

> *Do good, and more good will return to you. Do bad, and more bad will return to you.*

As with sowing and reaping, the reaping rarely occurs immediately. The consequences to your behavior may take months or even years to return to you. This is an extremely important spiritual law, as all decisions you make should be filtered through this law. There are consequences to your behavior, good or bad.

When you do the right thing, God will bless you bountifully. But if you decided to do things that go against God's will, the consequences of sin will be increased, again. So, simply do the right thing all the time!

THE LAW OF DIMINISHING RETURNS

Although this is not a biblical law, it is a spiritual principle that is important to understand. It is the principle of how sin affects our conscience. Each time we do something that we know we should not be doing or not doing something we should be doing, our consciences gets "seared" or calloused a little bit.

The first time we sin we will feel really bad for what we have done. Our conscience has been designed to convict us until we rectify the situation, but we often ignore our conscience. As we continue in sin over and over again, our conscience begins to convict us less and less. Eventually our conscience will stop convicting us altogether, we then try to justify our sinful behavior in some way or even begin to believe the lies from Satan that our sin is permissible.

Our conscience builds a tolerance to the sin just as our bodies build a tolerance to a drug or medication. The more of the drug we take, the more our bodies get used to the substance. Once this occurs the user will be required to take more and more of the drug to achieve the desired effect.

When our conscience stops convicting us for our sin, we often step up the sin a notch. Sin is often fun and gives some of us a rush or excitement. With no conscience, we need to increase the sin in order to obtain the same sensation or rush we experienced during the first time we sinned. This leads us to much greater sin. Some examples of this law include:

When we ride a rollercoaster for the very first time it is scary and exciting; adrenaline pumps through the body adding to the excitement. But after you have ridden that same rollercoaster ten or twenty times you will have built up a tolerance and the ride becomes boring. When this occurs, you will seek out a more exciting rollercoaster ride elsewhere. But when you do, the same thing will happen. You will never experience the same sensation after the first time you do something.

Another example is when you lie to a friend or a loved one for the first time, your conscience will tell you that you did wrong. You will feel uneasy and uncomfortable. But when you tell more lies, your conscience will convict you less and less. Eventually it will stop bothering you altogether. This may cause you to lie more with even greater untruths.

Most of us take office supplies from our place of work to use at home. A pen here, some computer paper there, and so on. After a while, we begin to believe we are entitled to these little extras because we work hard, are under paid and underappreciated. The truth is this is theft. As we continue to justify our behavior, we may even escalate our thefts by falsifying timecards or expense accounts, maybe even dipping into the petty cash box for lunch money. Sin becomes a slippery slope.

Lying, cheating and stealing are all behaviors where Satan influences us. The "world" and society even condone some of this behavior under certain circumstances. Video games and movies glorify thieves, drug dealers and promote worldly activities. As Christians we must resist the influences of this world that Satan controls.

When tolerance to sin has been built up, we remain in habitual sin. We are held in bondage to that sin and it begins to control our behaviors; we are a slave to the sin. We always want more. The "world" tells us to seek out fame, fortune, and power. This is not God's will. We see this in who the world idolizes; movie stars, sports stars, and reality television personalities. Why don't we idolize those who heal the sick every day or scientist who discover new drugs to prevent and heal illnesses?

Society influences us into believing that if we just had that new Corvette, we will be popular and meet the love of our life, if we just had that plastic surgery, people would adore us, and if we dressed and acted like the reality TV stars, we will be popular and influential. And when we get that Corvette or plastic surgery and we find nothing changes; we remain the same. Then we believe maybe if we got a Ferrari and liposuction, then things will get better.

We will always want more and more because nothing fills the void in our hearts. It is only God that can make our hearts whole. Satan wants us to believe that power, money, influence are the finer things in life, but due to the law of diminishing returns, possessions and power have no influence on our self-worth. Only God gives us our self-worth.

In Matthew 6:21 Jesus says, "For where your treasure is, there
your heart will be also."

The richest wisest man who ever lived, King Solomon said, "He who loves money will not be satisfied with money, nor he who loves wealth with his income; this is also vanity" (Ecclesiastes 5:10).

He is saying that man will never be satisfied with money, it only causes anxiety. Wealth and power feed pride. Wanting more possessions is not in and of itself sinful, it becomes a sin as we place the possessions and their acquisition above God that it becomes an idol. The very first commandment says, "You shall have no other gods before me" (Exodus 20:3). The god we idolize can be our job, our car, our family, our money, arts, or anything we place before the worship of the true God.

The only way to protect our conscience from callousing is not to enter into habitual sin. I know what you're thinking, "I am a sinner." Yes. We are all sinners. When we do sin, we must heed the Holy Spirit's warning to stop, confess and repent the sin before we become calloused to the sin that will eventually enslave us. It is that simple! Confess and acknowledge your sin to God, repent for the sin and be forgiven. When we listen to the Holy Spirit's voice, we remain in God's will.

HONORING YOUR PARENTS

Honoring your parents is another spiritual law that affects almost every one of us. The fifth commandment is to honor our parents (Exodus 20:12). The first five commandments are focused on God, the last five are on how we should conduct ourselves. Honoring our parents is first on the list of how we are to act. I do not believe God placed this commandment in this position by accident. This is an important commandment. The word "honor" is defined as showing great respect or to hold in high regard.

Deuteronomy 5:16 says, "Honor you father and your mother, as the LORD your God commanded you, that your days may be long and it may go well with you in the land that the LORD God is giving you."

Think about that! Honor your parents so that things will go well with you and you will have a long life.

Deuteronomy 27:16 adds, "Cursed be anyone who dishonors his father or his mother."

Paul tells us that this law is still valid in his letter to the church in Ephesus, "Children obey your parents in the Lord, for this is right. Honor you father and mother (this is the first commandment with a promise), that it may go well with you and that you may live long in the land" (Ephesians 6:1-3).

The first commandment with a promise! God promises you that when you honor your parents everything will go well with you and you will live a long life. How does this apply to those living with the pain of trauma? Healing!

For some of you, this law will be difficult to follow. Many parents do not deserve to be honored. Maybe your parent(s) have abused you, neglected you, abandoned you, or just never let you have a voice, so you are still holding onto unforgiveness, anger, hate, resentment, and judgments against them.

Maybe you have protected yourself with bitter root expectancies or inner vows so that they nor anyone else could harm you again. The pain you're feeling is from these sinful responses you committed against your parent(s). This sin has kept you in a cycle of pain and made you a slave to your sin.

The only way out of your pain to begin healing is to renounce the judgments on your parent(s), renounce the bitter root expectancies, inner vows, and forgive them for what you perceive they have done to you. Then confess and repent the sinful response. You will soon feel the weight of the pain lifting off your shoulders as your healing begins.

Honoring your parents does not require reconciliation or mean that you ever have to trust them again. It simply means that you acknowledge that they brought you into this world and gave you life. This alone deserves your respect.

I have talked with hundreds of inmates who told me their stories of what their parents had done to them, some horrific. If you could research your parent's childhood, you may find that they were also victims of your grandparents. They may have never learned how to raise a child properly because of their abuse.

If you look at it from this perspective, your entire attitude changes because you can see how they went through the same things that you did. They knew no better. If you have not yet realized a pattern in your life, look for it now. If we allow this cycle to go on unchecked, it will continue for generations.

Stop the cycle now before you become your parent(s) and model the same behavior. If you see this cycle, stop it now! Break the cycle today and accept God's healing.

I met a man from Texas who told me about what happened to him growing up with an alcoholic father who physically abused him. As this man grew up, he hated his father for the abuse he suffered. He judged his father as a bad man who liked to beat up children. He also judged his mother as a bad parent for not stopping the abuse and protecting him.

At a young age this man made an inner vow to never be like his father. As the boy grew to become an adult and had children of his own, he saw himself becoming his father. Due to his hateful judgments of his parents, he dishonored them. The laws of bitter root judgments and dishonoring parents were activated, as well as the law of sowing and reaping. He ultimately did the very same things as his father.

He became an alcoholic and physically abused his children and wife. These laws are absolute. It was not until he renounced this behavior, confessed and repented, that things turned around in his life. He stopped drinking and began to rebuild his relationship with his wife and children. He also started working on his relationship with his father. Things went better from that point on.

SOUL TIES

This spiritual law God instituted around marriage. Marriage is to be monogamous, a complete union of a male and female.

Genesis 2:24 says, "Therefore a man shall leave his father and mother and hold fast to his wife, and they shall become one flesh."

God is saying that when a man and a woman are joined together in marriage or a sexual relationship, the two are joined together spiritually; they become one. This applies to homosexual relationships also. Any two people in a sexual relationship will develop a soul tie. Their souls become bound together.

The seventh commandment is, "You shall not commit adultery" (Exodus 20:14). God's will is for a man and a woman to marry and remain together forever (except under certain circumstances).

A soul tie is created when a couple commits fornication (sex) or adultery (sex outside of marriage). They will be bound together until renounced. Fornication and adultery are sins. If they remain unconfessed, they open the door to Satan's oppression.

1 Thessalonians 4:3-5 says, "For this is the will of God, your sanctification, that you abstain from sexual immorality; that each one of you know to control his own body in holiness and honor, not in the passion of lust like the Gentiles [non-Jews] who do not know God. . . . "

"He who commits adultery lacks sense, he who does it destroys himself" (Proverbs 6:32).

We see that sexual sin is not God's will for us. Holding unrepented habitual sin prevents our sanctification. Our body is the residence for God's Holy Spirit, we are not to defile it. Paul explains this law in his letter to the church in Corinth who were committing sexual sin.

First Corinthians 6:13-20 says, "Food is meant for the stomach and the stomach for food—and God will destroy both one and the other. The body is not meant for sexual immorality, but for the Lord and the Lord for the body. And God raised the Lord and will also raise us up by his power. Do you not know that your bodies are members of Christ? Shall I then take the members of Christ and make them members of a prostitute? Never! Or do you not know that he who is joined to a prostitute becomes one body with her? For, as it is written, 'The two will become one flesh.' But he who is joined to the Lord becomes one spirit with Him. Flee from sexual immorality. Every other sin a person commits is outside the body, but the sexually immoral person sins against his own body. Or do you not know that your body is a temple of the Holy Spirit within you whom you have from God? You are not your own, for you were brought with a price. So, glorify God in your body."

The context here is about Christians engaging in sex with a prostitute, immoral sexual activity, and adultery. This unholy union is created between two souls and tied together. This union remains long after the sexual relationship is over. This sin is against our own body as well as God.

When we place our trust in Christ, we are given the Holy Spirit that resides in our body. Our body is then the temple of the Holy Spirit. We are to walk by the Holy Spirit and not glorify our sexual desires out of marriage.
"For the desires of the flesh are against the Spirit, and the desires of the Spirit are against the flesh . . . " (Galatians 5:17).

These two oppose one another and cause inner turmoil that not only keeps us in a cycle of pain, but allows Satan to keep us in sin and emotional distress. As you can imagine this will negatively impact every relationship and robs us of our peace and joy. Each soul tie must be renounced separately.
In prayer, renounce each illicit relationship separately. Confess the relationship to God and repent for it/them. You will feel the weight lifted off your soul.

STRONGHOLDS

> *"The LORD is my rock and my fortress and my deliverer, my God, my rock in whom I take refuge, my shield, and the horn of my salvation, my stronghold" (Psalm 18:2).*

A stronghold is a way of thinking and feeling that over time becomes a habit. The function of a stronghold is to keep us from thinking effectively or feeling repentant. Unchecked strongholds drive our behavior in the self-destructive direction.

As stated earlier, our belief system is learned from the environment we were raised in, as well as the traumatic experiences we have been through. Our feelings, decisions, and behaviors are based on those beliefs. When we respond to a traumatic event in a sinful way and hold onto this response, it becomes a habit engrained in us. It then becomes our default response.

If you exercise this habit long enough, a stronghold is established. God created us with the freedom of choice to respond to trauma in the manner we feel is appropriate. A stronghold removes this freedom of choice because the stronghold supersedes all other choices.

An example of this is alcoholism. It is very common that when some people go through extreme stress, they have a drink of alcohol to calm down. When this becomes a habit, it can become alcoholism.

This is a stronghold that is difficult to overcome alone because it is influenced by evil spirits. But with God all things are possible. As we overcome the stronghold, we must be vigilant and continue walking in the Holy Spirit to prevent the return of the stronghold.

Jesus tells us in Matthew 12:43-45, "When the unclean spirit has gone out of a person, it passes through waterless places seeking rest, but finds none. Then it says, 'I will return to my house from which I came.' And when it comes, it finds the house empty, swept, and put in order. Then it goes and brings with it seven other spirits more evil than itself, and they enter and dwell there, and the last state of that person is worse than the first."

To defeat a stronghold, we spiritually cleanse by confession and repentance. This cleansing and repentance is what Jesus refers to as the house has been cleaned. But if we don't fill our house (our heart) with the Holy Spirit, it remains empty, ripe for the stronghold's return. A stronghold's return is called a relapse. Often, a relapse is worse than the original stronghold. It is vitally important that after a stronghold of any type has been defeated, you must continue in your Christian walk with the Holy Spirit.

Satan uses and takes advantage of our strongholds to control our behavior. Strongholds include: unforgiveness, inferiority, addictions, homosexuality, hostility, and many more. Strongholds are an act of the flesh; without Jesus our flesh will control us.

Satan likes strongholds because they are based on fear as well as self-centered behavior. Strongholds prevent us from opening our hearts to God, they block God's truth and keep us in our pain. Strongholds keep us in bondage to the sinful way of thinking and behaving influenced by the stronghold.

Another type of stronghold is called a corporate stronghold. A corporate stronghold is difficult to dismantle because they are deeply engrained. A corporate stronghold is a way of thinking, feeling, and acting that results in a group of people possessing a common mentality that they share. Satan builds these strongholds with the lies he instills in people from different cultures, economic classes, political groups, religious groups, and certain careers.

An example is the career of a prison correctional officer. The majority of the officers are taught an us-vs-them attitude.

The lie from Satan is that all inmates are violent people who take advance of everyone they can. If accepted, this lie takes over the officer's thought process and influences their behavior. Their behavior results in aggressive abusive acts, oppression of inmates, an uncaring attitude for elderly or sickly, and often racists attitudes towards their common enemy.

Colossians 2:8 says, "See that no one takes you captive by philosophy and empty deceit, according to human tradition, according to the eternal spirits of the world, and not according to Christ."

This thought process is instilled into new recruits and hammered into their training programs and is said to be "traditional"—inmates are bad—lower than dirt. This is not what the Bible teaches. Satan uses corporate strongholds to imprison the minds of certain groups of people to destroy the conscience and blind them to logic, facts, and the truth of the gospel.

Strongholds can be destroyed, but this is a spiritual battle. We defeat Satan's lies with God's truths. We must renew our minds through the hearing of God's word, Christian fellowship, books like this, and Bible studies.

As we mature in Christ, we learn to take every thought captive and compare it to the word of God. Satan's lies are disregarded while godly thoughts are reinforced. When we learn God's truth and reject Satan's lies, we prevent new strongholds from forming and destroy the old strongholds that have kept us in bondage.

CHAPTER 9

SPIRITUAL WEAPONS YOU NEED FOR HEALING

> *"... Christ loved the church and gave Himself up for her, that He might sanctify her, having cleansed her by the washing of water with the word, so that He might present the church to Himself in splendor, without spot or wrinkle or any such thing, that she might be holy and without blemish"*
>
> *Ephesians 5:25-27*

As your relationship with Jesus grows, healing occurs and your mind is renewed. It is imperative not to return to the old ways of the world. Some of us may have to leave friends or family who are bad influences or just negative angry people, behind. We can find like-minded friends who can keep us on the right track in church.

It is God's will that we fellowship with other Christians. Upon regeneration we are in Christ and He is in us (2 Corinthians 13:5).

THE CHURCH

1 Corinthians 12:12-31 explains "the body of Christ." The body of Christ is the church. The head of the body or church is Jesus Christ (Colossians 1:18). The analogy is of a human body, Christ is the head, the leader, the shot-caller, the brains of the outfit. Paul says that there are many

members of the church body and adds that all Christians are baptized into one body through the Holy Spirit who is living in each Christian. Paul adds that the Holy Spirit is in ALL Christians, "Jews or Greek, slaves or free" (Galatians 3:28).

Then Paul relates each church member's position within the church. He describes the importance that all members work in the church in harmony, dependence on each other, and to care for one another. Paul emphasizes that each member of the church has been placed in the position by God. God chose the members and arranged them within the church. There should be humility, respect and honor for every job.

Paul gives an example of humility in verse twenty-one, "The eye cannot say to the hand, 'I have no need for you! nor again the head to the feet, I have no need for you.'"

Paul insists that all members of the church are just as important in the working of the church. There should be no division within the church. "If one member suffers, all suffer together; if one member is honored, all rejoice together" (v 26).

Paul goes on to describe the hierarchy of the church listing apostles, prophets, and teachers. One of Jesus' duties was to begin the earthly Christian church. He built a church that changed the world. This church will outlive Earth. Jesus loves the church and gave His life for her. Christ's love for the church should drive all Christians to become a member of a Bible believing church.

As we get involved in a local church, we meet other Christians with similar interests and goals. This fellowship helps us in our walk with the Holy Spirit. We are to encourage one another and to support one another (Hebrews 3:13).

As we support the church and its congregation, our faith in God increases. Through encouragement we are able to resist temptation. There is no better place to grow spiritually than in the church. The church should be a place where anyone can go and receive spiritual healing from the loving support of its members.

Today, this appears to be the exception rather than the rule. Pastor Jeff Kenney who led me to the Lord, but it was his church that made me stay and grow. The people there were kind, loving, forgiving, and compassionate. There are too many churches that believe sinners are not welcome.

I spoke to a lot of believers who were asked to leave their church after they went to prison. I spoke to three pastors who were asked not to return to their church after they were indicted. These were broken people who needed support and love. The church was meant to be a hospital for the spiritually and emotionally ill. There is no one in the church who is better than anyone else, even pastors and elders. We are all sinners.

The church needs to be a safe place for all people, a judgment free zone. This includes ex-felons, non-believers, people of any sexual orientation, the homeless, and those with emotional issues. Especially those from other religions seeking answers. NO ONE should be excluded. All humans are God's children. Churches must show the love that Jesus exemplified. When non-believers see the love we exhibit, they see Jesus in us.

The purpose of the church is threefold. The first purpose is the ministry to God. The church is a place where believers get together to worship God. In Paul's letter to the church at Colossae, he tells the church to, " . . . singing psalms and hymns and spiritual songs, with thankfulness in your hearts to God" (Colossians 3:16). This is the reason true Bible believing churches sing praise and worship songs prior to the sermon.

The church congregation is to minister to each other. Paul told the church in Ephesus that some people in the congregation were given gifts that,

" . . . equip the saints [Christians] for the work of ministry, for building up the body of Christ, until we all attain to the unity of the faith and of the knowledge of the Son of God, to mature manhood, to the measure of the stature of the fulness of Christ" (Ephesians 4:12-13).

As the members of the church build each other up, they mature in the faith. All members of the church are to nurture and minister to each other. The church must also evangelize. Jesus commanded his disciples to " . . . make disciples of all nations" (Matthew 28:19).

Jesus told us that our primary mission is to bring the gospel to our communities, our cities, our state, and country. This includes caring for the poor and needy in our communities through service.

Luke 6:35-36 says, " . . . love your enemies, and do good, and lend, expecting nothing in return, and your reward will be great, and you will be sons of the Most High, for He is kind to the ungrateful and the evil. Be merciful, even as your Father is merciful."

Often helping the needy turns into evangelism.

Bringing the truth of the gospel to non-believers can be frightening. Satan makes us believe that we do not know the Bible well enough or we are not articulate enough. He gets us to be embarrassed to be a follower of Jesus. Do not worry about these things. If you understand that Satan is trying to influence you, you can attack him with the word of God. We are given constant strength through our relationship with Jesus. Jesus provides us with the strength and the Holy Spirit will provide us with the words.

Moses was scared to speak God's word. When God called him to deliver the Israelites who were enslaved to the Egyptians, Moses tried to get out of his calling; Moses said,

"' . . . Oh, my LORD, I am not eloquent, either in the past or since You have spoken to Your servant, but I am slow of speech and of tongue.' Then the Lord said to him, 'Who has made man's mouth? Who makes him mute, or deaf, or seeing, or blind? Is it not I, the LORD? Now therefore go, and I will be with your mouth and teach you what you shall speak'" (Exodus 4:10-12).

There is no need to be frightened. God asks us to plant the seed of the gospel into someone's heart. God will lift the veil (2 Corinthians 4:3-4) and allow them to hear the gospel. You must not badger a non-believer because Satan has them blind to the truth. If you plant the seed, another will water the seed by talking about Jesus providing them their testimony. Then it is up to God to bring them to salvation.

First Corinthians 3:6-9 gives us an example of this process, "I [Paul] planted, Apollos watered, but God gave the growth. So neither he who plants nor he who waters is anything, but only God who gives the growth. He who plants and he who waters are one [the body of Christ], and each will receive his wages according to his labor. For we are God's fellow workers. You are God's field, God's building."

A church that teaches the Bible will ensure that these three objectives are met. Every Christian should seek out a church that is near them. Do not be afraid to go to several churches in an effort to determine which one provides the best fit for you. As you narrow down the list, do not be afraid to ask questions of the congregation or church administration. It's is very important that the pastor and board of elders believe that the Bible is the true and accurate word of God. And that the pastor teaches the Bible.

More and more churches are becoming "feel good" churches. They are uplifting, however, they seldom teach the true word of God. In order to mature as Christians, we must learn the scriptures and how to apply them to our lives. Once you find a church that suits you, stick with it. No church is perfect, just like no family is perfect.

Solidarity in the church is of utmost importance. When we have minor petty disputes, we break God's heart. I have two daughters. As they were growing up, they fought with each other as most siblings do.

I grew up as an only child, so when I watch my girls argue, it breaks my heart. God the Father feels the same way. The family of God must stand united. This does not mean we cannot have healthy debates. It is when we allow the debate to become personal that we become vicious with one another.

Matthew 18:20 says, "For where two or three are gathered in My name there am I [Jesus] among them." If we remember that Jesus is with us during fellowship, we will humble ourselves before one another."

Galatians 6:2 says, "Bear one another's burdens and so fulfill the law of Christ."

And Philippians 2:3-4 adds, "Do nothing from selfish ambition or conceit, but in humility count others more significant than yourselves. Let each of you look not only to his own interests, but also to the interests of others."
A Christian's church life is an important part of their walk. The fellowship with other like-minded Christians is essential to maturing as a Christian.

YOUR TESTIMONY

> *"Sing to the LORD, bless His name; tell of His salvation from day to day. Declare His glory among the nations, His marvelous works among all the peoples!" (Psalms 96:2-3)*

Your testimony is a very powerful tool. It is simply a story on what God has done in your life. Testimony is defined as a statement given as evidence. When you give your Christian testimony to a non-believer, you provide them evidence that we have a loving God. Testimonies often result from a difficult trial.

Your testimony may minister to someone who is in need, maybe even someone who is going through a similar trial than you have. It is the will of God to give your testimony of deliverance, redemption, and salvation.

King David shows this in Psalm 105:2, "Sing to Him [God], sing praises to Him; tell of all His wonderous works!"

Each one of us has many opportunities to tell others of how God moved in our lives. When you are given an opportunity, take advantage of it. Begin with telling about the difficult trial that came into your life and how painful it was. Describe how God intervened and gave you victory over the situation. How He healed your wounds. No need to write out a speech or use theological terms or doctrines. Just tell your story. What if God allowed your trial so that your victory would help one person make it through their trial? Without your help this person could be lost.

Do not underestimate the power of your story. Testimonies can change hearts and through your story, glorify God. The Apostle Mark describes a time when Jesus delivered a man from demon possession. This man was possessed by many demons and lived in a graveyard far away from the other people. This man must have been acting crazy because the people tried to bind him in chains and shackles, but he was so strong that he broke the chains and shackles.

This man lived in the graveyard and would cut himself with sharp rocks. Jesus ordered the demons out of the man. The text tells us that the man came into his right mind. The man was so happy that he wanted to follow Jesus as a disciple, he asked Jesus if he could follow Him. Jesus said, "Go home to your friends and tell them how much the Lord has done for you, and He has mercy on you" (Mark 5:1-20). Through your story, like his, God is glorified.

You may think that you are not good enough to talk to people about God. Your past is too messed up: too many poor decisions and mistakes. You may think that no one will listen to you. But God chose you to deliver His message to others through your testimony.

First Corinthians 1:26-31 says, "For consider your calling, brothers: not many of you were wise according to worldly standards, not many were powerful, not many were of noble birth. But God chose what is foolish in the world to shame the wise; God chose what is weak in the world to shame the strong; God chose what is low and despised in the world, even things that are not, to bring to nothing things that are, so that no human being might boast in the presence of God. And because of Him you are in Christ Jesus, who became to us wisdom from God, righteousness and sanctification and redemption, so that, as it is written, 'Let the one who boasts, boast in the Lord.'"

God often uses broken people: victims of abuse or abandonment, prison inmates, homeless, and other traumatized people to deliver His message to the world. Jesus chose His twelve disciples, they were not rich, powerful, kings, princes, priests, or even well-educated men; they were hardworking men. Each disciple had their flaws and faults, but God uses people like them—like us—to do His work.

The world calls us broken, flawed, damaged goods, and low lives. But God calls us His children, His chosen saints! He chose you through His grace, not because of the things you have done or how good you thought you were.

Part of our testimony is the way we behave. For sixteen years of my career, I worked undercover. The objective was to blend into the environment. I dressed like a "biker" to blend into that world. I dressed as a construction worker to blend into that scene. And I even dressed in a suit to fit into that world. It was like living a double life. On one hand I was me—a cop, but on the other I was "Gary"—drug dealer.

It's funny, but Christians are the same. They live a double life. Jesus' brother James describes this as being "double-minded" (James 1:8). On Sunday they go to church with the family carrying the Bible. But Monday through Saturday they are undercover Christians. No one would guess that they were Christians by watching them or listening to their speech.

They blend into the "world" which is led by Satan. Jesus spoke about these types of people in the Book of Revelation, chapter 3, verses 15-16, "I [Jesus] know your works: you are neither cold nor hot. Would that you were either cold or hot! So, because you are lukewarm, and neither hot nor cold, I will spit you out of My mouth."

Jesus said, "I know your works." He sees how we behave; He knows our hearts. Some translations have vomit instead of spit. This is how Jesus feels about those who do not fully trust in Him and submit to Him. If we are grateful for all that God has done in our lives, how can we not follow Jesus and submit to Him.

It is important how we behave. Non-believers are watching us constantly. If we do not act in a moral or ethical manner, then we are no different from anyone else and we have no testimony. But when we make every effort to do the right thing, we send out a message and people see Jesus in us, which glorifies God.

Stand proud! Do not be intimidated. Tell your story to those who God put in your path. God put them in your path for a reason, to hear what you have to say. Tell everyone about the wonderful things that God has done for you, to you, and through you.

When you share your testimony, you plant the seed of the gospel in their heart. In doing so you are fulfilling another command of Jesus. Acts 1:8 says, " . . . you will be My witnesses in Jerusalem and in all Judea and Samaria, and to the end of the earth."

This is called the "Great Commission." We are commissioned to spread God's word to all people. This can be done through evangelism and regular people who give their testimonies to non-believers.

BE BOLD! Share your testimony with someone today!

HEALING PRAYERS

> *"Is anyone among you suffering? Let him pray. And the prayer of faith will save the one who is sick, and the Lord will raise him up. And if he has committed sins, he will be forgiven. Therefore, confess your sins to one another, that you may be healed. The prayer of a righteous person has great power as it is working" (James 5:13,15-16).*

Once you have completed all the steps and have your journal ready and have evaluated your response to your trauma, you are ready to begin your healing through prayer. How do we pray? Jesus provided a prayer model that we all should follow in Matthew 6:9-13,

"Pray like this: "Our Father in heaven, hallowed be Your name. Your kingdom come, Your will be done, on earth as it is in heaven. Give us this day our daily bread, and forgive us our debts [sins], as we also have forgiven our debtors [those who sin against us]. And lead us not into temptation but deliver us from evil."

The Lord's prayer is a great prayer, but a lot of people memorize the prayer and after time recite it without thought. Prayer loses meaning when recited without thought. Jesus tells you not to pray with empty words (Matthew 6:7). God wants a personal relationship with you, He wants you to pray in a sincere manner in a personal way.

When we look at this model, we see that it begins with praising God, this is referred to as "adoration." We begin our prayer with praising God for who He is and what He represents. Use your own words telling Him how much you love Him and that you acknowledge that He is sovereign.

Verse eleven talks about supplying our daily needs. During biblical times, people had no way to store foods for a long period of time. They were required to prepare their food daily. The staple of that time was bread. You ask God to supply your daily needs whatever your needs may be. Remember God knows what you need even before you ask (Matthew 6:8).

The next verse does not refer to your financial debt, it refers to your unrepented sin. Repentance restores your relationship with God. Acknowledge your sins and repent for them. You must also consider whether you must ask forgiveness from anyone that you may have harmed. These are commandments from God.

We acknowledge there are temptations out there; God will never lead us into a temptation. He may allow one to test you. But through the strength of being in Christ we are able to resist those temptations. God will never allow you to be tempted beyond your ability to resist (1 Corinthians 10:13). We now can ask God to give us what is on our hearts. These are your requests. Remember He will only answer prayer requests that are in His will. Since you do not know His will and plan for your life, go ahead and ask Him for the things on your heart.

God wants to do great things for you. Do not limit Him by withholding prayers. He wants to show off for you. The Bible says that you do not have because you do not ask.

An important part of daily prayer is expressing how grateful you are for all God's blessings in your life. Thank Him for all He has done for you and your family. Even though you may be going through a difficult time right now, thank Him and praise Him. You must have faith that what you are praying for, God will do. Again, it must be in His will.

Matthew 17:20-21 says, " . . . if you have faith like a grain of mustard seed, you will say to this mountain, 'Move from here to there,' and it will move, and nothing will be impossible for you."

A mustard seed is among the smallest of the seeds, but it grows into a big plant. When you have faith that God not only hears your prayers, but is faithful to answer them, we know that you can ask Him to remove any obstacle (mountain) that stands between you and your healing—His will for you.

Obstacles include: emotional pain, strongholds, sin, physical ailments, anxiety, depression, or spiritual oppression. Hebrews 11:6 says that without faith you cannot please God. When you lose your faith, you slip into a sinful behavior.

In Matthew chapter fourteen, there is a story of when the disciples were on a boat in the Sea of Galilee while Jesus went off to pray. Between three and six a.m, the wind and waves were pounding the boat. The disciples were all frightened. They saw Jesus walking on the water towards the boat, they reasoned that the vision was a ghost.

Jesus identified Himself and told them not to be afraid. Peter called out to Jesus, "Lord, if it is You, command me to come to You on the water." Jesus said, "Come." Peter got out of the boat and walked on the water, all the while looking at Jesus ahead of him.

But when the wind and waves came, Peter took his eyes off of Jesus, he became afraid. He focused on his surroundings, not Jesus. His faith was in doubt. Peter cried out for help, Jesus saved him and said, "O you of little faith, why did you doubt?"

Peter was walking on top of the water! But he took his eyes off of Jesus and reasoned that what he was doing was impossible. He focused on the storm instead of his Lord. We do the same thing. We have great faith when everything is going good, but when a difficult time pops up, we doubt our faith and begin to focus on ourselves, not Jesus.

Keep your eyes focused on Jesus not only through the good times but it the trials in your life also. Never doubt the power and love of God. God will never leave you. He is always with you.

Praying in faith brings up a theological debate whether we should pray for something more than one time. Some churches believe that you should make your request to God for something just one time, then every prayer thereafter will be a prayer of thanks for making it happen. If you have enough faith, God will answer any prayer request.

This is based on Matthew 21:22 that says " . . . whatever you ask in prayer, you will receive, if you have faith."

If your faith is strong enough, you can pray for ***anything*** and God will do it for you. If your request did not come to pass, you simply did not have enough faith in God.

Most pastors agree that this is a false teaching. I believe it is not only permissible to pray for something repeatedly, but it is often God's will for you to do so. You still pray in faith that God is able to answer any request made, but we must understand that we will receive nothing that is not in accordance with His will (James 4:3).

An example: if your prayer request is to win the multi-million-dollar lottery, and you have great faith in God's power, and it does not come to pass, it is obvious that it is not God's will for you to be a millionaire, even if you have the greatest faith in the world. God sees all, it may be that He sees that by becoming rich you will fall away from Christianity and return to worldly activities. This is not His will for your life. However, it may be His will for you to win the money so you can give it all to charity. Again, you do not know what God's will is for your life.

I say, go ahead and pray for that winning lottery ticket, but if you do not win, realize it has nothing to do with your lack of faith. I am saddened to see this happen in faith healing churches. A church member has cancer and is on their death bed, the congregation begins to pray in faith believing that the patient will be cured by divine intervention. They possess great faith. But it may not be God's will to heal this person.

When the patient is not healed and they die, that family, and maybe even other church members will be let down and actually lose faith or become angry at God. God has a plan and purpose for our lives and everything that happens in our lives. See 1 John 5:14 and James 4:1-3 for praying in God's will.

The Bible teaches that it is permissible to pray for the same thing earnestly and regularly. There is an example of this in Luke 18:1-8. Jesus tells this parable, "And He [Jesus] told them [Pharisees] a parable to the effect that they ought always to pray and not lose heart. He [Jesus] said, 'In a certain city there was a judge who neither feared God nor respected man. And there was a widow in that city who kept coming to him and saying, 'Give me justice against my adversary.' For a while he refused, but afterward he said to himself, 'Though I neither fear God nor respect man, yet because this widow keeps bothering me, I will give her justice, so that she will not beat me down by her continual coming.' And the Lord said, 'Hear what the unrighteous judge says. And will not God give justice to His elect [Christians], who cry to Him day and night? Will He delay long over them? I tell you, He will give justice to them speedily'"

This is a fictitious story because Jesus uses no names. We see that there is a woman who wants justice from a judge, most likely from a civil suit. The judge is a non-believer and obviously self-centered. The woman returns to this judge over and over again. The judge finally relents just to get her off of his back. Jesus then tells us that God will do the very same thing for those who cry out to Him!

This scripture confirms that it is permissible to pray day and night for a certain request of God. We see the same teaching in Luke 11:5-8. God wants us to call out to Him when we are in need and to praise Him in all time.

There are four types of prayers:

1. **Corporate prayer.** This is when two or more people get together and pray for someone or something. A church congregation may pray for a member who is sick or injured. James 5:13-18, Matthew 18:19-20 says that if two or more believers agree on any prayer, it will be done for them. And where two or more are gathered in Jesus' name, He will be there with them. There is power in corporate prayer.
2. **Intercessory prayer.** This is where we pray for others. We can pray for non-believers to be saved, or for the welfare of children around the world, or even pray for others to have more faith (Luke 22:32). We can pray for our enemies (Luke 23:34), or we can pray for the safety of our military and first responders.
3. **Personal prayer.** This is the prayer model that was laid out above. Prayer can be done at any time day or night and in any position (kneeling, standing, sitting lying prone on the ground, driving a car, and even in bed).
4. **Private prayer.** This is the same as personal prayer, however, it is done in a private place like a prayer closet (Matthew 6:6).

New believers often ask what the proper position is for prayer. The Bible teaches that any position is proper, so the answer is "any position you want." Christianity is a relationship with God, not a set of rules where you must do something in a proper way.

The traditional position for prayer is on the knees with the head tilted down to the ground, it is a position of submission. We are showing our submission to our God. The Bible mentions a variety of positions in where people prayed. The position is not important, it is the dialog with our heavenly Father that is important.

When do we pray? When is the best time to pray to increase the chances for having the prayers answered? Any time is good, all the time is better.

Psalm 55:17 says, "Evening, morning, and noon I cry out in distress, and He hears my voice."

1 Thessalonians 5:16-18 says, "Rejoice always, pray without ceasing, give thanks in all circumstances; for this is the will of God in Christ Jesus for you."

The bottom line is—pray as much as you can. Pray in any position you want. And, pray at any time you want.

God answers prayers in three different ways. God can say "yes," "no," or "not yet." Never forget God has a plan and purpose for your life. You may have a great walk with God and have been doing everything right, but it seems like God has left you and is not answering your prayers. Why?

God knows what is best for you. He may be saying "no" because He knows the results. Maybe if you get what you're asking, it will not turn out good. It may be that the timing is not right at this moment in your life. Maybe you must wait for other things to occur to complete God's plan for your life. You may have to wait until the time is right.

The Book of Daniel has a good example of another reason why we must wait for our prayers to be answered. In Daniel 10:12-14, we learn that Daniel had prayed for God's intervention in a crisis. Daniel waited three weeks and still no answer. On the twenty-first day an angel came to Daniel and told him that God heard his prayer on first day and dispatched an angel to help him. But the angel was delayed by a demon that prevented the angel from arriving at a timely manner. The angel sought assistance from the Archangel Michael for help. The delay of your prayer may be because of the unseen spiritual world.

God often says "no" to our prayers. As we already discussed we may be praying out of God's will; or maybe we are out of fellowship with God due to our sin. Or the motives of our prayers maybe wrong. God knows our hearts and motives.

James 4:1-3 says, "What causes quarrels and what causes fights among you? Is it not this, that your passions are at war within you? You desire and do not have, so you murder. You covet and cannot obtain, so you fight and quarrel. You do not have, because you do not ask. You ask and do not receive, because you ask wrongly, to spend it on your passions."First Corinthians 4:5 says that God brings to light those things hidden in darkness and exposes the purpose of the heart.

Proverbs 27:19 says, "As in water reflects the face so the heart of man reflects the man."

And Matthew 6:21 tells us that whatever we treasure, that is where our heart will be also. God may say no to a request because He is trying to teach us something that is for our own good. Second Corinthians 12:7-9 talks about the Apostle Paul being oppressed by a messenger of Satan. Paul prayed three times for God to remove this oppression. But God said, "My grace is sufficient for you, for My power is made perfect in weakness."

Paul said that God did not answer his prayer because God did not want Paul to become conceited. So, Paul rejoiced in his weakness and praised God for it.

Always stay in faith. Do not lose hope. What God said no to in the past, may change to a yes very soon. Maybe your being prepared for a trip or a ministry and once you're well prepared, God will say yes.

If we try to do things on our time, we tend to rush because we are impatient. When we get ahead of God's timing, we can lose faith and become angry and bitter, then, the "not yet," may turn into "no."

When I first began to pray, I felt that I was bothering God, and annoying Him by praying to Him too much. But the more I studied the Bible, the more I realized that He wants us to go to Him for help. He is our creator, our Father, He loves us. We can go to Him with any problem.

He is always there for us. Pray all you want. This will please Him.

I recommend that you keep a prayer journal. Every day write down what you prayed and what you prayed for. Look back and see how many of your prayers were answered. You will be amazed and your faith will grow.

CHAPTER 10

6 STEPS TO START YOUR HEALING

The Christ-centered approach to healing a wounded heart has six steps. Each step is vitally important. As you read on and begin the steps, before you move on to the next step, make sure you fully understand the step you have just read. The steps are:

1. First and most important, you must understand who God is and who you are in Christ. This is done through studying the Word of God. You do not need to be a biblical scholar or a theologian, but you must understand the Gospel, who God is, and who you are when you place your trust in Christ.
2. You must be familiar with the spiritual laws and principles that build strongholds keep you in a cycle of sinful behavior. You must understand how these laws affect your life.
3. You must determine the initial wound: the place where this all began. Once the initial incident has been identified; you must determine your response to that wound. This identification can be done through journaling the event and its after-effects or confide in a trusted friend. You want to identify the sinful responses to the wound.
4. Using your journal, it's time to determine if any of these spiritual laws or principles came into play during the response to your wounding. If you were honest and detailed in your journal you can pinpoint each violation of God's law. Once these are determined, you must renounce the sin, confess and repent the sin to

restore your relationship with God. This is done through a loving relationship with God.

5. Once you are realigned with God's will by following the first four steps, you ask for God to heal your heart. This can be done through your own prayer or using the prayers in the appendix as a guide. Remember prayer is just a conversation with God. You ask for healing of the wounds you suffered and to restore your heart.
   NOTE: If through this process you have not pinpointed the initial wounding and still believe that you have endured a traumatic event due to the outward character traits you exhibit and your uncontrolled emotions, use the "Starting Prayer" that asks God to reveal the wounding to you through His Holy Spirit. When the time is right, and He knows you are ready for the incident to be revealed, the Holy Spirit will reveal it to you. The Holy Spirit is the Spirit of truth (John 16:13). And through the truth of what happened to you, you will be set free from the pain that you're going through (2 Corinthians 3:17), and this freedom will give you life (John 6:63).
6. Lastly, you must learn how to remain in God's will by walking in the Holy Spirit. When you stay aligned in God's will, you will receive continual blessing and healing.

These steps may appear simple. Do not be deceived, they are not. You must acknowledge your pain, evaluate the initial wounding, take responsibility for your role in your wounding, determine your sinful responses to the wound, determine who must be forgiven and forgive them, ask for forgiveness where necessary, renounce your sin, confess and repent your sin.

It is always difficult to acknowledge our role in an incident and forgive those who we perceived harmed us. We like to hold onto our unforgiveness and seek revenge. We like to hold on to bitterness because it's easier than to forgive. This may seem daunting but through Christ's strength, He will get you through this.

Take your time to ensure you thoroughly understand each step before moving on to the next section. If you feel uneasy or fearful, stop and begin on another day. Take your time, do the work, and accept God's healing. Joy and sorrow meet at the cross of Jesus Christ.

After all the research, self-reflection, and journaling, you're ready to begin the final step towards healing. This is when we ask God to heal our trauma. Have your journal and/or your notes ready. Chose a safe place to begin the prayer. In the appendix are prayers for the subject matter we spoke about in the book. They are used with permission from Elijah House Ministries written by Sandra Sallmar-Kersten. They are from a DVD series and study manual called, "Healing Trauma." These are the best prayers I have found.

Elijah House Ministries was founded by John and Paula Sandford who were pioneers in the healing of trauma. Their book series called the, "Transformation Series" was instrumental in my journey of healing. I utilized some aspects of their teaching but added some things and changed others. I could not have developed better prayer outlines.

These are just a guide. They must be personalized to your specific circumstances. Prayers cover different points that will not apply in all situations. Prior to beginning your prayers, personalize each prayer to suit your situation.

These prayers are just a template. Each prayer has a specific purpose. If the topic of the prayer applies to you, use it; if not, disregard it. Please do not incorporate multiple prayers into one single prayer. This type of "blanket" prayer does not work.[26]

List of prayers:

1. **The Sinner's Prayer:** Dedicate your life to Jesus Christ.
2. **First Step:** Take the first step to healing.
3. **Choosing to Trust:** Sample prayer to choose to trust God.
4. **Prayer of Invitation:** Invite God into your heart.
5. **Starting Prayer:** We ask God to reveal to us our trauma and our sinful responses. Good prayer to use prior to beginning journaling and if the traumatic event is not known. This prayer adapted from "Healing Trauma."
6. **Prayer to Forgive:** Sample prayer to ask God to help us forgive our offender.
7. **Renouncing Bitter Root Judgments, Expectancies, and Inner Vows:** Sample prayer to renounce sinful responses.

---

[26] Sandra Sellmar-Kersten, *Healing Trauma*, (Spokane Valley: Elijah House Ministries, 2013) 47.

8. **Prayer for Repentance:** Sample prayer for repentance.
9. **Prayer to Remove Guilt or Shame:** Sample prayer to ask God to remove your guilt or shame.
10. **Prayer to Renounce Generational Sin:** Not from "Healing Trauma." Unknown author. Not required for Christians. Prayer to proclaim to Satan that you belong to God.
11. **Prayer to Choose Life:** Sample prayer to Renounce thoughts of suicide.
12. **Prayer for Release of Unholy Ties:** Sample Prayer to renounce ties resulting from neglect, physical, or sexual abuse.
13. **Prayer for Release of Soul Ties/Unholy Sexual Ties:** Sample prayer to denounce ties resulting from sex outside marriage. Not for sexual abuse.
14. **Prayer to Release Fear Bond and Ties of Control:** Sample prayer to renounce ties that develop when someone has manipulated us through threats.
15. **Prayer for Healing Shame:** Sample prayer to ask Jesus to heal our shame.
16. **Prayer to Remove Trauma:** Sample prayer to ask Jesus to remove our trauma and heal our heart.
17. **Prayer of Affirmation:** Prayer letting God know that you belong to Him and that He is your Lord and Savior.
18. **Prayer to reveal and renounce fears:** Prayer asking God to revel any fears that place the focus on yourself, then a prayer to renounce those fears.
19. **Prayer to reveal and renounce wrong priorities:** Prayer asking God to reveal any idolatry in your life, then a prayer to renounce idols.
20. **Prayer to reveal and renounce prideful behavior:** Prayer asking God to reveal any prideful motivations holding you back, and a prayer to renounce those motives.
21. **Prayer to renounce Performance Orientation:** Prayer renouncing low self-worth due to seeking the praise of others.
22. **Prayer to renounce behavioral Addictions:** Prayer renouncing the use of behaviors as a coping mechanism.
23. **Prayer renouncing Substance Abuse:** Prayer renouncing the use of substances as coping mechanism.

It is important to note again that these are all just sample prayers. There is no formula for everyone. They are meant as guide to direct your prayer.

Each prayer must be personalized to fit your situation. If a portion of the prayer does not apply to you, do not use it. If something needs to added, add it.

As you begin this process, wait and be led by the Holy Spirit. Note: Prayer to remove trauma has been changed by me to enable you to pray the prayer alone. It was originally written to be read by a Prayer Minister. A Prayer Minister has been trained in the healing process to recognize your sinful responses to your trauma. They lead you through the prayers to renounce, repent, forgive, and heal.

It is important to understand that your emotions will come out during this process. Do not suppress your emotions—let them flow out. As you finish reading each prayer out loud, sit silently and listen for the Holy Spirit's voice.

He may reveal to you more things that need to be addressed. Any thoughts that come to mind during this time should be noted, even if you think they may be unrelated, write them down. Take the prayers slow. One at a time then take a break. See how you feel after a few hours, if you feel good, continue to the next prayer. If you do not feel at ease, wait a day or so and repeat the prayer. All healing is directed by the Holy Spirit. It is common to have to repeat the prayer a few times until you feel it in your heart.

God wants to heal you. Work through the process and accept the healing. As you move forward make every effort to walk in the Holy Spirit for continual healing.

CHAPTER 11

CASE STUDIES IN HEALING

To fully understand the process, I have included two examples of people who went through the *Christ-Centered Healing* process. These people realized that they produced poor fruit in their lives. The suffered emotional pain and were enslaved to their strongholds. They wanted more that God had to offer. The names and some details have been changed to protect the identity of these individuals.

TIMOTHY

I met Tim in prison. He was a forty-one-year-old ex-police officer. He was serving a sentence for Driving Under the Influence (DUI) causing injury on federal land. This was his third DUI. Tim had been a decorated police officer in a medium sized city of about 150,000 people. He had been a cop for about fifteen years and had been involved in several critical traumatic incidents during that time. He was divorced with two daughters.

One hot summer day Tim was working patrol during a dayshift. It is common practice for the officers who work dayshift to take care of minor personal business while on-duty. This is because they normally work a ten-hour shift. Most officers do this during their coffee or lunch breaks.

On this afternoon he went to the bank to cash a check. He had been in the bank for five to eight minutes when he received an emergency dispatch of a report of a young child who was drowning. The call was in his beat. The house was close to the bank. He responded with his emergency lights and siren on.

It took him six minutes to get to the residence due to heavy traffic. Upon his arrival he saw a female holding a toddler in her arms on the front lawn of the residence. He arrived before the fire department.

The victim was three-year-old girl. She was unconscious. Tim began CPR, her mother was screaming for help. The paramedics arrived about two minutes later and took over the medical rescue.

The girl's mother told him that she was in the backyard with her daughter. She told her daughter to stay out of the pool while she went into the house for a few minutes. When she returned, the little girl was under water. She jumped in the pool and got the girl out of the water. A neighbor heard the screams and called police.

The child died at the hospital. Tim had handled many death investigations before, but never a child this young. At that time, his own daughter was four years old. He stayed with the family at the hospital until more family support arrived.

Tim was bothered by this call. Death calls are never easy, but this really got to him not only because the age of the victim, but the fact that he was not in his patrol car at the time of the call. He felt guilty for not getting to the scene faster.

This began to affect him at work and at home. He never showed emotion. That's what cops are taught, never show emotions! He sensed something was wrong with his emotions because sometimes when he was alone, he cried.

Cops are never supposed to cry, this is considered a sign of weakness. Cops also never seek out help. If he were caught seeing a counselor, the other cops would shun them.

He began to drink heavily, mostly off-duty but sometimes he brought alcohol to work so that he would keep his buzz going. His performance at work suffered. A few months later he was arrested for DUI in another city. He was placed on leave.

He isolated himself from everyone, including his wife and kids. He tried to stay strong denying his grief and emotions, but this brought him more pain. He was taught to be a "warrior."

While on leave he got another DUI. He resigned from department. He went into alcohol rehabilitation. There, he was diagnosed with PTSD. His marriage fell apart because he refused to communicate.

He continued to drink, even during rehab. He had extra time on his hands, so he began to gamble. One night after gambling and drinking at a casino, he drove home. He crashed into another car totaling both cars. A person in the other car was seriously injured. Tim was arrested for the third time, this time a felony. This occurred on federal land, he was charged in federal court. Since the collision he has remained sober mostly because he was in jail.

He isolated himself in prison. He got into fights when confronted and was having a difficult time emotionally. He had nightmares, suffered from depression and suicidal ideation.

I worked in the chapel. Tim came into the chapel off and on, and soon became a Christian. He began to open up, I could relate to him for what he has been through. I had taken several child death calls and responded negatively to them. I did not seek help either. We spent some time together and he finally told me his story.

Tim was not a Christian at the time of his trauma. He blamed himself and God for everything that happened. He blamed himself for conducting private business during work hours. As he opened up and told his story we learned that he had made an inner vow to never let his children out of his sight while he was with them. He thought about that day every day.

The only way to cope was to numb his pain through drinking. When he was sober, his mind would be filled with thoughts of what he could have and should have done different on that day. These intrusive thoughts infiltrated into his dreams and caused nightmares. He felt angry and bitter all the time and had difficulty focusing on daily activities.

His guilt was the traumatic seed that was planted in his heart. He blamed himself for this little girl's death. He truly believed that if he were not in the bank of personal business, he could have saved the girl's life. He made the judgment that he was selfish. He grieved that he could never be an officer again. I asked him to journal all these things he was telling me. I asked him for complete honesty and to include as much detail as possible. I even asked him to describe the drive from the bank to the victim's residence. This took him several days. When he felt he needed a break, he took one and we prayed.

When he completed the journal, with permission, we went over it together. When he spoke about his response to the emergency call, he realized something did not match with his internal feelings. He realized that something was wrong with the timeline. As he analyzed the timing of this event, he saw that by the time the mother called the police, the girl had already been in the pool for four to five minutes.

By the time she was able to get the girl out of the pool, another two minutes elapsed. Emergency dispatchers do a wonderful job but the calls normally take up to a minute or so to go out to the patrol units. The time that the girl was unconscious without CPR was anywhere between six to nine minutes. Even if he were in his patrol car just two minutes away from the house, the girl would still have died because she would have been without air for to eight to nine minutes.

If the mother or a neighbor knew CPR, that might have had a chance to save her. However, a child without air for five minutes or more has little chance of survival. It was impossible to have saved the girl. He was not at fault.

Although he still grieved, it gave him a sense of relief knowing that he was not responsible for the child's death. This was a huge step forward but he still had a lot of work to do. His marriage failed due to his negative response to the trauma that changed his character structure. It was not the girl's death, it was his guilt, anger, bitterness, drinking, isolation, and his over-protectiveness that kept him oppressed and in emotional pain.

He began by renouncing his belief that he could prevent what God ordained. He renounced the vow that only he could protect his children to such a high degree. He renounced his judgment and the blame he placed on himself and God. He repented for his vows and sinful judgments.

He saw that he needed to ask forgiveness from a lot of people. He began with his victim, wife and family. He wrote letters to his supervisors and co-workers explaining his actions. He realized that the spiritual laws are absolute, he reaped what he sowed; with increase. Using the attached prayer as a template we prayed for his healing.

As he went through this process, he found a few more events in his life that kept him in pain. He worked on those also. This was indeed a traumatic event. This is what police officers go through every day. But few ask for God's help.

There were many different components to this event. Tim's story is a great example of the benefit of having a friend or family member confide in. But I do believe that Tim would have come to the same conclusions if he proceeded alone. He was the one listening to the Holy Spirit's guiding.

VIOLET

I met Violet in a while facilitating a trauma group counseling setting. Violet is a beautiful 23-year-old Christian woman who was being oppressed by her broken heart. She told me that she feels depressed all the time and life seems hopeless. Her relationships seem to implode prior to moving to the "next step." She does not know why but all her relationships break up over petty arguments or minor incidents.

Each of her last three boyfriends were kind and compassionate men, even her parents liked them. She now avoids potential relationships. She told me that she had a normal childhood. When she was thirteen years old her parents divorced, her father left them for another woman. She saw him every other weekend. In her senior year in high school, she was a popular cheerleader. She dated a boy for over a year. He was her first love.

Early on in the relationship, he accused her of cheating on him. She never gave him a reason to feel that way. One night after their team won a football game, they celebrated and she came home late. He was waiting in front of her house. He accused her of cheating on him, they argued, he slapped her and threw her to the ground. She did not tell anyone.

The next day he apologized for his actions and promised to never hit her again. A few weeks later he hit her again and apologized again. She did not want to leave him because she loved him and also didn't want to look like a loser. Things went good for a while. She later caught him cheating on her. She was devastated, and broke up with him. She felt like a failure. She went to college and never saw him again.

As she went deeper into her story, she admitted that she believed it was her fault for his abuse. She believed she caused him to hit her. She was always very confident but after they broke up she felt no self-worth. She felt that she could no longer trust men to do the right thing. Her father left her. Her boyfriend betrayed her with abuse and an affair.

She finally realized that she resented her father for hurting her mother. She developed the expectancy that all men would hurt her then leave her, she expected that every man would treat her poorly because she deserved it.

Violet saw how inner vows and expectancies were strongholds in her belief system and behavior because she herself sabotaged her relationships with men even when they treated her well. She did this because in her heart, she believed that that all men would soon abuse her and abandon her. She wanted to cut it off before they could hurt her. She would subconsciously blow-up small arguments or even invent an argument to be used as an excuse to break up with the man.

Whenever possible we need to deal with the chronological trauma first. Violet forgave her father for leaving them and hurting her mother. Using the prayers in the appendix, she renounced her judgment of her father for being a poor father and husband to her mother and repented for not honoring her father.

She renounced the inner vows that she made after her first love betrayed her. She renounced her bitter root judgments and expectancies she developed from her heart break. And finally, she forgave her ex-boyfriend for the abuse and betrayal. She then prayed the attached healing prayer.

As she studied God's word, she learned who God is, and who God says she is. She now understands that her self-worth is not based on what other people say about her, but her value is based on who God says she is.

As she moved through the process; strongholds were being broken one-by-one. She soon began to feel better. As she studied the word of God and began to walk in the Holy Spirit, she began to experience the peace and joy that only God can instill. Her demeanor changed. She began to open up and not fear meeting new people, especially men. I heard through a mutual friend that she had met a new man and was beginning a relationship with this new guy.

CONCLUSION

Through these two examples, we can see there can often be several layers of trauma that have built character structures. We must allow Jesus to deal with each layer separately, beginning with the first initial trauma if possible. Healing trauma is like peeling an onion, each layer must be slowly removed. Expect tears. It is important to take time within each layer.

As we break Satan's stronghold by placing our sinful responses at the foot of the cross, we allow Jesus to transform our character into His likeness. Our repentance restores our relationship with God the Father who gives us the peace that is beyond all understanding. This allows the healing to begin.

If you went through the process and do not believe you are feeling any better, make sure you DIDN'T do any of the counterproductive mistakes listed:

1. Did not carefully and methodically go through each step of confession, renouncing, and repenting your sins.
2. You are not being completely honest in self-examination and/or journaling the initial events. Or holding back the most painful part of that event.
3. You have returned to your sins.
4. You do not believe or accept Jesus Christ is Lord.
5. You do not believe who Jesus says you are.

There may be more layers of trauma that require attention. Pray for God to reveal any other events that have not yet been resolved. If you believe that you have resolved all painful issues in your life, it may help to have a trusted friend or prayer partner to help you. Share your journal with them, have them review it and ask clarifying questions. As you answer their questions you may obtain a different perspective on the events, a fresh set of eyes and ears will; help you obtain that different perspective. You will be able to dive deeper in your pain. If you are honest with yourself and put in the work, God will heal you.

APPENDIX

The Sinner's Prayer
Father,

I confess that I am a sinner. I repent of my sins. I want to make / reaffirm that Jesus Christ is my Lord and Savior. He died on the cross for me so that my sins could be forgiven and that I would be healed. I believe that He was resurrected and now sits at Your right hand. Father, I love You and I thank You for calling me, loving me, and forgiving me. Thank you for Your mercy, grace, and healing.

In Jesus' name I pray, Amen

Affirmation
Father,

I affirm that there is only one true living God, our Heavenly Father. I now proclaim Jesus Christ as my Lord and Savior. I place my trust in the triune God and submit to Him.

I believe that Jesus was crucified and died on the cross for my sins. I believe that after three days in the grave, Jesus was resurrected disarming Satan. Through Jesus' death and resurrection, I am forgiven of all sins, past, present, and future. I am now dead to my sins and sin, nor Satan has power over me.

I affirm that I am a new person, spiritually alive in Christ Jesus. I am a child of God and a co-heir with Jesus. My citizenship is now in heaven. I am deeply loved and accepted. I reject all the lies of the evil one telling me otherwise.

I choose to put on the armor of God everyday. I choose to take every thought captive and compare it to the Word of God. If that thought does not match the Word of God, I will reject it. I resolve to stand firm in Christ and to resist the devil. I declare that I have authority over Satan and his demons. They are subject to the authority of Jesus Christ; Jesus has given me that authority.

I declare myself dependent on God, I cannot do anything apart from Him. I choose to abide in Christ, I believe that He will abide in me.

I understand that I will be exposed to trials and endure suffering. But I know that I am victorious in Christ. I will overcome all obstacles and trials and come out of them stronger than before. All things work for the good for those who love God.

I choose to obey the two greatest commandments: to love God with all my heart and love all my neighbors. Thank You Jesus or Your work on the cross.

In Jesus' name I pray

Choosing to Trust and Let Go
Father,

It's not easy recognizing all the different traumas that I've experienced but thank You for helping me. Thank You for suffering for me. Thank You for paying such an incredible price for my healing and salvation.

I admit that sometimes I have wondered where You were and why You didn't help me why You didn't stop what was going on. So many things have felt so unjust and unfair! But right now I choose to trust You. I choose to let go of the things that I don't understand and take hold of Your hand instead.

I've been bound and held captive in my pain and shame, and I want to be free. I want to begin living the abundant life that You promised me. I hear you calling me, and I'm choosing to step forth into life.

Give me courage to allow people around me to help me. It can be hard for me to open up my heart and my life, and my first response is to run and hide! But help me Lord, to run to YOU instead!

There are things that I have done, and things that have been done to me, that I'm ashamed of. But I'm tired of the hiding. I'm tired of trying to bury my pain. I'm tired of the shame.

Please continue to walk with me and help me through this process of learning and healing. And Lord, if there comes a time that I feel that I cannot walk one more step, will You carry me? I choose to believe that You began a good work in me, and that You will complete it.

In Jesus' name I pray, Amen.

Used with Permission. *Healing Trauma*, Sandra Sellmer-Kersten

Prayer of Invitation
Jesus,

I open the door and invite You into broken places of heart. I ask You to heal the pain, gather up all the shattered pieces, and make me whole.

I open my heart to receive the healing balm of Your love, and ask that You cleanse me from the disappointment, confusion and shame I've felt, and set me free. I receive your comfort in the places where I have refused comfort, or have been unable to receive it.

I tell my heart to **beat again**, to begin to **hope again**, to begin to **trust again**—to **embrace life**, to **embrace this healing process** and to **embrace you!**

Thank You for loving me, thank You for choosing me. Thank You for healing me! Thank You for restoring honor to me. May I truly live like the oak of righteousness You have created me to be, for the display of YOUR splendor.

In Jesus' name I pray, Amen.

Used with Permission. *Healing Trauma*, Sandra Sellmer-Kersten

Prayer to Reveal Unrepented Sin
Father,

I confess and repent for my fleshly behavior. I live in the world, however, Jesus told me not to be conformed to it. I confess that I am a sinner, my sin has separated me from you. I want to restore my relationship with you. I want to live a Christ-Centered life. Please bring to mind any and all unrepented sin that keeps me from being close to you. This unrepented sin is producing bad fruit in my life and I want to repent of it.

In Jesus' name I pray, Amen

Note: unknown author

SAMPLE PRAYERS

Sample Prayers are not formulas. Rather they offer ideas and direction. Be led by the Holy Spirit and use the substance of these prayers as a guide.

Starting Prayer
Heavenly Father,

Thank You for who You are and what You represent. Thank You for being a healer. I ask that Your Holy Spirit be with me today as I seek Your healing balm.

I ask You to search the depths of my heart and soul, I give You permission to search the dark corners of my heart. Please shine Your light to expose the areas which have been hurting or any area where the enemy has a stronghold. Bring those wounds to memory so that I can place them at the foot of the cross.

I ask You to bind any demonic spirits that may seek revenge on me or my family members. Please send warring and guardian angels to protect me.

I recognize that I have exhibited poor fruit in my life that is affecting my relationship with You and others. This bad fruit is also affecting my health and the ability to live the abundant life that You have given me. I ask You to reveal the initial wound that caused this poor fruit in my life. I ask You to reveal any bitter roots, and expectancies, inner vows, and any area where I need to forgive or ask for forgiveness. I ask You to reveal any unhealed trauma, sinful responses, or any unresolved issue that keeps me in my pain.

I give You permission to work deeply in my broken heart and heal me spiritually, emotionally, and physically. Lead me to genuine repentance in areas where I have sinned.

I know that You are gentle and compassionate, loving and kind, and I know that this healing process will not be easy, and may be painful, but it will not be overwhelming.

I trust You to guide and protect me throughout this process. Allow me to experience and feel only that which is necessary for healing. I open the door of my heart and say, "Come Lord Jesus, Come!"

In Jesus' name I pray, Amen.

Used with Permission. *Healing Trauma*, Sandra Sellmer-Kersten, changes made by me

Prayer of Repentance
Father,

I stand before You undone by the damage I have caused (*name the person specifically*).

I confess that I have hurt him/her in this way: (*name the sin, and how it has affected the person*).

I confess that I have also grieved Your heart by hurting Your child in this way, and I repent.

I repent for and renounce all denial, self-justification, self-defense, minimization of my sin (*and minimization of how it has hurt others*) and blame. I make no excuses; I take full responsibility for what I have done.

My sin has resulted in broken trust and broken relationship. Father, I am so very sorry for the pain and grief I have caused. Help me continue feeling the pain until the cost of my sin is written deeply into my heart, so that I will not be tempted to sin in this way again.

May the strength of this experience sustain and empower me to do and say the things needed to rebuild trust and bring healing, and if possible, reconciliation. Show me what restitution needs to be made, how it is to be done and the timing involved.

Please give me patience and sensitivity to honor this person's heart in all I say and do. Help me give them time to process, and heal and to respond, I release to You any demand that they respond to my repentance and/or restitution in a certain time frame or in a certain way.

I release to You my insecurity, my "need to be right," or my need to "look good" in the eyes of others. I repent for the ways I have placed my need to be right above relationship, and for the times I've allowed shame or a "desire to save face" to tempt me to hide or cover up my sin.

Create in me a clean heart. May my motive for restitution and reconciliation be pure and for other's sake . . . and for Christ's sake, not so my life will be easier, or to escape the consequences of my sin. Fill me so full of Your love that I will be willing to lay my life down and pay the cost for relationship.

I ask you to bless and heal (*the person you have wounded*).

Pour the oil of your Holy Spirit into the wounds I have caused. Bless (*him/her*) with Your presence and bring Your perfect comfort and healing to (*his/her*) life.

In Jesus' name I pray, Amen

Used with Permission. *Healing Trauma*, Sandra Sellmer-Kersten

Inviting Jesus to Heal Shame
Jesus,

It's not easy to look at and acknowledge the shameful events of my life. But I want to be healed, and I want to be free to live the life that You have called me to, I choose to open up the door to my heart and invite You into my memory, into the broken places in my heart. I ask that You heal the pain, draw to the cross all shock, trauma, fear, terror and shame, and gather up all the shattered pieces of my heart, and make me whole.

Please cleanse me from the disappointment, confusion and shame, and set me free. I receive Your comfort in the places where I have refused, or been unable to receive comfort in the past.

Sometimes I've felt like David's daughter Tamar, when she asked ***"What about me? Where could I get rid of my disgrace?"*** I've felt that there was no place for my shame, the disgrace that I've felt. But now I know there IS a place, and it is on Your Cross, I release the shame to You now.
In the places where my heart has been filled with shame, fear, and distrust. I ask that You replace it with your tender mercies and great abounding love. I ask that You remove my shame and reproach and restore me to honor and dignity, which is my true inheritance as a child of the Most High God.

I thank You that you are a kind, loving and gentle God. I thank You, Jesus, for dying on the Cross for me, and for paying the price for my sin and shame. Lord, I confess that I need You I need Your love, protection, power and deliverance. First John 1:8 proclaims that You came to undo the devil's work. I know that devil's work is to kill, steal and destroy. Shame has been a way that he has stolen from me, and has brought destruction.

But You promise to give me life, and life in abundance. So, I choose this day to receive Your promise of fullness of life, and I ask that You set me free from the bondage of sin and shame. I invite You into every area of my heart, mind and spirit. Set me free from the lies that I have believed about You, others, life, and myself And let me know your truth in my inmost being.

I receive by faith the healing balm of Your love, and thank you for restoring honor to me. May I truly live like the oak of righteousness You have created me to be . . .for the display of YOUR splendor.

In Jesus' name, Amen.

Used with Permission. *Healing Trauma*, Sandra Sellmer-Kersten

Release from Fear Bonds and Ties of Control
Lord Jesus,

I repent that I have allowed (name) to control me. I take full responsibility for relinquishing my will and placing (him/her) in a place of power and domination in my life. I ask that You forgive me and cleanse me of my sin.

Choose to forgive (*name*) and I choose to sever and come out of agreement with the (*tie, union bond, agreement*) I have made with (*him/her*).

In the power and authority of the Name of Jesus Christ, I break the power of this (tie, union bond, agreement). I ask the Lord Jesus, that You set me and my descendants free from any effects, curses, and consequences that have come upon us from this negative soul tie.

Lord Jesus Christ, please free me from any covenant agreement—written, verbal or implied—that I have made with this person. Thank You for the New Covenant which supersedes every other. I embrace Your New Covenant and the sacrifice You made on the cross to establish it.

In Jesus' name I place the cross between (name) and myself, and release (him/her) into Your care—body, soul and spirit, thought, word and deed.

Please cleanse me from anything that was transferred to me; cleanse and restore anything that was stolen from me. I ask that You supernaturally gather up all my loose ends and restore me to my original design—the person you create me to be.

Lord Jesus, restore my discernment, my conscience and my ability to hear you through the Holy Spirit. Forgive me for the way I yielded my will to another human being and allowed fear to dominate me. I now declare that You are only Lord and Savior, and I choose this day to yield my will to You and you only. Strengthen me in my inner man/woman, strengthen my will, and give me wisdom, knowledge and understanding that I may choose wisely from this moment on.

I make the decision now to renounce all unnatural authority, manipulation, domination or control exercised over me by this person. I renounce all covenants, pacts, promises, curses and every other work of darkness to which I have been exposed or made liable by my own actions or the actions of others. As a volitional act and by the decision of my will, I loose myself from every soul tie and from every form of bondage of my soul or body to Satan or any of his agents being either human or demonic. I choose also to present my body to the Lord's as a living sacrifice, as the scripture recommends, and to walk in holiness as you, Lord Jesus, enable me.

Please free me from the trauma and fear, and continue to heal the wounds and reveal any un-confessed sin that tempts me to allow others to manipulate, dominate and/or control me. Please deliver me from any force of darkness that gained a foothold in my life through this sin and/or tie, resist the enemy now in the Name of Jesus. Please escort away any force of darkness that seeks to oppress, hinder or affect me in any way. Please sever any bond that would give this person or any evil spirit access to me, or any of my descendants in any way that I have been connected to this person. I choose now to disconnect from them and to connect in every way to You, that I might love You with my stole heart, soul and mind. Thank You, Lord Jesus.

In your name I pray, Amen.

Used with Permission. *Healing Trauma*, Sandra Sellmer-Kersten,

Release from Unhealthy/Unholy Ties of Habitual Masturbation and Pornography

(Adapt this prayer as needed)

In the name of Jesus, I ask forgiveness for each instance of masturbation (evil fantasy, or viewing of pornography), and speak directly to my body, soul and spirit, loosening them from this habit.

I break any identification of peace, comfort and emotional release with this sin, and say to my body, soul, and spirt that I have chosen to find release now in prayer at the foot of the cross, not in sinful physical or visual stimulation.

I command my body, soul and spirit to come into alignment with the Spirit of God and with His Word.

In the name of Jesus, I break any unhealthy or unholy tie with masturbation (fantasy/pornography). In any way that I have become tied to this habit, I choose now to break that tie, connecting instead to the Holy Spirit of God, who strengthens me and enables me to withstand temptation.

Father, I ask that you strengthen my body, soul, mind, will and emotions, and strengthen my spirit.

Forgive me for yielding my will to this temptation. I choose now to yield my will to your Holy Spirt.

Father, I give you permission to reveal any unhealed wound, unmet need, inner vow, bitter root judgment or bitter root expectancy that may be at the root.

Father, please cleanse me from any shame or false guilt that I carry because of my sin, and free me from any generational iniquity associated with this sin.

Father, I repent for fantasizing, and/or gazing at pornography during masturbation, and repent for entertaining any lustful, perverse or adulterous thoughts. I break any ties that have developed as I have lusted after another. Father, in Your name I resist and send away any force of darkness that has gained a foothold in my life because of my sin.

Father, please rightly divide that which is normal and holy from that which is not. Grant me wisdom to know the difference, and to walk as the child of God you have called me to be. Please continue to heal the wounds that make me vulnerable to this temptation. I give you permission to reveal any sin, judgment or inner vows that "sets the stage" for this sin. Enable me to bring them to death on the Cross of Christ, and strengthen me to resist temptation.

I have acted shamefully, and I repent. Thank You cleansing me from my sin and from my shame.

Thank You for restoring the honor and dignity that is my rightful inheritance as your child.

In Jesus' name I pray, Amen.

Used with Permission. *Healing Trauma*, Sandra Sellmer-Kersten

Release from Unhealthy/Unholy Ties Resulting from Abuse
Father,

For so long I have felt the shame and pain of what happened to me. My heart has felt overwhelming and so heavy, I ask You to heal me and free me from the trauma, fear, pain and shame that have bound me for so long. Wash me clean—body, soul and spirit, and restore every portion that has been shattered, fragmented, broken or defiled.

Please cleanse and free me from the shame that has bound me. At times I have felt so desolate and lost, but you are God who restores and redeems. Thank You for washing me whiter than snow, and for restoring to me the honor and dignity that is my rightful inheritance as Your child. I choose to receive that honor and dignity now.

Forgive me for any unforgiveness, bitterness or anger I have harbored. I give You my desire for revenge, and release any demand for justice that I still cling to and ask You to bring justice into this situation. Even though I don't understand why this happened to me, or why You allowed it to happen, I know that You are the one true and just God, and that You love me, and will work all this together for my good.

Please reveal any judgment or inner vow I may have made, any bitter expectations that I have developed in my life and any lies I have believed. Give me the courage to bring each one to Your cross through confessions and repentance. Renew my mind, and give me new ways of thinking, acting and responding. I sometimes feel "marked" by what happened to me, and seem to draw abusers to me. Please wash me clean from any defilement, and remove and "mark" or residue of pain and shame. I repent for every bitter judgment of my abuser and for every bitter expectation of further abuse and dishonor. Set me free from every pattern of sowing and reaping that is at work in my life, and give me new life experiences.

Thank You, Jesus, for enduring the pain and shame of the cross so that I can be free.

As an act of my will, I choose to forgive the person who hurt me, the people who didn't help or rescue me, and myself. Holy Spirit, I need your help! Please accomplish this forgiveness in me.

In any way I have been connected in an ungodly way to this person who abused me, I choose to disconnect from them now. Set me free from any unhealthy, unholy tie/bond/union/ covenant that was formed between me and (*name person, or if you do not know the name, simply "this person"*). If anything was transferred to me from this person, I ask You to remove it from me and cleanse me.

Please cleanse and restore to me everything that was stolen, and make me whole. Deliver me from any evil that passed from this individual to me, and close any door of access that was opened to the enemy.

In the Name of Jesus Christ, I take authority over any spirits tormenting me, and command them to leave me now. Heavenly Father, please send heavenly hosts to come and escort away any higher levels of darkness or familiar spirits that may have been given a foothold in my life. Scripture says that Jesus came that I might have abundant life. I receive that abundant life now, and choose to fully embrace my destiny and purpose.

In Jesus' name, I pray, Amen.

Used with Permission. *Healing Trauma*, Sandra Sellmer-Kersten

Release from Unhealthy/Unholy Sexual Ties
(This prayer is not for sexual abuse victims; there is a specific prayer for sexual abuse.)

Lord Jesus, I repent for being sexually involved with (*name of person*). I take full responsibility for this sin, and I ask that You forgive me and cleanse me.

I know that by committing this sin, I have broken Your law and deserve to reap the consequences. I ask You to forgive me for disobeying you and Your commandments, and that You set me and my descendants free from the consequences and curses resulting from my sin and disobedience.

I ask for Your grace, mercy and blessing for (*name*) and (*his/ her*) descendants. Set (*him/her*) free from any consequences, effects and curses that may have resulted from this sin. I release (*name*) in Your care—body, soul and spirit, in thought, word and deed. Forgive me for the harm I caused this person and (*his/her*) future generations.

I willingly gave myself to (*name*), and as a decision and act of my own will, I entered into sexual relationship with (*him/ her*). According to your Word I became one with (*him/her*) and entered a covenant relationship with (*him/her*). I repent of my willful disobedience and my sinful choices.

I choose now to obey the Word of God and come out of agreement with the tie, covenant, union, bond, agreement that I made with (*name*). As an act of my will, I sever the tie that has been established, and I ask You to break the power of it over me, placing the cross of Christ and the resurrection power of Chris between us.

Cleanse me from all defilement and from anything that was transferred to me from this person. Deliver me from any evil that passed from this individual to me, and I close any door of access that I opened to the enemy. Please send heavenly hosts to come and escort away any higher levels of darkness, or any familiar spirits that may have been given access to me. Please deliver me from any forces of darkness that gained a foothold in my life through this sin and/or soul tie. In the Name of Jesus Christ, I resist the enemy and take authority over the spirits tormenting me.

(Take time to listen. If the Lord reveals a demon, proceed with)
I bind you, you spirit of ________, and I command that your power over me be broken and that you leave me right now in Jesus' name.

Heavenly Father, please free me and cleanse me from the shame that has bound me because of what I have done, and the shame that *was inputted to me* by this person. Please restore to me the honor and dignity that is my rightful inheritance as Your child.

Lord, please heal my heart and restore to its proper place every portion of my body, soul or spirit that has been fragmented, torn or broken, and restore everything that was stolen. Heal my heart, and guard it by Your power and love. Restore me to my original design—the person You created me to be. Renew my mind in accordance with Your Word, and supernaturally gather up all my loose ends and make me whole.

I choose to disconnect from (*him/her*) now, from the ungodly ways that I was connected to this person, and I choose to connect in every way to You Lord Jesus, that I may love You with my whole heart, mind and soul.

In Jesus' name I pray, Amen.

Used with Permission. *Healing Trauma*, Sandra Sellmer-Kersten

Renouncing Bitter Root Judgments, Expectancies, and Inner Vows
Father,

I recognize I have judged (*name of the person*) for (*name of the offense*) and have locked myself into that same behavior/ attitude.

I choose to forgive (*him/her*) for hurting me, and I choose to release my "right" to hold this offense against them, knowing it is up to You alone to judge.

Please forgive me for the sinful ways I've reacted and for the ways in which I have done the very same to others. *(Be specific in naming those you've hurt and how.)*
Forgive me for judging (*name*). I repent for the judgment and dishonor.

Now I see I am reaping the same pattern throughout my life. Forgive me for my part in tempting other to do the very thing I hated, by the power of my bitter root expectancies and judgments. Place the Cross between me and the sowing and reaping of my judgments, and consume on the Cross everything that I am due to reap because of my sin. Thank you for replacing it with your blessing

I ask that You give me new ways of expecting, believing and responding that are in accordance with your Word.

Please forgive me for me trying to protect my heart by making the inner vow to: (*Name the vow specifically*). I repent for making this vow, renounce it, and ask that you break the power of it over me.

I command my body, soul and spirit to forget the vow and I declare that I am no longer required to act, think or feel according to this inner vow. I am set free to my original design; the person you created me to be.

I repent for, and tear down the following habitual ways of acting out this vow: *(i.e., withdrawal, fears, isolation, angers, resentments, denial, etc.)*.

I bring my sin to death on the Cross of Jesus Christ, and consider myself dead to those old ways. Show me how I can "pursue peace" with those whom I have wounded, and help me to restore relationship where possible. Fill me afresh and anew with your Holy Spirit.

In Jesus' Name I pray, Amen.

Used with Permission. *Healing Trauma*, Sandra Sellmer-Kersten

Prayer to Forgive
Asking God who you need to forgive
Father,

I thank You for the riches of your kindness, forbearance, and patience towards me, knowing that your kindness has led me to repentance. I confess that I have not shown that same kindness and patience towards those who have hurt me. Instead, I have held on to my anger, bitterness, and resentment towards them. Please bring to my mind all the people I need to forgive in order that I may do so now.

In Jesus' name I pray, Amen

Unknown author

To Forgive
Lord, I don't know how to make forgiveness happen. I can't cleanse my heart or change my feelings. I don't know how to trust, and I'm afraid to hold my heart open.

You have told me in Your Word that forgiveness is not an option. You simply said I have to choose, yet I often have difficult even choosing to forgive. By Your grace, please do for me what I cannot do for myself! Thank You for accomplishing forgiveness for me.

As an act of my will, in obedience to Your Word, I make a choice to forgive. I know that I may have to choose again and again until you make forgiveness real and complete in me. Please give me the willingness and strength to persevere in choosing until forgiveness is accomplished in me by Your power.

I choose to forgive (*name the person who wounded you, and what you are forgiving them for again, be as specific as you can*).

I give You any "right" that I've felt was mine to blame. I surrender what I felt was my "right" to be paid back for my loss; they owe me nothing. I declare my trust in You alone as the Righteous Judge, and release to You any anger, resentment and bitterness that I've held in my heart.

Forgive me for the ways that I've wanted those who hurt me to hurt like I do. I wanted them to know the enormity of what they have done to me, and I wanted them to be sorry, but that is vengeance, and that is Your territory. Forgive me for my desire for vengeance, and for trying to take your place.

Thank You that I do not have to pretend it is all right, or that it did not hurt or matter. Thank You for always listening to me, for hearing my cries and expressions of pain, and that my tears are important to You. Thank You for wiping the tears from my eyes, and for healing me and making me whole. Forgive me for all the condemning judgments I have made. Give me a new and right spirit that will enable me to hate sin but look with your compassion and love upon sinners. Heal the wounded heart of the child within me and pour Your love in. I know that my emotions will heal in time, and that I will be able to feel the emotion of being forgiven and of extending forgiveness, but until that time, I will continue to make the right choice to forgive and continue to release this person to You. Help me to learn to forgive the way You have forgiven me. I choose to walk in your mercy and grace.

I choose to bless (*name the person*), and I sincerely ask You to richly bless them as well.

Prayer to Remove Trauma

Lord Jesus, I ask that You come as the Prince of Peace and bring your peace to me. Come establish your dominion of peace in me, and manifest yourself in such a way that I will know that you are here. Enable me to feel the depths of your love.

Lord, I ask you to rebuke every force of darkness that seeks to harm me and my family in any way, or has tried to keep me locked in this prison of trauma. You have not given me a spirit of fear, but love, power and soundness of mind, and that is what I claim for me today. Hide me under the shadow of Your wings, and keep me safe. I break every assignment of trauma against me, and bind and send away every "guard" assigned to me.

I ask that you be like poultice, drawing all the pain, trauma, shock, fear, terror, and shame from me, bringing it all to death on your cross. You suffered and died for me, and we appropriate all that you accomplished for me.

Put your love and grace, and by the power of the Holy Spirit remove any trauma that has been stored in my body. Restore the cells to perfect order and vibration.

Lord, I ask You to remove any shock, trauma, fear, terror, or shame experienced at conception, in the womb during birth. Bless the moment of my conception, the moment of my birth, and the newness of my life. I know that You have a purpose and plan for my future, and to provide me a hope for my future and to prosper me in every way.

Lord, I ask You to heal my DNA and remove all the shock, trauma, fear, terror, and shame that has come through my generational flow. I plant the cross of Jesus Christ firmly between me and my ancestors, and I ask that all iniquity be stopped at the cross of Christ. Forgive those in my generations who traumatized others or manipulated, dominated or controlled through fear and torment. Release Your precious blood and heal all unresolved grief and pain.

I ask You to heal the "fear center" of my brain and every place where memory is processed and stored. Remove all shock, trauma, fear, terror, and shame from the conscious and subconscious memory, and draw from me all the pain that has caused me so much torment. Turn off the alarms that have been ringing for so long, and replace the fear dread, hypervigilance with godly discernment. Let me know when there is truly danger and give wisdom to know how to respond. Bring peace and rest to the part of the heart that has always had to stand guard and be alert. Remove and pervasive low-level anxiety.

Please fill up every area of unmet need with your love and peace. Establish new neurological connections to the joy center of my brain. Enable me to have a full range of emotions as You have purposed for me.

Heavenly Father, please remove the trauma from my eyes and ears. With the blood of Jesus Christ, wash over any images "seared" upon the soul. Remove trauma that has come from any harmful or harsh words spoken, and remove any disharmony, disease, or disorder that these words or images have caused. Remove any trauma associated with scent and remove any trauma from the skin.

Sing Your song of love over me and bring everything into agreement to Your original design. In the name and blood of Jesus Christ, I declare order and healing to my spirit, soul, and body.

Trauma has shaken me to the very core of my foundation, I ask that You heal every crack with Your love. Restore trust and grace to believe in You and receive Your promises and to trust others.

Please remove all shock, trauma, fear, terror and shame from my will and spirit. Restore my will, and strengthen it in every way.

Please remove all shock, trauma, fear, terror and shame from the muscles, ligaments, tendons, bones and bone marrow. Bring Your healing power to everywhere my spirit has been crushed or broken, and restore health, vitality and vigor. Make my bones and connective tissue strong. I ask that You remove all shock, trauma, fear and terror off the organs and the rest of my body.

Please heal the immune system and remove all toxins that remain from any chemicals or hormones that have poured through my body for so many years. Cancel any and all effects they have had on the spirit, soul or body, restore all neurochemical balance.

Please sever all fear bonds, trauma bonds, and unhealthy and unholy soul ties that have been created through my response to trauma.

Lord Jesus, help me recognize and bring to death all the old ways of responding and reacting to shock, trauma, fear, and terror. Empower me with wisdom and power to dismantle the ungodly structures of defense, and rebuild godly new structures of defense based on scripture. Help me come to true understanding of my spiritual authority as a child of the Most High God.

Please fill every cell with Your peace and healing grace. Displace any darkness with your light. Keep me in Your perfect peace, especially in the night seasons, and bring Your rest. Surround me with Your protection and love.

In Jesus' name I pray, Amen.

Used with Permission. *Healing Trauma*, Sandra Sellmer-Kersten. Modified by me to make in the first person

In Jesus' Name, Amen.

Used with Permission. *Healing Trauma*, Sandra Sellmer-Kersten

Prayer to Choose Life
Father,

I do want to know You and the abundant life that You paid such an incredible price for. This day I choose that abundant life!

I specifically repent for my sin of ________. Please forgive me for agreeing with your enemy and participating in such darkness.

I repent for the times I have wished for death. I break every agreement and/or covenant I have made with death and renounce every death wish and thought of suicide I have had. I break the power of every command I have given my body to die. I speak to my body, soul and spirit and say, "live!" I embrace You, Jesus, as the Way, the Truth and the Life, and I embrace the abundant life You died for!

Please sing over me and restore my song, my ability to love and receive love, my hope and my passion for life. Restore me to my rightful design, the person You created me to be. Forgive me for every way I've turned from life. I turn to You now, and I embrace the life, purpose and destiny You have for me.

In Jesus' Name I pray, Amen.

Used with Permission. *Healing Trauma*, Sandra Sellmer-Kersten

Prayer to Reveal Generational Sin
Father,

I ask You to bring to mind now all the sins of my ancestors to the fifth generation that are being passed down through family lines. I make Jesus

Christ my Lord and Savior. The curse has been broken. I want to be free from the influences passed down to me and my family. I want to renounce familial sins.

In Jesus' name I pray, Amen

Note: Make a list in your journal of all the sins that come to mind, then pray the below prayer out loud. Each sin must be renounced separately.

Prayer to Renounce Generational Sin
Father,

I renounce and disavow all the sins of my ancestors. I specifically renounce the sin of (*name each sin*) I also renounce their sins that have not been revealed to me or that I did not hear. Any sin that has been passed down and is producing bad fruit in my life as well as my family's life I renounce. In the name of Jesus Christ, I command Satan and his demons to release any foothold or stronghold that were achieved by sinful behavior. In the name of Jesus Christ, the curse is broken through His work on the cross, the blood of Jesus cleanses me and my family. In the name of Jesus Christ, I command Satan and his demons to release any influence on me or my family and to leave our presence.

In Jesus' name I pray, Amen

Unknown author

Some behavioral addictions include:
Gambling, excessive eating, excessive physical fitness, extra-marital affairs, excessive dieting, excessive church, masturbation, self-mutilation, excessive shopping/spending, lustful behavior, being a work-aholic, excessive gaming

Prayer to Renounce Behavioral Addictions
Father,

I confess and repent that I have used sinful behavior specifically (*name each behavior separately*) for the purpose of pleasure, to cope with overwhelming life events, or just to escape from life's stresses. I understand that this addiction has harmed my mind, body, and soul. I renounce the addiction of (*name each addiction*) and repent from making it a priority in my life. In the name of Jesus Christ, I command Satan and his demons to release any foothold or stronghold that were achieved by my sinful behavior. I commit myself to no longer allowing this behavioral addiction to control me. I choose to be controlled by the Holy Spirit.

In Jesus' name I pray, Amen

Unknown author

Prayer to Reveal Prideful Behavior
Father,

I confess and repent that I have been prideful and self-centered. I have sinned by believing that I can make better decisions than You. I ask you to please bring to mind now all the ways which I have lived my life in pride. I want to renounce my prideful practices.

In Jesus' name I pray, Amen

Unknown author

Note: make a list of all things that come to mind in your journal. Then pray the below prayer out loud to renounce prideful behavior.
Some prideful behaviors include:

1. Not admitting I'm wrong
2. I care more about others than God
3. I consider myself smarter than others
4. I rely on my own ability instead of God
5. I tend to manipulate others
6. I seek out praise from others
7. I seek out wealth and status
8. I believe that I am more religious and spiritual than others

Prayer to Renounce Pridefulness
Father,

I confess that I have been prideful. Your Word says that pride comes before destruction and not to be wise in my own eyes. I have placed my will before Yours. I renounce my pride in the area of (*name each separate incident*). In the name of Jesus Christ, I command Satan and his demons to release any foothold or stronghold that were achieved by my sinful behavior. I choose to humble myself before You and I claim Jesus Christ as my Lord and Savior.

In Jesus' name I pray, Amen

Unknown author

Prayer to Reveal Fears
Father,

I confess and repent that I have allowed Satan to instill fear into my life. I have focused on myself, my feelings, needs, and circumstances. I ask You to please bring to mind now any and all fears that make me question my faith in You. I want to renounce my fears.

In Jesus' name I pray, Amen

Unknown author

Note: Make a list of the things brought to mind and write them in your journal. Then pray out loud the prayer to renounce fears.

Some fears include:

- Fear of death
- Fear of illness
- Fear of relationships
- Fear of death
- Fear of loneliness
- Fear of embarrassment
- Fear of rejection
- Fear of losing salvation
- Fear of crime
- Fear of future
- Fear of failure
- Fear of financial loss

Prayer to Renounce Fears
Father,

I confess that I have allowed fear to master me. My fear has made me focus on myself, not You. I renounce the spirit of fear. You have not given me a spirit of fear, You have given me the power to overcome. I renounce the fear of (*name each fear separately*). In the name of Jesus Christ, I command

Satan and his demons to release any foothold or stronghold that were achieved by my sinful behavior. I claim Jesus Christ as my Lord and Savior.

In Jesus' name I pray, Amen

Unknown author

Prayer to Renounce Performance Orientation
Father,

I know that my self-worth is not based on who others say I am, but who You say I am. I confess and repent that my self-worth was dependent upon my ability to earn love and respect. My identity is not found in my mistakes or poor decisions, but in the truth that I am a child of God and deeply loved. I choose to place my faith and trust in Jesus. Based upon my faith alone, I am forgiven, not by what I have or have not done, but by Your grace. There is no need to strive for protection. I renounce my efforts to earn love and respect from others. I choose to walk in the Holy Spirit and he truth of being in Christ.

In Jesus' name I pray, Amen.

Unknown author

Prayer to Renounce Substance Abuse
Father,

I confess and repent that I have used substances specifically (*name substance*) for the purpose of pleasure, to cope with overwhelming life events, or to just escape life's stresses. I understand that these substances have harmed my mind, body, and soul. I renounce my use of these substances and I repent for making them a priority in my life. In the name of Jesus Christ, I command Satan and his demons to release any foothold or stronghold that were achieved by my sinful behavior. I commit myself to no longer allow these substances to control me. I choose to be controlled by the Holy Spirit.

In Jesus' name I pray, Amen

Unknown Author

Prayer to Reveal Wrong Priorities
Father,

I confess that I have allowed people or things to become more important to me than you. Your simple command is to place You first, I have not followed this command. I have sinned against You. I repent and turn away from my idolatry. I am going to make every effort to make you first in my life. Please bring to my memory now any and all things or people that I have placed above You. I want to renounce all idols.

In Jesus' name I pray, Amen

Unknown author

Note: Make a list of the things brought to mind and write them in your journal. Then pray out loud the prayer to renounce idols. Some idols include:

- Work-aholic Spouse
- Family
- Finances
- Work
- Power
- Possessions
- Ministry
- Food
- Control
- Ambition
- Video games
- Television
- Sports

Prayer to Renounce Idolatry
Father,

I confess and repent that I have placed (*idols list separately*) above You. I renounce the worship of (*idols list separately*) and choose to worship You only. In the name of Jesus Christ, I command Satan and his demons to release any foothold or stronghold that was achieved by my sinful behavior. I claim Jesus Christ as my Lord and Savior.

Prayer to Reveal Occult Activity
Father,

I confess that I have participated in occult and/or satanic activity. Please bring to mind now any and all occult activity that I had knowingly and unknowingly participated in so that I can renounce this activity.

In Jesus' name I pray, Amen

Unknown author

Note: Make a list of all things that come to mind and write them in your journal. The pray out loud the prayer to renounce occult activity.
Some occult activity includes:

1. Witchcraft / Sorcery
2. Palm reading
3. Seances
4. Mediums
5. Fortunetellers
6. Satanism
7. Blood pacts
8. Spirit guides
9. Ouija boards
10. Spells / Curses
11. Hypnosis
12. Cutting
13. Mental telepathy
14. Magic eight ball
15. Trances

Prayer to Renounce Occult Activity
Father,

I confess and repent that I have participated in the occult practice of ________. I renounce my involvement in ________. In the name of Jesus Christ, I command Satan and his demons to release any foothold or stronghold achieved due to my sinful participation in this occult activity. I claim Jesus Christ as my Lord and Savior.

In Jesus' name I pray, Amen

Unknown author

AUTHOR BIO

NORM WIELSCH was a law enforcement officer for over twenty-five years. Norm spent Sixteen of those years as an undercover narcotic agent. He experienced many traumatic incidents during his career. Norm was a police academy instructor and is an expert in PTSD, police tactics, narcotic enforcement, and the first responder culture. In 1998, he was diagnosed with PTSD and an incurable neuro-muscular disease that caused the loss of feeling, mobility, and strength in his hands and feet. After over 30 surgeries he became addicted to opioids. Due to his sinful responses to his trauma, Norm made a series of poor decisions that landed him in federal prison. It was during the most intense trial of his life, that he answered the calling of God. God was calling him to minister to people who were suffering from trauma.

While in prison, he obtained a Master's Degree in Theology, a Doctorate Degree in Christian Counseling, and a Drug and Alcohol Counseling Certificate. In prison, Norm counseled inmates, preached God's word, and taught Bible studies. Norm Counseled many inmates who experienced severe trauma. They experienced God's healing power and transformation through the biblical principles taught through Christ-Centered Healing process. Norm is a Registered Addiction Counselor a credentialed Chaplain.

Go to www.Christ-CenteredHealing.com or @ChristCenteredHealing on Facebook to book Norm for your church or other speaking event.